Topic Books

Lucy Calkins ✦ Casey Maxwell

Photography by Peter Cunningham and André Martins

HEINEMANN ■ PORTSMOUTH, NH

Heinemann • 145 Maplewood Ave., Suite 300 • Portsmouth, NH 03801 • www.heinemann.com

Offices and agents throughout the world

© 2023 by The Reading and Writing Project Network, LLC

EDITORS: Jessica Chadbourn, Natalie Chapman, Anna Cockerille, Dana Dillon, Havilah Jespersen, Zoë Kashner, Jean C. Lawler, Katherine Love Miller, Jennifer McKenna, Julia Mooney, Felicia O'Brien, Molly Picardi, Shannon Rigney, and Shannon Thorner

PRODUCTION: Rebecca Anderson, Carole Berg, Kerri Cardone, Kate Lennon, Vanessa Richards, Elizabeth Valway, and Richard Weed

COVER AND INTERIOR DESIGN: Jenny Jensen Greenleaf

PHOTOGRAPHY: Peter Cunningham, André Martins, Nadine Baldasare, Elizabeth Franco, and David Stirling

ILLUSTRATIONS: Marjorie Martinelli

COMPOSITION: Publishers' Design and Production Services, Inc.

MANUFACTURING: Gerard Clancy

Printed in the United States of America on acid-free paper
1 2 3 4 5 6 7 8 9 10   MP   29 28 27 26 25 24 23

February 2023 printing / PO# 4500866381

CONTENTS

ACKNOWLEDGMENTS

E.B. White wrote at the end of *Charlotte's Web* that "It is not often that someone comes along who is a true friend and a good writer." The two of us are so grateful that we, and this book, are surrounded by people who are true friends and good writers—and good artists as well.

In writing this book, we stood on the shoulders of those who came before us. How grateful we are to Kristi Mraz and Barb Golub, coauthors with Lucy of the original *Nonfiction Chapter Books*, a unit that brought immeasurable joy to so many classrooms and launched an entire generation of young information writers. Rewriting such a wonderful book felt like an enormous responsibility: How could we possibly rewrite a unit that kids and teachers already adored? We have moved heaven and earth to do justice to that earlier work.

Every page of this curriculum carries the brilliance of our colleagues—and by that, we refer not only to other staff developers and writers at the Teachers College Reading and Writing Project (TCRWP), but also to the scores of teachers who have problem solved in ways that have deepened our work. The powerhouse of primary staff developers at TCRWP is led by Amanda Hartman, who imbues everything she does with joy, high standards, and an incredible ability to make everyone feel seen and valued, and we thank her. For this writing, we leaned heavily on Shanna Schwartz, who always reminds us of the importance of intentionality, scaffolding, a sense of humor, and social-emotional learning. Natalie Louis and Rebecca Cronin have influenced our thinking about phonics and early writing in countless ways and this book echoes their wisdom.

We are also grateful to the Project's senior leaders. Mary Ehrenworth and Laurie Pessah do so much to both hold this organization together and push it forward, and we are all so privileged to learn from and work with them. None of this would have been possible without Kathleen Tolan, our former Senior Deputy Director, whose beautiful teaching still serves as a model today.

There is perhaps no truer friend than Katie Clements. Her gentle but powerful feedback (and rewrites!) helped us bring this book to fruition. Katie is joined in the writer's suite by Valerie Geschwind and Liz Franco, primary writers and staff developers extraordinaire who shaped our thinking and contributed to our writing throughout the entire process.

Everyone at TCRWP is supported by an incredible office team. Special thanks to Lucy's assistant, Mary Ann Mustac, and to Lisa Cazzola and Rebecca Godlewicz who lead the office staff. Much of this book was written as the COVID-19 pandemic shut schools down, and from that situation emerged several heroes. Shannon Ballou and Brittany Nocito were virtual teaching pioneers, and their students and the writing they collected made the unit come to life. Molly Picardi and Sara Berg shared the pen with us and contributed mightily to this book's work-time sessions. Heather Kessel and Kristen Sampino joined us at the eleventh hour to put the finishing touches on student work.

When we work with teachers, we are so frequently asked to show them "how to draw people the Teachers College way." Marjorie Martinelli invented the "TC way" of drawing, and her art fills this series. Katie Lindner joined Marjorie by illustrating this book's many demonstration texts and one-day charts. Invisible to the reader are the many, many drafts that Katie and Marjorie went through.

The entire team at Heinemann took our work from its original format in Google Docs to the beautiful book that it is now. Thank you to Julia Mooney for pushing us across the finish line, and to Jen McKenna and Natalie Chapman for ensuring that every detail was just so. Elizabeth Valway and Carole Berg meticulously laid out every word, and we are amazed at what this team has produced. Jessica Wollman led this entire team, and we are so thrilled that the final product—that all of our final products—are in Lisa Bingen's capable and enthusiastic hands.

Although we were supported by so many people—true friends—at work and in the writing of this book, our families were the ones who made this book possible and our gratitude to them goes beyond words.

WELCOME TO THE UNIT

Welcome, colleagues. We are so glad that you'll bring *Topic Books* to life. In this section, we want to share the thinking that informs this unit and help those of you who taught the earlier iteration (*Nonfiction Chapter Books*) to understand how and why this unit is different.

This genre is especially close to the coauthors of this unit and to our colleagues—after all, this book itself is informational writing, as is most of the writing we do. So yes, this genre is dear to us. But the important thing is that this genre should also be dear to you. As someone who has taken teaching as your profession, you are, in a way, an informational writer. It's just that your teaching occurs mostly real-time, in-the-air, while the teaching that informational writers do is on-the-page. But writers of informational texts are teachers, and all the techniques that work when teaching live are also important when teaching through writing. And of course, teaching involves far more than imparting facts.

But we write and teach not only for those who are taught—for our readers and our students—but also for the way in which this work changes our own relationship with our lives and with our knowledge. It is an extraordinary, beautiful thing to learn, as Faulkner put it, that one's "own little postage stamp of native soil is worth writing about." Faulkner said, "I can never live long enough to exhaust it." Something transformational occurs deep inside a person when you realize that yes, indeed, you have knowledge to share, expertise to convey to others.

Do you remember when you first taught—the time when you began to live as a teacher, when everything you did became grist for your teaching mill? I so recall my first months as a teacher, being out to dinner and spotting a menu I could bring to the kids. I remember watching shows, thinking, "I've gotta tape this for the kids!" I recall realizing that, for the rest of my life, I'd live differently because I am a teacher. And it is true that I have found the stuff of my life so much more precious because it is all grist for my teaching mill, my writing mill. Writing, like teaching, turns a person into a student of one's own life, making everything in life seem more interesting, more precious.

We want all of that and more for first-graders. We want this unit to induct youngsters into the work of teaching on paper, and we especially want youngsters to know that their own local knowledge is worth writing about.

How—and Why—Is This Unit Different from the Original?

We've tried to maintain the most engaging and age-appropriate parts of the original unit, while working to make sure that the instruction is more precisely aligned to children in the fall of first grade. As part of that, we have built very carefully on the previous information writing unit, *Show and Tell Writing*, taught in the fall of kindergarten, and we've set children up for two informational writing units in second grade. We have been careful to avoid stealing the thunder from second-grade units. To do this, we clarified the developmental progression between kindergarten, first-, second-, and third-grade instruction, aiming to not teach content to first-graders that we actually think is beyond the reach of most of them. Our thought is, "Why not save that for second grade?" while we meanwhile devote more time to the skills and dispositions (including phonics) that are essential for first-graders.

It was this thinking that led us to decide to save nonfiction chapter books for second grade. Most first-graders are not yet reading nonfiction chapter books, and there is plenty of elaboration and development work they can do prior to writing chapter books. By second grade, kids will need ways for information writing to feel new, and inviting them to write chapter books can be important to seven year olds.

Across this unit, students will write what we're calling "topic books." These books will be approximately five pages in length. You'll want to teach that every page teaches about a different part of the topic. Your instruction will channel students to think about what, exactly, they'll teach on every page. A topic book about crayons might have a page about the colors of crayons, a page about what kids color with crayons, and a page about caring for crayons. This focus on structure is highly intentional. It lays the foundation for all of the information writing that your students will do in the future, and the teaching of structure in writing instruction has been proven to have a consistently positive, statistically significant effect size (Graham, McKeown, Kiuhara, and Harris 2012).

Your students will develop many different *ways* to elaborate. The elaboration chart from the previous version of this unit was an absolute favorite of teachers and students; we've borrowed parts of it and added new strategies, expecting that this new version will become a favorite too.

We know that these are tall orders for first-graders, and we've put lots of thought into how you'll support your students' independence across the unit. First and foremost, you'll want to consider your expectations for children's volume of writing. Students should produce about a book a day across this unit, and that can be true for more and less proficient writers. Your most sophisticated writers might spend a bit longer on each book, whereas children whose writing is less complex will probably produce more books. John Hattie's work has taught us that transparency around goals and visibility of goals are among the most powerful strategies that we, as teachers, have to increase student achievement (2012). We've made sure that these strategies are folded across this unit's work times to promote independence and volume in your students. Writing partners, too, are well backed by research, and you'll see that we channel you to pay attention to this important scaffold.

OVERVIEW OF THE UNIT

This unit, like every unit in the series, is divided into parts. Those parts, called bends, each offer a new portion of the journey you'll take students on.

Bend I: Writing Teaching Books with Independence

You'll launch this unit by telling your kids that their own small corner of the world is worth writing about, and you'll get them started writing information books about their classroom, that is, their own special place in the world. On this day, you'll provision all of your kids with a "topic wand" (made from a craft stick), and they'll walk through the classroom with a partner, thinking, "Hey! I could write a book about . . ." therefore generating tons of possible topics. Once they've come up with some ideas, they'll engage in a process similar to that from *Small Moments*: they'll make a stack of "ideas-in-waiting" by filling out some covers. This time, though, you'll also channel your students to generate subtopics. The paper you supply for covers can contain four squares into which children can sketch subtopics—although they may start by anticipating just two subtopics.

Students will begin writing their books in Session 2, and that first piece of writing will serve as their on-demand assessment for this unit. Expect that students will write approximately a book a day for the rest of the bend, and these books will show remarkable growth across the bend—they will get longer, more structured, and more detailed. A favorite session for our pilot teachers featured the kids looking at a book that contained almost no information at all, declaring it to be a letdown, a bummer, and resolving to not write bummer books. With that in mind, you'll teach students to create little puppets with their hands that prompt them to add more details that can be easily missed.

In Bend I, you'll teach students to use the word wall both effectively and quickly, in the service of getting more down on the page. You'll also show them how to reread, asking themselves, "Is my book ready for a reader?" Those readers will arrive at the end of the last lesson in this bend. We suggest you invite a class of kindergartners to visit your classroom so that your students may read their books to them.

A few notes. In this first bend, you initially channel students to write about a topic within the classroom as a way of making this work particularly accessible. Then, mid-bend, you'll invite students to bring objects from home. By writing about things close to them, students have all of the necessary information at their fingertips. They can focus on their writing work, instead of the information-getting work. However, although we're provisioning students with topic wands and sending them off to hunt for topics in the classroom, you may have some students who want to write about their cat, their little brother, or a favorite fast-food restaurant. Don't worry so much about this. You'll want students to have at least one book about a classroom topic to share at the celebration, but students can still accomplish the work of this bend—writing with structure, volume, and independence—regardless of the topic they choose.

Prior to the launch of Bend II, it'd be great if you can set up your nonfiction library with bins that represent high-interest titles: big machines, water and weather, dinosaurs, people who invent and discover, animals, space, and the like. It will be important to title your categories before the start of the next bend.

Bend II: Writing about the Whole Wide World

You'll begin this bend by opening up students' topic choice. You'll encourage them to look through the classroom library, browsing different bins, thinking about books that they could write. You'll hope that by seeing what someone else has written, they will be reminded of topics they know and care about. Youngsters may not know a lot about planets and dinosaurs, soccer and video games, but they probably know enough to fill books on these topics. They can also use books and each other to learn about the topics they choose to write about.

The second session of the bend focuses on spelling. We intentionally moved this work to be earlier in the bend to convey that writers focus on spelling while they draft, not just as they prepare for publication.

The remainder of the bend will feel familiar to those of you who taught *Nonfiction Chapter Books*. You'll spend the next days using a mentor text to teach your students about the concrete ways that information writers write and revise. You'll particularly focus on elaboration, teaching students that writers say more by adding examples, comparisons, diagrams, introductions, and conclusions.

You'll wrap up this bend with a celebration that circles back to its start. Students return to the same shelves and bins that sparked ideas for writing, and now they add their own books to the library. The new bin of books by and for kids is sure to become a favorite of all of your students, so make sure that it stays in the library, and give your students lots of opportunities to learn from each other!

PHONICS, SPELLING, AND CONVENTIONS

There are phonics, spelling, and conventions lessons in each bend of this unit, all aligned to first-grade standards. If you haven't read *A Guide to the Writing Workshop, K–2*, we recommend you do that before teaching this unit, since it describes how phonics, spelling, and conventions are supported across the series, and also provides recommendations for assessment. Phonics experts agree that writing is one of the best ways for students to solidify their phonological awareness and phonics skills. This is perhaps especially true as your students write information books and work to include fascinating, domain-specific vocabulary in their writing. At the end of each session, save for the final one in each bend, you'll see a phonological awareness and phonics extension that you can teach at any time. These extensions are not specifically connected to that session's writing work, rather they present a research-based sequence of instruction that will support children's writing development across the unit.

Each bend in this unit has minilessons that teach spelling to the entire class. These minilessons aim to help students transfer their phonics knowledge into the writing workshop. Because we often find that first-graders' ideas come to them faster than their ability to write the words, we've included a session in Bend I on writing high-frequency or snap words—those that are apt to be on your classroom word wall—quickly, drawing on frequent encounters with them. At the end of Bend I, your students will publish their pieces. Before doing so, they will find and fix up places where their writing could be confusing to readers. Many of the confusing parts will involve misspelled words, and you'll channel students to listen carefully, making sure that they record every sound. This work aims to solidify your students' phonics skills while also strengthening their phonological awareness as they segment words by phoneme and syllable. You will also remind your children that the classroom is full of tools that can help them spell words.

Bend II channels students to focus on spelling, both while writing and as they near publication. Session 2 nudges youngsters to spell using analogy. The words on the word wall contain word parts that can help with other words. Session 9 fits tongue-and-groove with the unit *The Mystery of the Silent* e, from the Units of Study in Phonics. After receiving a letter from the Super Secret Detective Agency, you'll teach your students about making sure that they signal to their readers when a word has a long vowel. You'll model listening for a vowel, adding a silent *e* or including a vowel team, and then confirming that the spelling looks correct. Remember that you are not striving for perfection and mastery yet. For now, you are reminding students to slow down, listen carefully, and draw on everything that they've learned about vowels.

ASSESSMENT

Session 2 of Bend I does double duty. It will feel like a normal workshop to your children, but the writing they produce will serve as their on-demand piece for the unit. As your students write on that day, you'll want your approach to be as hands-off as possible so that you can observe them and take anecdotal notes. As in other units in this series, we use the anchor chart as the visual that kids can rely on as they write on the on-demand day. We also provide a printable on-demand prompt in *A Guide to the Writing*

Workshop, K–2, which you might display as a reminder on the on-demand day, or use if you decide to give an on-demand assessment at another time, such as at the end of the unit to assess growth. Whatever visuals you provide, instead of reminding students to use classroom tools, it'll be far more informative for you to observe who does and does not use them. After you've collected students' work, photocopy or scan and return the original to students' writing folders, then use the rubrics in *A Guide to the Writing Workshop, K–2* to norm, assess, and score, if necessary. Those scores serve as only part of your assessment, though. To assess, draw also on your observations from that day and every day as well as from the treasure trove of information on your students that you will have accumulated by this point in the year.

You'll continue assessing throughout this unit. Your goal will be to form the most complete and comprehensive picture of each child and his or her progress over time.

We've tried to also make sure that this unit contains ample opportunities for students to self-assess. Work times in both Bend I and Bend II feature goal-setting sticky notes that students can use to set and work toward specific, individual goals. There are also several shares that invite students to locate places in their books where they did the work you have taught them to do. Although your students' self-assessments may not always be as accurate as you wish, honor them and push your students to act on their self-assessments.

GETTING READY

As with any unit, there are some materials that you'll want to prepare ahead of time. You'll particularly want to ensure that your writing center is provisioned with the paper choice that best supports students' information writing. See the online resources for the varying paper choices. We suggest that, across both bends, your students write in premade, stapled five-page booklets. It'll be particularly beneficial for these booklets to include a cover page with four small boxes, which can channel children to plan the subtopics they'll cover. The other pages in the booklet can reflect your judgment. How many lines of writing can your youngsters do at this point in the year? Be sure there are blank booklets in which the pages support more drawing, as well as some that leave little space for pictures. You might also want to place single sheets of a few different paper choices, along with a stapler or tape, in the writing center so that students can add pages to their books if they choose to.

In the first session, students will generate topics for information books by walking around the classroom with topic wands—you can use a package of craft sticks, and you might make them extra fancy by placing a star-shaped decal or sticker at the end.

You'll also invite your students to bring in a special object from home, which they'll write about across the second part of the bend. Consider having some other objects on hand for those students who do not supply things from their homes. In this first bend, your children may write a chapter on paper designed to show how their object looks on the outside and on the inside. The online resources contain directions to help you construct that special paper. You'll also introduce students to special pages that will teach readers how their objects work, feature questions and answers, and list different types of whatever it is they are teaching about. You'll want to make sure that those choices, along with some lined paper, are all in the writing center.

As you launch Bend II, your students will look toward the nonfiction section of your classroom library as a way to generate new ideas for topic books. They will again use the topic wands from Bend I, and this time they'll use them to look through the nonfiction section of your library.

In this series, we've added digital tips in green to support you and your students in incorporating technology and digital tools throughout the writing process. In the early grades, we don't suggest students spend much time writing digitally. Instead, many of the digital tips suggest ways that you can draw on technology as an instructional tool or as an alternate mode of publication. For example, you might record students reading their final information books and share these videos virtually with caregivers and family members.

MENTOR AND DEMONSTRATION TEXTS

There are two mentor texts for this unit: *Cake* by Hareem Atif Khan and *Now You Know How It Works* by Valorie Fisher. In addition, you'll write a small pile of books that the kids will learn from, including books about the trash can and your teacher closet! These demonstration texts can be found in the online resources.

You will also want to invite kids to study nonfiction books, noticing all that the authors of those books did so they can try those same things in their books. Don't underestimate the power of art in those books. You'll see zoom-in pictures, art that includes numbers or arrows, and lots of other easy-to-replicate things.

If you teach writing workshop in Spanish, or if you have students who speak and write in Spanish, you might use Spanish mentor texts. Be sure to check the online resources for the most up-to-date recommendations for Spanish mentor texts. This list includes *Pasteles* by Hareem Atif Khan, which is used regularly across the unit.

Even if you aren't fluent in Spanish, you can make these texts accessible for kids by inviting others—colleagues, families or caregivers, and older students—to read them aloud or by sharing an audiobook, for example. Reading these texts aloud prior to the minilesson will help kids focus on the writing analysis during the minilesson. If you have students who speak and write in other languages, we encourage you to find mentor texts in those languages, keeping in mind your students' identities, cultures, and languages. You can even recruit the kids to help, saying, "Can you help find an information book you just love, one you think you could learn from as a writer?"

We tend to assume that a first-grader's natural position is that of learner and lover of learning. When students have obstacles to learning, we owe it to them to make learning more accessible. You'll see Ensuring Access sections at the beginning of each session, which give specific tool and strategy ideas. We encourage you to try these whether or not a student has an identified learning need. If after a few weeks you do not see much change or growth, we suggest you ask a colleague to come in and observe or study the student's work. You might also want to request an informal evaluation from a member of your school's evaluation team if that is a possibility to see if a student could be a candidate for intervention or else a formal evaluation. Writing, because of its very visible nature, can bring to light learning needs that might not be easily seen in other forums.

MULTILINGUAL LANGUAGE LEARNERS

Topic Books is especially accessible to multilingual language learners (MLLs) because the unit sets students up to write about topics of personal expertise, including cherished objects and places they can see and hold. How important it is that kids know their knowledge and passions will be honored and valued in your classroom! It is equally important that kids know their multiple languages will be honored. Encourage MLLs to draw on all the languages they know when they teach information. For example, a child might first touch and teach across the pages in a language other than English or create bilingual labels for a diagram.

When a child doesn't yet have the English vocabulary or the linguistic structures to produce grade-level work in English, it is critical to remember that the child's stage of English acquisition is not the child's stage of cognitive development. Encourage students' volume through detailed pictures first. You or a peer can then help the youngster label their drawing with English words, which will become a little glossary when it's time to write. Later, prompt them to say more with questions like: "What makes this special? How does it work?" Use the opportunity to learn words in another language too.

To support your students' success in information writing units, offer exemplar pieces that represent familiar topics and accessible language structures. Launching the unit by writing a shared class book can be a helpful way to teach new vocabulary—concrete nouns in the earlier stages and more sophisticated describing words for later stages—and to practice language structures that MLLs are beginning to approximate. You can also support these skills by inviting students to orally describe pictures of people, places, and things that are important to them.

Above all, keep in mind that your most important job is to create an environment where students feel supported as they take risks. MLLs will speak and write with increased complexity about their topics when they feel comfortable. Accepting approximations with language, drawings, and spelling is the best way to encourage students to make the attempts that will help them grow as information writers.

You'll see MLL coaching notes in blue within the margins of this unit and often the Ensuring Access sections will be helpful. You'll also want to read *A Guide to the Writing Workshop, K–2* to learn more.

 ONLINE RESOURCES

A variety of resources to accompany the Units of Study in Writing are available via the online resources platform. For details on how to access the online resources for this grade-level set, visit unitsofstudy.com/resources.

Writing Teaching Books with Independence

Finding Topics in the World at Your Feet

In This Session

TODAY YOU will launch information writing by channeling students to choose topics from right inside the classroom. You'll teach them that ordinary topics like the class trash can may yield exciting information writing, and you'll plan books about your teacher closet and the trash can. By suggesting that everyday things are worth writing about, you celebrate children's funds of knowledge. You'll set students up to walk through the classroom with topic wands to find worthwhile topics that they can use to make several covers today. Mid-workshop, you'll suggest that writers also find topic ideas by talking to other people. In the share, you'll introduce students to their new partners and rally them to share their topic ideas.

TODAY YOUR STUDENTS will notice a world of writing ideas right at their feet as they walk through the classroom with wands, and then use these topics to make several covers for some of the books they'll write in the upcoming weeks. Each cover will contain a drawing of a few specific things that the writer might teach about the topic. In the share, students will meet their new writing partners.

Getting Ready

YOU WILL NEED . . .

- two blank booklets with cover pages to start two demonstration books, one titled, "The Teacher Closet," and another titled, "All About Trash Cans." If you don't have a closet, choose another topic. Examples of the covers can be found in the online resources.

- to create a new chart, "How to Write a Teaching Book," and add the first sticky note.

- to make "topic wands" using straws or craft sticks with a special sticker at one end.

- to assign long-term writing partners. Write both partners' names on sticky notes or other paper and assign each a number (either 1 or 2). You'll place these in the meeting area right before the share.

STUDENTS WILL NEED . . .

- their writing folders with red and green dots, from which you have cleared out the *Small Moments* writing.

- a place to gather for the minilesson, and a system for gathering quickly. (see *A Guide to the Writing Workshop, K–2*).

- one topic wand for every two students.

- five-page blank booklets (one cover and four writing pages), plus a stack of blank booklets on each table. Be sure to stock these in the writing center as well.

Ensuring Access

YOUR ULTIMATE GOAL TODAY is to get your students ready for the upcoming weeks of information writing by helping them make covers and plan the books they'll write soon. You send the message that writers write information books to teach others about the things that are closest to them.

- Asking students to come up with the different aspects of their topic that they'll write about is new. Remember that the students in your class are young, and structure is something that they'll develop over the next several years. It's okay if their subtopics aren't really subtopics.

- You may have MLLs who aren't yet ready to name things in English. You might support their vocabulary development by saying something like: "I see that you drew a picture of those tools that we use during math. These are called pattern blocks!" and "You're writing a book about the sink! I know it's called a *lavabo* in Spanish. The English word for it is *sink*. Do you want to mention that there is *soap* next to the *sink*?"

- Remember that whenever you switch writing partnerships, it's a chance to take stock of your MLLs' oral language development. Some students who had been in triads may now be ready to work in a partnership because they are regularly joining the conversation. Consider pairing these students with a friend—if possible, one who speaks the same language—as this creates space for students to strengthen academic language across both languages.

- Pre-teaching the minilesson can provide increased understanding of key vocabulary and content, especially for MLLs. Spanish video introductions to each minilesson across the unit are available in the online resources.

Finding Topics in the World at Your Feet

CONNECTION

Launch the new unit by announcing that students are going to write teaching books about things in their own corner of the world.

Once kids had gathered with their folders, I said, "Do you notice that your folders are awfully light? Are you asking, 'What happened to my writing?' I've put away the stories you wrote to clear out space for a whole new kind of writing. Starting today, you aren't writing Small Moment stories. Instead you are writing teaching books—books that teach other people about things you know. Right now, think about the things you know a lot about." I gave the children a moment to think.

"Did you think, 'I know about the shoes that we wear?'" and I pointed to my shoes. "'I know about our coat closet.' 'I know about our fish, Bloopy.' 'I know about our writing center.' No? None of those things? Why not? Sure, teaching books can be about whales and outer space and volcanoes, but they can also be about shoes and pets and hobbies. You see, all writers need to learn that their corners of the world are worth writing about. This classroom is worth writing about. Your home and your street and your kitchen sink are worth writing about."

Remind children that, earlier, they came up with book covers for story ideas. Suggest they do something similar with information books.

"Do you remember how, at the start of our last unit, you thought of lots of stories you could write and made lots of covers for those stories? You tucked them away in your folder and then, every day, you took out another cover, remembered that idea, and wrote a new story? You can do the same thing today, only this time, you're going to make book covers that capture ideas for information books you can write!"

◆ **Name the teaching point.**

"Today I want to teach you that getting ready to write information books is a lot like getting ready to write Small Moment stories. You think of *lots* of possible books you could write. To get ideas, you look around and think, 'This reminds me that I could write about . . .'"

TEACHING

Demonstrate the process of looking at something to spark an idea for a book. Then grab a blank booklet, write the title, and sketch a few subtopics.

"Will you help me look around our classroom to think about topics I know about, topics that I could teach about in a book? Hmm, . . ." I looked around the room, and then placed my hand above my eyes, as if I was scanning the horizon. I looked toward my own teacher coat closet. "I could write about my teacher closet! I use it every day. It's important to me. I could definitely write about my teacher closet!"

I took hold of a blank booklet and made a super-quick sketch of a closet door in the first box. "I could tell about the door—I keep it locked since it's just for teachers."

Then I said, "Wait, the closet has lots of hooks and a mirror inside," and I sketched a picture of the inside of the closet in the next box. I muttered that I might write about things that go in my closet and sketched a bag.

"What other topics could I write about? Hmm, . . . oh yes! Now I remember. It helps to look at things around you." I scanned the room for a moment, then continued, "Well, I'm looking at our trash can. It might not be a very fancy topic, but it's important. And we have three in this room, don't we? I could definitely write about our trash cans." I grabbed another blank booklet and started to draw and write on the cover.

"There are also loads of small things in the classroom that I could write about." Putting up a pretend magnifying glass to show students I was looking closely and carefully, I said, "Like the stapler! Or the pencil sharpener! Or even something as tiny as . . . a crayon box! Later, I'll make covers for books about these topics too!"

List the steps of the process that you just demonstrated. Start an anchor chart.

"Wait, I shouldn't keep making *my* covers with *my* ideas. I should let you come up with *your* ideas and *your* covers, right? So, let's list out what you need to do and then you can get going." I started the "How to Write a Teaching Book" anchor chart and added the first sticky note.

ACTIVE ENGAGEMENT

Give pairs of students a topic wand, and ask them to move around the room, touching things they could write about for their teaching books.

"Are you ready to think about what topics you could teach? Great! Pair up with the friend you've been working with for the past few weeks. I'll give the two of you a topic wand to help you find topics to write about." I held one up. "Here's how they work. You move around the room and touch something with your topic wand. When you touch something, you could say, 'This reminds me that I could write about . . .' and then you say the thing, like . . . *coats*!

"Then, say a few different things you could say about your topic. Like this: 'Some coats are furry, with big collars that are soft and puffy. A few kids have coats that go with a sports team, like coats that say. . . .' After you say what you could write about the first topic you pick, pass the topic wand to your partner, touch something else, and say aloud what you can write about that. Get started!" I gave each pair a topic wand and gestured for kids to get started.

LINK

Disperse your kids, charging them to make the covers for a few teaching books. Invite them to move around the room in their minds if they need more topics.

"Oh my, hurry back!" Once the kids were back, I said, "You looked around our classroom, and you came up with so many great ideas that could become book topics! Head off to your work spots and put those ideas onto covers for booklets. I left a big stack on each of your tables.

"And if you need *more* topics to write about, you can move around the room in your mind with your topic wand. Everywhere you look, the classroom can inspire tons of topics!"

You'll use the cover about the trash can to write a demonstration text in Session 3. Make sure to include sketches on your cover that reflect different people using a trash can, the types of things that are thrown away—lined paper, apple cores, and juice boxes—squishing trash down to fit more, and someone taking out the trash. You'll also write a book about the stapler in Session 5, so make sure to prepare that cover too.

If sending the kids around the room feels like too much, ask partners to pretend they're moving around the room, touching things, and to instead whisper what they see and are pretending to touch. They can still say, "This reminds me that I could write about . . ." to each other's ideas.

MLLs in the early stages of language development can work with a triad or a partner to support vocabulary development for the objects around the room. They may point to objects and ask their partner for support. You may also invite MLLs to name (and label) objects around the classroom in their own language.

Voiceovers ✦ Generating Momentum

- *"Wow!* You are thinking up so many books that you could write."

- "You haven't finished one yet? Sketch like the wind, so you can get started on a second."

- "I can't wait to read this book. I bet that you could teach me so much about . . ."

- "What a fascinating topic you've chosen. I'm thinking of all you could teach about that!"

- "I love that you found the word on our walls and are using it to help you spell."

- "You're filling up your folder. I bet that by the end of the day, you're going to have tons of books-in-waiting, all ready to be filled with your words."

- "A lot of other students are planning books about ______. Maybe you could be a writing club. We have so many experts on ______!"

- "What might you put into that book? Draw that—just a super-quick sketch to remind you."

- "Try going and sitting in the library area and see if you can think about three books on just the library. Go super-fast since you just have five more minutes."

- "Wait! You haven't yet written about art stuff? And you are our Class Artist! Go look at the art corner and get some ideas."

- "You drew a book and labeled it *kitaab*—you must be writing about the books in the library. What a great idea!"

Conferring Supports ✦ Predictable Challenges

If you notice . . .	Then you might . . .
Kids signal that nothing in the room is interesting enough to make into a book	Bring a few students on a sort of "Pied Piper Tour" of the room, acting enthralled with ordinary things. "Wait—look at this display of books. Some are so tall, and some so tiny! Fascinating how differently they are shaped." Make your enthusiasm contagious.
Kids have a title and only one picture on each cover	Say, "You can only think of *one* thing to put in your book? Here's a trick. Think about what you see" (I touched my eyes), "about your topic, what you say" (I touched my mouth), "what you do. So one page could be what you see when you look at our fish, one page could be what you say to the fish, one could be what you do with the fish (like feeding him). Try thinking, 'What do I see, say, do?' about your topic."
Kids are prematurely "done" after having written one cover	Channel them to make another cover by looking around the room and naming more things they could write about. "Remember the strategy of looking around the room with your topic wand, noticing things you see. Like . . . do you see the daily schedule? You could write a book about the daily schedule, right? That'd be fascinating."
Kids spend lots of time creating elaborate drawings, rather than quick sketches	Say, "Writers, when you are planning a book, you make super-quick sketches of things you might put into the book, but just with one color, and not every single little detail. Take just a minute to sketch what you might put into your book, because you want to spend time thinking up *lots* of books you can make."

■ RESEARCH/DECIDE

Study the student's work, noticing trends.

I pulled up next to Abby. She had a stack of booklets in her folder, with titles such as "Tables" and "Class Schedule." None of her covers included sketches.

"Wow, Abby! You've come up with tons of topics." I counted her books. "You've come up with one . . . two . . . three . . . four books you're going to write!"

"Yup!" Abby said. "I'm going to teach about the tables and about the class schedule and that the schedule shows us the order that we are going to do things on that day."

"Wow! That idea about the schedule would be a great detail to put in that book. Why don't you sketch that part in one of these picture boxes so you don't forget?"

■ TEACH

Merge complimenting and teaching in a way that helps the writer feel understood, and that teaches toward tomorrow.

BEND I FIG. 1–1 Abby's revised cover produced after the conference

"Abby, you're the kind of information writer who is so full of information that you never run out. You look around and—poof!—you've got tons of ideas. Sketching a picture or jotting a word or two to hold some of those zillions of ideas will really help you remember them when you actually write."

Show your covers from today's minilesson to reinforce your point.

"Abby, do you see how I made sketches on the cover of my book to remind myself of my ideas? You can do this too! You already started to do this with your class schedule book. Before you think about the other books you will write, think about the other things you will teach in your schedule book and sketch those ideas too."

Channel the student to try the work herself as you coach in.

"Point to each of the boxes on the cover and say what you will teach."

Abby pointed to the next box on the cover page and said, "Lunch and recess are together. We eat lunch and then go out and play in the yard." I nodded and she continued pointing to the other boxes and saying more.

"You've got it. Go ahead and finish planning this book, sketching the big things you want to teach. And remember, this is something you can do in all of your books. You can think about what you will teach and sketch your ideas! Which cover will you add to next?"

> *Since Abby only has a title on each of her covers and barely any sketches, I come to the conference with a theory that she'd benefit from sketching her subtopics. As research, I confirm my theory.*

> *Make sure that you compliment something that builds the student's identity as a writer. To do this, you might link a compliment and teaching. My teaching, here, builds on an area of strength.*

> *Having an example to show (of even just your own writing) can help solidify your teaching.*

> *Notice how I encourage the student to do the specific strategy, see that it is well within reach for her, and therefore don't persevere on this. If she needed coaching, this might have been a bit more prolonged.*

MID-WORKSHOP TEACHING ✦ Getting Topic Ideas from Friends

"Writers, my grandmother always used to say something to us kids. She'd say, 'I'm so proud of you, I'm pleased as punch.' That's how I feel right now. All over this room, I see kids thinking, 'What could I put in my book about building blocks or chairs or cubbies?' And then you are drawing little sketches on your cover in ways that show the specific things you will write about in the book. Like if you are writing about cubbies, you draw some of the stuff that is in your cubbies to remind you what to write, and you draw the whole line of cubbies too.

"Right now, will your table share ideas you have come up with for topics? Start with the person sitting closest to this door. Show one of your covers and talk about the pictures you drew to remember what you will talk about."

After the kids did this for a minute or so, I said, "I bet you have even *more* ideas for things you can write about, am I right? Your friends' ideas spark ideas in you, right? So make another cover, using an idea you got from a friend. Go!"

Q&A ✦ Teaching about Classroom Objects

Q **I'm worried that my kids won't find it interesting to write about the word wall or the math manipulatives in our classroom. Why can't they write about their favorite sports team or movie star?**

A Thanks for thinking hard about the plotline of this unit and every unit. Know, always, that you are the boss of your teaching and you can adapt this curriculum so that you can endorse it wholeheartedly. But yes, it's also important to understand the rationale for decisions in a unit. We want units to begin with more constrained and scaffolded work, then move toward more complex work and higher expectations. The writing-about-what's-underfoot at the start of Bend I both supports and places a special demand on students. It requires that students look carefully, think a lot, and push themselves to produce lots of language and information. At the same time, the plentiful information in front of them provides a level of support.

Young students are malleable. You can rally them to think it's fantastic to write about the coat rack or the fish tank by acting utterly convinced that this writing is fascinating. And remember that, in the next bend, students will write lengthier books about topics of personal interest.

Q **How can I help kids to say more about the classroom objects they see every day?**

A You'll find it helps to teach kids "kinds of things" one can notice when observing anything. You might teach them to use their senses, think about the parts and the uses for the object, or think about things that are in close proximity to their object. They can recall stories related to their object. When actually writing, kids can reach for precise words or use comparisons. It can also help to have some endlessly interesting topics in mind—the nonfiction books in the library, the kids themselves, the student teacher.

 New Partners, New Energy

Frog and Cherry Sue

Introduce students to their new partners, and channel them to share the books they might write over the next few days.

As students put the finishing touches on their covers, I set out name cards around the rug and asked the children to gather with their writing folders, find their name card, their new partner (their new number, Partner 1 or 2), and shake hands with each other.

"Writers, I know you all had really great partnerships going, and you probably are wondering why I'm suggesting new partnerships. That's a *great* question. And it is true that often in books, there are two characters that stay together, forever it seems—like Frog and Toad, Henry and Mudge, Ling and Ting, Poppleton and Cherry Sue.

"But first-graders, I have always been longing for a book that would be Poppleton and Ting. Or Frog and Cherry Sue! I think that people can learn all kinds of brand-new lessons when we partner up with different people.

"So, I have thought and thought about new partnerships that I think will be surprising ones for you, hoping the two of you end up learning some surprising things together. To become good helpers for each other, start by showing each other some of your covers and talking about what you might write."

Remind students about how to organize their writing.

After partners talked, I called them back together. "Your partnerships have changed, but the red and green dots on your folders haven't changed! What do they show?"

Kids called out that they showed whether the work was finished or not finished. Nodding, I said, "So where do your covers go now?" Soon I nodded, agreeing. "Right. Put your booklets on your 'not finished side,' the green-dot side, and they'll be waiting for you tomorrow."

BEND I FIG. 1–2 "The Art Center"

BEND I FIG. 1–3 "All About the Classroom Door"

PHONOLOGICAL AWARENESS AND PHONICS EXTENSION ✦

For this extension, show a phonological awareness video.

This first video welcomes your students to a new unit of phonological awareness work. Students begin by stretching words, isolating the medial sound and determining if it is a short-vowel sound or a long-vowel sound. Students will next read CVC and CVCe words, focusing particularly on identifying and listening for short- and long-vowel sounds. Next, the instructor leads students through dictation, where your students will segment words that end in blends, then write the word. The last activity is a round of making words. To play making words, students will first write a word, then manipulate the vowel sound, and finally record a new word.

Touching and Teaching before You Sketch, Then Write

In This Session

TODAY YOU will rally students to believe that they are the experts, the professors, on their topics as you set them up to write an entire book. You'll demonstrate how you rehearse by touching and teaching on each page, then quickly sketching across the pages. You'll channel students to rehearse the book they'll write today in the same way. You'll then send them off to write a whole book, which will qualify as the on-demand assessment for this unit. Your coaching will be minimal as kids work so you can see what they do independently. During the mid-workshop teaching, you'll remind students to write up a storm and finish a whole book. In the share, you'll invite them to reread their writing and "fix it up" before they share with a partner.

TODAY YOUR STUDENTS will write a teaching book from start to finish. First, they'll choose a topic from the covers they prepared in the previous session. They'll touch and teach across the pages during the minilesson, then sketch and write at their seats. If students finish one booklet, encourage them to start another booklet so that other kids have the time they need to write an entire book today.

Getting Ready

YOU WILL NEED . . .

- your demonstration text, "The Teacher Closet," that you made a cover for in the previous session. An example of this demonstration text can be found in the online resources.

- to add two new sticky notes to the "How to Write a Teaching Book" chart.

STUDENTS WILL NEED . . .

- their writing folders, containing topic covers from the previous session, along with something to write with.

Ensuring Access

YOUR ULTIMATE GOAL TODAY is to help all your children have success writing an entire information book. They'll touch and tell, sketch, and write. This should feel accessible to everyone. Since today serves as your on-demand assessment, you'll want to keep your coaching and teaching minimal.

- If you have some children who struggle to use invented spelling to record the words they want to write, be sure that you encourage them to stretch out words, segmenting them into component sounds. Refrain from getting into the role of saying "*Sneaker*, /sn/ /sn/ . . . which letters make the /sn/ sound?" since you'll then be doing the all-important work of breaking a word into component sounds for the child. Remember that your goal today is to collect data, so, if you have students who are having difficulty doing this, take note so you can provide more directed teaching on future days.

- Prior to giving the on-demand assessment, review your students' IEPs for testing accommodations. Those same accommodations apply here. It's important to establish consistent testing routines with these students to help them learn how to use their accommodations well.

- Channel students who are still acquiring English to point to things in their pictures and say what those things are. Go ahead and supply words if a child needs that. If the child is speaking in one- or two-word labels, repeat those words, and add to them: "Yes! These are sneakers. They are blue sneakers, aren't they? These are laces." If the child is not speaking at all, you might name out what you see in their picture. The student may need more language input from you first.

Minilesson 

Touching and Teaching before You Sketch, Then Write

CONNECTION

Announce that kids will have the chance to write one of their planned books. Do a symphony share to celebrate topics.

"Bring your writing folders and come join me," I said, and after most children had settled, I began. "You've learned to get topics in a jiffy, haven't you? Right now, will you go through your pile of covers and decide on the one you want to write first? Put that booklet on the top of your folder." The kids sifted through their booklets and settled on one. "I can't wait to hear these topics! When I signal to you, say your topic, loud and proud. Our classroom will be full of the sounds of your beautiful topics."

I gestured one at a time to about half of the class. As I pointed, each child named out their topic.

"Writers, the way you said your topic, loud and proud, was very writerly. And that's important because you can't write a teaching book if you act like this." I opened to the first page, threw my hands up, and in my whiniest voice, squeaked, "'Oh no, oh no, I don't know what to say. Help me, help me, I'm so stuck! What do I say, what do I say?'

"Nonfiction books are teaching books, and it takes *chutzpah* (khŏŏt-spə) to teach. Do you know what *chutzpah* is? It is a beautiful Yiddish word that means courage. It means that you can talk, loud and proud, and you can write that way too."

◆ **Name the teaching point.**

"Today I want to teach you that when you write an expert book, you need to remember that *you are the expert*. You become Professor of Trash Cans, or Captain of the Block Area, or Leader of the Water Fountain. You touch and teach, touch and teach, touch and teach, across your whole booklet. Then you are ready to sketch and write."

TEACHING

Convey respect for the local experts in children's own lives and invite kids to role-play being Professors of the Coat Closet, or of whatever topic they choose.

"So writers, if you want to write a teaching book, you can't come at that project like this: 'Who me? Write something? Me? No way!' To write a teaching book, you have to step into the role of being an expert, a professor, teaching all the little kids. You may know someone in your community who's a professor of sorts. Maybe it's your abuela, or your big brother. To write an information book, *you* need to become an expert.

"Can you imagine the person in your life who acts like an expert? Think of how that person looks when she or he teaches. Does that person sometimes use a teaching voice, and sometimes even a teaching finger, to teach? You are going to discover your teaching voice, your teaching finger."

Demonstrate the way you first touch the pages and teach your topic before sketching and writing the book.

I pulled out my booklet about my teacher closet. "So, watch me sit up and act like a professor of my teacher closet. Hmm, . . . what am I going to teach?" I looked at my cover to get ideas from the pictures, then nodded. I cleared my throat, raised a teaching finger, and then

One of the qualities of good writing that matters most is voice. Ideally, the voice of the author shines through in a text.

Note that I'm just dictating these pages. Nothing has been written out yet. You definitely do not want to do this amount of writing while kids sit and watch and wiggle.

turned to the first blank page, touched it, and began, turning the blank pages as I dictated what I would later write:

[Page 1] My teacher closet is full of private stuff. Kids are not allowed in it.

[Page 2] My teacher closet has a hook for my coat. There's a mirror for me to check if I look okay. I keep things in my closet in case I need to fancy myself up when we have a publishing celebration or special visitors.

[Page 3] There are bags of secret stuff in my teacher closet. I'll give you a hint: some of it is tasty.

[Page 4] It's too bad every kid doesn't have a Kid Closet in school. I hope backpacks and cubbies are just as good!

"Writers, now that I have touched each page and taught what will go there, I'm ready to sketch and write the words." I started sketching the first page, super-quickly, then turned to sketch the second, but paused to continue the minilesson.

ACTIVE ENGAGEMENT

Channel students to step into the role of professor and to touch and teach as a way to rehearse the book they'll write today.

"Writers, now that you've decided which book you're going to write first, it's time to plan what to teach about your topic. Look at your cover to help you think about what you'll teach."

After a moment of silence, I said, "Now, get ready to write by touching and teaching across the pages. Use a teaching voice and your teaching finger to teach about your topic, and that way, you can all get practice saying your book aloud. You ready? Start with your title—touch and teach that, then move to the next page."

Each child will practice saying aloud his or her book at the same time. Often, we feel obligated to give kids an audience for their rehearsal, but the truth is that in life, writers often say their writing to themselves without an audience.

LINK

Set students up to sketch and whisper-write the first pages of their books. Then send them off to their writing spots to write.

"Writers, are you ready to write? Yes? Can you show me your pen?" I lifted up my pointer finger to show that I meant for fingers to be pens. "Open your book to page 1." I waited. "Now, use your pen to sketch your picture, then whisper-write your words for page 1." I gave the kids a few moments to get started, then said in a stage-whisper, "When you finish that page, turn the page, and use your pen to sketch and write your second page. If you need a reminder of what goes on each page, look back at your cover and check your sketches. Go!"

After a minute, I said, "How about you go off to write? Off you go—and I'll add to our chart so that we can remember to touch and teach on every page before we sketch and write."

I added two new sticky notes to the "How to Write a Teaching Book" anchor chart.

BEND 1

Try a "Silent Sweep" as Writers Leave the Meeting Area

Move around the room, using gestures and your presence near children to get them started. You might give a thumbs up to some who have gotten started, shrug dramatically for students who aren't yet sketching, tap the paper of a student who isn't writing yet.

Add Teacher Talk as Necessary

If gestures aren't enough, voice over with quick compliments and reminders that name the behaviors you'd like to see.

- "I notice you are getting right to your writing!"
- "So many people already have a book out. Some of you have started to touch each page and say what you'll write."
- "Remember: put what you want to teach first on your first page!"

If Kids Keep Asking for Help

- "If you are stuck—just give it a try! You can do it!"
- "If you are not sure what to do, remember everything that you already know about writing, and try your best!"
- "If you forget what you wanted to say, the picture can remind you. Study your picture, and you'll remember."
- "If you aren't totally sure of an English word that you want to write, you can add it in later. Keep writing and drawing as much as you can!"

To Keep Kids Working Productively during Writing Time

- "Look at all of those labels!"
- "Your writing is full of details. Your readers will really be able to learn about your topic!"
- "After you write one expert book, you can write another one! Pick the booklet from your folder that you want to write next. Then, get started writing."

MID-WORKSHOP TEACHING ✦ Channel Students to Complete Entire Books

"Writers, you have fifteen more minutes, and the hope for today is that you really truly do write a *whole book*. So shake your hands out as a way to rest them up, then put those hands and minds back to work! Write up a storm. Aim to not only get to the end of your book, but to fill up all of your pages with lots of information. Today just might be the day you write the most you've ever written!"

ASSESSMENT TOOL ✦ Writing an Information On-Demand

Today is meant as an assessment of writing. We suggest you observe and collect data on your students, using a data collection grid like the one below.

	Getting Started	Drawing	Writing Stamina	Writing Fluency	Revision and Editing	Using Resources
★	Writer has difficulty getting started.	Writer doesn't draw at all, or their drawings are not representational.	Writer sustains writing/drawing for only a short time.	Drawing and/or letter formation appears strenuous. Child pauses after each individual letter.	Writer does not reread or return to writing.	Writer does not yet use the tools around the room.
STUDENTS	______ ______	______ ______	______ ______	______ ______	______ ______	______ ______
★★	Writer takes time to get into writing but eventually works with independence.	Writer draws using bare-bones representational drawings. Writer may (or may not) draw across all the pages.	Writer sustains writing and drawing for only 10–15 minutes.	Writer writes and then pauses after every few words.	Writer rereads and makes small changes. Writer attempts to make writing readable.	Writer rarely uses a chart or tool (e.g., looks at the word wall once or twice).
STUDENTS	______ ______	______ ______	______ ______	______ ______	______ ______	______ ______
★★★	Writer gets started right away—either sketching, writing, or planning.	Writer makes elaborate drawings across pages that teach about a topic. Drawings include details, labels, or arrows.	Writer sustains writing and drawing for over fifteen minutes.	Writer writes fluently and continuously, stopping at the ends of sentences.	Writer rereads and makes big revisions. Writer does intentional edits to make writing more readable.	Writer uses different charts or tools in the room (e.g., the word wall, the anchor chart, and the writing center) throughout the writing workshop.
STUDENTS	______ ______	______ ______	______ ______	______ ______	______ ______	______ ______

STUDENT WORK ✦ On-Demand Strengths and Next Steps

As you study student work today, you'll want to notice individual students' strengths and needs to plan for future teaching. See Jordan's strengths and needs chart below.

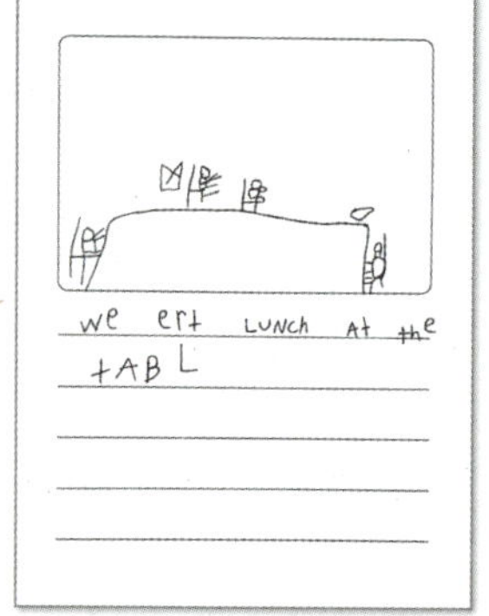

We eat lunch at the table.

We do writing at the table.

We read at the table.

We do math at the table.

BEND I FIG. 2–1 Jordan's book about the table 

Jordan's Strengths	Jordan's Next Steps
Jordan's topic is a wonderful one—so much happens at a table, and she's captured many of these activities in her list.	Jordan could write about other places in the classroom, creating a whole series of books about places in the classroom where life happens. Will she write about the meeting area, or the math corner?
Jordan's book is structured. Each subtopic has its own page.	Jordan could easily tell more on each page. She could use "For example, we . . ." and tell a detail.
Jordan shows a lot of consistency and accuracy in spelling high-frequency words: *we*, *do*, *at*, and *the* are consistently spelled correctly.	Some spelling next steps for this student: vowel teams (*ert* for *eat*, *red* for *read*), beginning blends (*witing* for *writing*), and silent *e* (*tabl* for *table*).
Jordan spaces words correctly, showing an understanding of the concept of a word.	Jordan's book lacks punctuation, and she uses capital letters throughout words and sentences. Sentences begin with lowercase letters.

 Writers Work Hard to Fix Up Their Writing

Channel students to reread their writing and "fix it up" to get ready to share it with partners. Then set partners up to respond to each other's writing.

"Writers, stop, look, and listen!" I waited until I had everybody's attention: "In a minute, you'll give your writing to your partner to read. But first, will you reread your writing and do any quick little fix-ups it needs? If you left out a word or things don't make sense, don't go, 'Oh well!' and just let it go. No! Fix it up. If you are trying to write a long tricky word, clap it out, then say just the first syllable and write that part, then say the next syllable . . . In that way, you tackle your hard words, part by part. Do that rereading and checking now.

"Ready to share? I know you have new partners and are doing new writing, but you'll still work with partners in the same way you did when writing Small Moment stories. Sit next to your partner and put a book in the middle. Can everybody scoot next to your partner and set yourself up?"

Once students were sitting with their partners with a book in the middle, I continued. "Now the writer will give a little book introduction, just like you did when you wrote stories. Since we're writing information now, you might tell your partner things like, 'My book is about the block area,' or 'Here is a book about the water fountain.'"

I gave students a moment to introduce their books. "Now get to reading, and listening partners, make sure that you respond with interest. Say 'Wow!' or 'Huh?' or ask questions." I collected students' books when they were done sharing.

PHONOLOGICAL AWARENESS AND PHONICS EXTENSION ✦

For this extension, show a phonological awareness video. 

The video revisits many of the same activities from the previous video. The video begins by asking students to stretch words and isolate the medial sound, focusing in particular on the short and long *E* and *U* vowel sounds. Students will then move on to reading CVC words and CVCe words and changing the vowel from the short to long sound. Next, the instructor leads students through dictation, where your students will segment words that end in blends, then write the word. The last activity is a round of making words, where your students will write a word, then add or delete a sound, and record the new word.

Predicting What Your Reader Will Want to Learn

In This Session

TODAY YOU will teach kids to elaborate right from the start by imagining what their readers would want to learn. To encourage them to do this, you'll show them that they can make their hands into little puppets that prompt them to add more and more information. In the mid-workshop teaching, you'll set partners up to ask questions of each other's writing, as another way to elaborate and add more. In the share, you'll demonstrate how you add "wow" facts to each page of your writing, and channel students to work in partnerships to do the same.

TODAY YOUR STUDENTS will practice teaching more by conversing about their topics with an imaginary hand-friend. Because the books students wrote in Session 2 will have been collected to serve as their on-demand writing, all students will write a new information book today, choosing from one of the booklets with covers containing subtopics. Students will work with their partners during the mid-workshop teaching, giving thumbs up for specific information their partner has included and asking questions to help their partner add more. In the share, students will reread a partner's book, helping that partner add interesting information to each page.

Getting Ready

YOU WILL NEED . . .

■ the "All About Playgrounds" book, or another example of a bare-bones information book.

■ your "All About the Trash Can" demonstration text from Session 1, with the cover prepared. You'll plan this book aloud in the minilesson, but you'll need the first page written before the share. You'll need to write the rest outside of writing class before the next session.

■ to add a sticky note to the "How to Write a Teaching Book" chart during the minilesson, with a replacement sticky note ready to be added in the share.

STUDENTS WILL NEED . . .

■ to choose a booklet to write from their writing folder.

Ensuring Access

YOUR ULTIMATE GOAL TODAY is to encourage students to teach as much as possible on every page. Kids can access this work in many ways.

■ Writers who are more emergent can say more through drawing in addition to writing. Also, remember that these students can sometimes talk more than they can write, so encourage volume and sophistication of their spoken language.

■ This session is chock-full, which makes it a lively and interesting session for some students but could make it feel overwhelming for others. Notice that there are lots of bits of cuteness that are expendable or adaptable. For example, we chose to teach kids to talk about their topic to a make-believe person, created out of each child's fist (we model with a fist turned into a person named Sasha). That fun twist could obviously confuse some youngsters, so you may want to tell those children about this at an earlier time.

■ This session relies heavily on questioning and answering, which is a sophisticated language skill. Encourage particularly talkative partners to support MLLs' oral language by starting a sentence for their partner.

Predicting What Your Reader Will Want to Learn

CONNECTION

Set students up to write a new book.

As children convened, I said, "Check that you remembered to bring your folders—always bring your precious writing to the rug!"

Once children had settled, I said, "Last night I brought home all of the books you wrote yesterday and holy moly, I learned a lot from you! I'm making copies of those books so I can save them forever and I'll return them to your folders soon, I promise. But meanwhile, each of you will write a new book today, so pull a booklet out of your folder, one with a cover that you made earlier. For a second, will you touch the pages of your blank booklet and teach aloud what you *might* write on those pages? Do that quietly."

Share a "book" that someone gave you that contains little but hot air. Convey your disappointment. Rally students to write with information.

"Writers, our principal gave me a new book teaching all about the playground. This could be a great book if we have new kids come to our school, right? I was thinking we could read it together." I displayed and read the book, with increasing despondency, as it said very little.

[Page 1] Playgrounds are great.

[Page 2] Playgrounds have stuff.

[Page 3] Playgrounds are the best.

"Hmm, . . . there's not much here." I reread the book, even more dubiously. Then I put it down, shaking my head. "This book reminds me of a box of candy I got once. It was a big huge box. Then I opened the lid . . . and the box was mostly empty. That huge elaborate box held almost no candy. I was so disappointed, I thought, 'What a bummer!'

"You know what? Sometimes, I read books that are supposed to be information books and I think, 'What a bummer! There's almost no information!' It's just words like 'playgrounds are great, playgrounds have stuff.' And I haven't actually learned anything about playgrounds!"

✦ **Name the teaching point.**

"Today I want to teach you that writers of information books don't want their books to be bummers. To make sure their books aren't bummers, writers teach *a lot* on every page. To think of more to say and write, writers might get people to ask them questions. They might also imagine what readers would want to learn."

TEACHING

Pretend to teach an imaginary friend, using your hand to bring this friend to life. Say words you later write. Dramatize finishing the book prematurely.

"Today I want to be sure you know that you can ask a friend, or a writing partner, to hear your ideas for what you'll say across the pages of your book, and your friend can ask you questions that get you to say more. You can also pretend to be your own readers and ask the questions you think readers might ask—what they might want to learn. Let me show you.

As you show this "nonexample" of an information book, make sure to focus on the lack of interesting information in the book rather than its simplicity and/or length. Some of your MLLs might be proudly writing very short and simple sentences or phrases.

"I'm going to teach my pretend friend about my topic before I even start writing." I held up my "All About the Trash Can" book with one hand, and with my other hand, I tucked my thumb into the fold of my first finger, to make a little hand puppet. "Here she is! Her name is . . . uh . . . Sasha!" I turned my hand (now a puppet) toward my face and said. "Sasha, may I teach you about . . . the trash can?" Sasha—my fist—nodded a vigorous yes.

"Okay, let me take another look at the cover for a reminder of the different parts of my topic that I'm going to teach about." I intensely studied the cover of my booklet, then flipped to the first blank page. I touched it and then started to dictate (writing-in-the-air):

> Kids, teachers, and visitors all put things in the trash can.

I flipped to the second page and thought aloud:

> People throw away things like lined paper and drippy old food.

"I guess—the end!" I closed the booklet and looked thoroughly done.

Allow your imaginary friend to coax you into saying more. Say aloud the next few pages you could write.

I looked down at Sasha (my fist) who moved in a fashion that signaled she wanted to hear more. "Wait a minute. Sasha wants to hear more. She's right! I don't want my book to be a bummer. Hmm, . . . What else can I teach Sasha about the trash can that she might want to learn?" I thought for a moment. Sasha knocked on my head, as if signaling, "Think, think." I did, and acted as if a light bulb turned on. "Ooooohhhh, I know! Let me look back at my sketches on the cover and see if that gives me any ideas." I flipped back to the cover page. I pointed at each item in my sketch as I thought aloud. "Oh, apple cores and juice boxes, gross! I also remember seeing a lot of half-eaten sandwiches. All those things end up in the trash can. So maybe this second page could say:"

> People throw away things like lined paper and drippy old food. There are apple cores, old juice boxes, and half-eaten sandwiches.

Sasha prompted me to keep going. "More, Sasha? You want me to teach more? Let me go to a different part." I flipped to the next page and thought aloud.

> [Page 3] When the trash can gets really full, you can squish things down and fit more in it.

> [Page 4] I don't know how our trash in our class gets dumped. In *my* house, I sometimes take a big bag to all our trash cans and dump all the trash into one big bag. I don't know who does that in our school.

"Wow. I thought of a lot to say in this book. Now it definitely won't be a bummer. Next I have to write it. I'll do that later on."

Debrief in a way that helps the kids learn a strategy that will help them another day with another topic.

"Writers, when you write a nonfiction book, you don't want it to be a bummer. Sometimes, after you write a page or two, you think, 'I don't have anything else to say. I'm done.' You can pretend your readers are near you as you write. You can think about what *they* would want to know and push yourself to teach more for them. Readers are hungry to learn, learn, learn, and if you *think*, you can come up with more to say."

I added a new sticky note to the "How to Write a Teaching Book" anchor chart.

Note that you are simply saying aloud the book, although after the minilesson, it would be good to have this version in print. You'll at least want to jot down page 1 prior to today's share.

You'll return to the book that you began during Session 1, and you'll reference the prepared cover as you teach this session.

ACTIVE ENGAGEMENT

Channel students to rehearse their books by reminding themselves of the topic they chose yesterday, then teaching that topic to an imaginary friend.

"Are you ready to try this? Right now, read your title, then open your booklet to page one, and make yourself an imaginary friend." I held up my Sasha-friend to remind them how to make a fist-friend. "Tuck your thumb into the fold of your fingers. That makes your friend's face and mouth! If you look with imagination, you can see eyes right under your knuckles. Tell someone the name of your friend.

"Now, whisper-write your book in the air, teaching your friend all that you can about your topic. Think about all your imaginary friend might want to learn from you. Get started! Remember to teach your imaginary friend as much as possible!"

LINK

Send students off, reminding them that the important work for the day is not to just teach a lot of information, but also to write a lot of information.

"I just saw tons of whisper-writing! Here's the thing, though: whisper-writing is something that writers do to get ready to write, but now is the time that you're going to go off and start filling your books with real, not just whispered, writing!

"You've taught so much, though, that you'll probably fill up pages and pages today. Your words are ready to be put down on the page. Off you go!"

Remember that forming questions and their answers in a second language is much more challenging than using declarative sentences. Consider channeling MLLs to tell more information by using sentence frames such as "I know that . . ."

Possible Coaching Moves:

- *"Make your friend say, 'Come on, come on. I want to hear more.'"*
- *"Make your friend tell you to think!"*
- *"Make your friend say, 'Tell me everything you see.'"*
- *"Tell more! Don't stop talking! Your imaginary friend wants to learn."*

CONFERRING SUPPORTS ✦ Starting a Second Book

If you notice . . .	Then . . .
Writers write stories or some other type of piece, not information writing	• Say, "Hmm, . . . that's a lovely small moment. Remember that our class is writing *information books* right now. Why don't you put this wonderful small moment aside for now, and you can work on it later? Here's a brand-new booklet to use to write an information book." You might have the student plan and rehearse their book with you. • It might be possible to prompt them to turn their story into an information book: "Wow! I'm so fascinated by your story about playing on the playground. Do you think you could write an information book teaching about the playground? What might you teach on the first page?" • Show an example of information writing. "Let's look at this information book. We can notice how it sounds because information books are different from stories, and you have a story there."
Writers write their entire book on one page, rather than across pages	• "Oh my goodness, it looks like everything you know about the math center is jammed onto just the first page. Can we think about how to take all of that information and spread it out across all the pages of your book?" • "Next time when you start a book, will you come to me? I want to show you how you can plan your book so it goes across all the pages."
Writers spend a brief amount of time on each page, drawing something quickly, writing just a sentence, and then moving on	• Remind them that to get more writing, it helps to go back to the picture and draw some more, then write some more. Have students look at their pictures and think, "What else could I add?" • Try changing their paper choice. Paper choice conveys expectations, and giving more lines and space to fill communicates to students that they should write more.
Writers tackle gigantic topics (for example, "All About First Grade" or "Students in the Classroom")	• Coach them to focus their writing. A child writing "All About First Grade" might instead make one book about Choice Time, one book about reading workshop, one book about math workshop, and so on. • Say, "Wow! You have so much to teach about your topic. I bet you could write a bunch of books about the different parts of this topic. What books could you write? Look at your cover for ideas." Then, pull out a few new booklets. "Yes, that could be its own book. Jot that down on a new cover so you remember."
Writers are unsure of the English words to add information about their topic	• Encourage them to add more to their pictures, then touch and tell what they can. You can teach two or three explicit vocabulary words that might help their piece by extending what they are saying. Say something like, "Yes! The coat rack is big. I see a lot of *hooks* there too—can you try to write that?" • Use the classroom as concrete vocabulary support: when you teach a word, point to the actual object and have the writer say the word.

MID-WORKSHOP TEACHING ✦ Listening Partners Ask Questions

"Writers, eyes up here." I waited. "Writers, today you learned that you can write more by imagining your reader and thinking about what they will want to know. Another way to write more is to get your friends, who are right here, to ask you questions.

"Partner 1, read your book aloud to Partner 2, and Partner 2, will you be the listening partner? Listening partners, give a thumbs up every time you learn some specific information. If your partner's book doesn't yet have much information, you know your job. Ask questions that help the writer add more information. You can start by asking 'who?' 'where?' 'when?' 'why?' 'how?' questions.

"I'm not going to suggest that Partner 2 shares writing—not today. For now, though, this means that Partner 2, a lot is being expected of you. Today, help Partner 1—and then . . . and this is really important in life . . . later, help yourself."

CONFERENCE ✦ Transitioning to Information Books

◼ RESEARCH/DECIDE

Celebrate the writer's strengths.

Emma told me that she'd written a story about a time the class went on a field trip to the history museum. "Wow! It sounds like you've chosen a topic you know a lot about, which is one of the things expert writers do. You even included some special words that teach about your topic like *permission slip* and *Museum of Natural History*."

Emma responded, "I love field trips."

Sometimes, I immediately notice an important need. In this case, I notice Emma wrote a story, not a teaching book. Rather than researching more, I move right to my compliment and teaching point.

◼ TEACH/LINK

Suggest a way the writer can strengthen her writing. Set her up to teach orally.

"Can I give you a tip for how you can become a stronger writer of teaching books?" Emma nodded. "This sounds more like a Small Moment story than a book that *teaches* about field trips. You could take this topic—it is one you know and care a lot about—and write a teaching book about it.

"Pretend to be my teacher, and I'll be your student. Teach me about the Museum of Natural History."

Emma was quiet, so I asked, "What about it? Tell me the interesting part, right?"

Emma launched in. "Well there were a lot of glass cases, they were the size of rooms, that had animals that were dead but stuffed and standing up. It showed the bugs crawling near them and the trees around them."

I nodded. "It sounds like they were lifelike, is that true? And the cases showed where they live?" Emma nodded. "Can you give an example?" I asked, and Emma explained about the polar bears in an Arctic scene.

Whenever possible, I link my compliment to the tip I'm going to teach. In this instance, I help Emma see how she can use what she already created to start a new book in the correct genre.

With an entire class of students, there isn't time to sit next to the student as she writes her book. Instead, I get her orally rehearsing how her new piece might go. I listen in and provide feedback.

Channel the student to work.

I handed Emma a blank booklet. "When you want to make big changes, it is usually easier to start a new book. Touch and teach each page, then sketch and write!"

Sometimes I give more choice in the link. Here, I set Emma up with exactly what she should do next.

If you notice . . .	The next step might be . . .	And you could say . . .
A student with no labels or words on the page, or strings of letters	To begin saying words slowly and recording the sounds that they hear. Students will probably start with a beginning sound, move to an ending sound, and only then move toward including middle sounds. Celebrate the steps!	• "Can you say that word slug sl-ooow—ly?" (Avoid the temptation to stretch words out for the child. If the child cannot stretch words out, teach that!) • "Say that word slowly. What is the first sound? Write that down. Now reread what you wrote and keep going." • "Say the first (or last, or middle . . .) sound again. Find the letter that goes with that on your alphabet chart."
A student whose writing includes salient consonants, but is missing vowels	To incorporate vowels into their writing. Fluency with vowels takes a long time, so you aim to see students "using and confusing" vowels.	• "Every word that you write needs a vowel. Check to make sure that there's a vowel in every word!" • "Say that word slowly again. Make sure you put down a letter for each sound. You are missing some letters here." • "Keep your vowel chart near you as you write and make sure you use it to help you decide which vowel to use."
A student who represents digraphs or blends with one letter only	To listen for, and then begin recording, blends and digraphs.	• "Say the word again and listen for that beginning sound. Check your blends and digraphs chart. What goes there?" • For blends: "You wrote the first sound. I hear another sound when I say the word slowly. Say the word again. What else do you hear? Add it." • For digraphs: "Hmm, . . . you wrote an *S* there. I don't hear /s/. I hear /sh/. How do you show the /sh/ sound?"
A student who leaves off word endings	To listen through to the ends of words and make sure to include those endings in their writing.	• "Check the ending." • "Say the word and listen to the *whole* word. Push all the way through to the end!"
A student who misrepresents the CVCe spelling pattern	To work toward a more accurate representation of the CVCe spelling pattern, using known words that contain the same pattern.	• "You are spelling by sound and that is how you came up with *cak* for *cake*. Think, 'What other words do you already know that have the same word part, *ake*?' Use those words to help you."

 On Every Page, Add Information that Wows Readers

Explain that writers want to wow their readers on every page. Demonstrate by doing this with your book on trash cans.

"There's one thing I have been working on that you'll want to work on too. I'm trying to make my book *really interesting*. I want my readers to say, 'Wow! I didn't know that!'

"So, when I reread, I ask, 'What on this page will wow my readers?' If there's nothing there, I squeeze my mind and come up with something interesting to put on that page. Let me show you what I mean." I opened to the first page of my trash can book, and read it aloud:

> Lots of things go into a trash can at school. Kids, teachers, and visitors all put things in the trash can.

I shook my head, disappointed. "There is nothing on that page that will make anyone say 'Wow!' So kids, help me think what I could add. Hmm, . . . how about this?" I dictated:

> People make so much trash that we have three trash cans. The cafeteria has ten trash cans!

I turned to the students and said, "Doesn't that make you say 'Wow!'?"

"So, writers, will you try this with your partner? Partner 2, read your book to Partner 1, and Partner 1, be honest with your partner. Is there something on that page that makes you say, 'Wow!'? On the next page? If you find a page with nothing interesting yet, then squeeze your minds together, and think, 'What could we add here to make this page more interesting?'" I replaced the fourth sticky note on our "How to Write a Teaching Book" anchor chart to include this new strategy.

PHONOLOGICAL AWARENESS AND PHONICS EXTENSION ✦
Sorting by Short- and Long-Vowel Sounds

For this extension, you'll need a copy of the vowel chart and short- and long-vowel picture cards.

Engage students in a picture sort to help them isolate the vowels in a set of words, and identify whether those vowels are short or long.

"Friends, you've been working really hard at listening for vowels in the middle of words. You've also been working hard to think about whether the vowels that you hear are short or long. We're going to practice that today, but let's quickly warm up by reading our vowel chart. Let's make sure we read the short-vowel sounds and the long-vowel sounds!"

Once we'd finished reading the chart, I continued, "Now, I have some pictures here. I'm going to hold up a picture and say what it is. Your job is going to be to say the word slowly after me, then say the vowel sound, and think about whether you hear a short vowel or a long vowel. Then point on the chart to show whether the vowel is short or long."

I held up a set of pictures one at a time. Students repeated each word after me, then isolated the vowel sound and pointed to the chart to show whether the vowel was short or long. Soon, we'd sorted all of the pictures into a pocket chart.

Short Vowels	Long Vowels
crab	say
apple	stage
rat	rake
rash	plane
mask	game
crack	maze
flag	gate
tag	snake

Researchers Look Closely to Discover and Add Details

In This Session

TODAY YOU will teach students that information writers explore, research, and investigate to learn more, and therefore teach more. One way they do this is by looking closely at their topics, seeing little things that others might not even notice. You'll look closely at the trash can, noticing the tiniest details and then channel students to do the same work in their mind with their topics. In the mid-workshop teaching, you'll rally kids to see and think more through "writers' eyes" as you invite them to study their hands closely, and then their topics. In the share, you'll emphasize the importance of adding details to your writing for your readers and invite partnerships to notice where they've tried this.

TODAY YOUR STUDENTS will decide which information book they want to write next and will write that book, making sure to include visual details. You'll help students know that they don't actually need to observe their subjects up close; they can create a mental image of their subject and study that picture, zooming in on the details. Expect your students to write about a book a day or every other day, depending on how detailed their writing is.

Getting Ready

YOU WILL NEED . . .

- the "How to Write a Teaching Book" chart, with a replacement sticky note ready to be added. 

- your demonstration text, "All About the Trash Can," ready to add to the third page. An example of the revised demonstration text from this session can be found in the online resources.

- the "Ways to Start an Information Book" chart.

STUDENTS WILL NEED . . .

- blank booklets, if they are starting a new topic.

Ensuring Access

YOUR ULTIMATE GOAL TODAY is to rally kids to write a new information book, or to finish the one they started in the previous session, writing with more details as they closely observe their topic. This work is multilevel and has scope enough to be challenging yet doable for all your writers.

- In the link, you introduce several sentence stems students can use to begin their books. These are presented briefly and without much support, so don't expect that most students will pick up on that teaching today. These sentence stems can be helpful, so revisit them with small groups of children who could benefit. You'll return to beginnings in more depth in Bend II.

- For your MLLs, remember to teach vocabulary related to the content they have chosen to write about. When introducing learners to a new word, encourage them to do lots with it: say the word in another language, see if it sounds similar to the English word, use the word repeatedly in a sentence, study the way it is spelled, chunk the word, and try spelling it independently. Encourage them to include the word in their writing.

- You may find some kids, especially MLLs, can use help with high-frequency words that will be dominant in this unit. Children will be doing a lot of observation; expect them to need prepositions (without knowing the term) such as *under*, *over*, *near*, *beside*, *inside*, *around*. You might gather a small group and teach into some of those words, getting kids to move objects or their bodies to match each preposition. You'll also want to model the accurate use of these words as you study kids' writing, perhaps saying, "Oh, the snake lives *inside* the tank. The snake slithers *around* the rocks. The tank is *near* the snake food."

Researchers Look Closely to Discover and Add Details

CONNECTION

Channel writers to choose a new book to write and place it on their folder. Tell students that they have new work to do to become stronger information writers.

Once children had gathered with their folders, I began. "Writers, will you look through your folder and decide which teaching book you'll write today? Put that book on top of your folder and sit on the whole thing—that way you'll be ready to grab it when it's time. If you don't have any books in your folder with covers already made, I'll give you a fresh book to start today." I handed out booklets to the students who needed them.

"Okay, first-graders. Wait, I mean writers. Hold on, I mean teachers. Oh my, you are many things, aren't you? You're doing so much information writing, and wearing so many hats, that I don't even know what to call you anymore! Now that you're getting so good at writing information books and wearing so many hats, I think it's time for me to tell you another secret about nonfiction writing: to be really great at nonfiction writing, you don't just write down the information that you already have in your back pocket."

✦ **Name the teaching point.**

"Today I want to teach you that to write books that teach people things, you need to become someone who investigates, who explores, who researches. You need to look *really* closely at your topic, seeing little things that others might not even notice. By looking closely, you can discover all sorts of interesting things to teach."

I replaced the fourth sticky note on our "How to Write a Teaching Book" anchor chart to include this new strategy.

TEACHING

Help students to gather up their "research kit," telling them about the things they'll need to do this important work.

"Today, then, you become not just a writer, not just a teacher, but . . ." I paused and did a drumroll on my lap . . . "a researcher! And researchers need a few special things. Let's gather those things." I whispered to the students, "Don't worry! We won't have any trouble finding them!

"The first thing you'll need is . . . your eyes!" I pointed to my eyes, and a few students did the same thing. "You'll need your eyes to help you look really closely and carefully." I next held up my hands, wiggling my fingers a bit. "You'll need your hands . . . to hold things up and study them carefully." I tapped my head. "And you'll need that big powerful brain of yours to think about what you're seeing and how you're going to tell your readers about it." I took a deep breath and paused. "Do you have any of those things? I thought so! Now you're ready to research."

As you go through today's minilesson, regularly repeat the word researcher *with a consistent gesture, like holding up a magnifying glass to study something. Slip in quick explanations like "someone who studies things closely" to make it stick.*

Explain that looking closely allows you to add details to your writing. Demonstrate how you examine the trash can to get details to add to your teaching book.

"When you look that closely at your topic, you can see even more details that you can add to your writing. I'm going to look *really* closely to see more details about the trash can so that I can teach my readers more!" I opened to the third page of my book, and read it aloud:

When the trash can gets really full, you can squish things down and fit more in it.

"What can I add here?" I pulled the trash can closer and looked inside. "Hmm, . . . I can say that our trash can is black . . . but no. That's not a *detail*. That's a big obvious thing. Let me look more closely to see details that others might not notice." Holding my nose, I peered into the trash can. "There is some paper in there, sandwich baggies, marker tops, oh, and some food too. Yuck! When I put my hand in there to squeeze the trash down, I'd want to avoid touching those banana peels and apple cores, gross! Maybe I should add that to my writing." I picked up my marker and quickly added to my writing.

When the trash can gets really full, you can squish things down and fit more in it. Be careful! If your trash can has food in it, like banana peels and apple cores, you want to try not to touch those when you are squishing the garbage down. Yuck!

Debrief, emphasizing that students can do this all the time, with any topic.

"Did you see how I looked *really* closely at what I was writing about, seeing little details that others might not notice? By looking closely, you can discover all sorts of interesting things to teach."

When the trash can gets really full, you can squish things down and fit more in it. Be careful! If your trash can has food in it, like banana peels and apple cores, you want to try not to touch those when you are squishing the garbage down. Yuck!

ACTIVE ENGAGEMENT

Channel students to think of the thing they are writing about, and imagine looking at it closely. Then, set them up to teach a partner.

"Okay, researchers, writers . . . I think I should just call you all of those things. Get your teaching book out from under you. Now, imagine you are looking at whatever you are writing about—you're looking *really* closely and noticing little details. In your mind, do that looking. What do you see?"

I gave students a minute to think. "Now, turn to your partner, touch a page in your book, and teach all you can about the little details you just noticed!"

LINK

Share a few sentence starters that help kids write strong beginnings.

"Put a thumb on your knee when you're ready to go off and start adding those details to a book you already wrote or writing a new book that includes these details." Many signaled.

"In case it is hard for you to start a new book, I'm going to share a bunch of beginnings that people use for information books, just to help you get started quickly." I displayed the "Ways to Start an Information Book" chart. Once kids began to write, I sent them off to their work spots.

CONFERRING SUPPORTS ✦ Adding More in Pictures and Words

If you notice . . .	Set a goal, say . . .	Leave a resource . . .
Writers with pictures, who are able to talk about information, but who don't have any writing	"Make sure to add some words to your picture. That'll teach your reader more!" "Touch your picture, say the word slowly, then write the word."	Add labels! table top leg chair
Writers with pictures that lack details	"Your picture can teach your reader too. Think, 'What else can this picture show?' Add it!" "Did you include everything about your object in the picture? What about the _____ and the _____? Check your object, then add what you're missing!"	Draw more — show details.
Writers with lots of information in the pictures, but not in the words	"You know, I'm seeing _____ and _____ in the picture, but you didn't write about those things in the words. It looks like you are all set to add information to the words, am I right?"	Study the picture say more add words!
Writers with some information and some elaboration, but who could do more	"There are still some empty lines here. It's important to push yourself to fill as much of the space as possible. What else can you add?" "Let's see what else you can teach. Reread and see what you can add!"	Reread + think. What else can I add?
Writers who've elaborated a bit, but who haven't included any sensory details	"Are you wondering what else you can say to help people picture your topic? One thing that helps me is to think, 'Would it help to tell what this looks like? Feels like? Smells like? Sounds like?'"	Think! What do I... hear see feel smell

"First-graders, did you know that you can see everything in the world with a writer's eyes? One author, Katherine Paterson, said that if you're a writer, you're the type of person who pulls close and watches while a bug sheds its skin, spreads its wings, and then tumbles off a branch like an acrobat. You know what? *You* are becoming that kind of writer, that kind of person. You see things in this classroom that others wouldn't even notice.

"Just for a minute, practice using your writer's eyes by looking at your own hand. Really truly study your hand. See things others might not even notice."

I studied my hand with rapt attention while students did the same. "Teach your neighbor what you see, using sentences that begin, 'When I look closely, I see . . . I also notice . . . I wonder . . .'" I gave students a moment to talk, and made my way through the room, listening in. After just a few moments I called the group back together.

"Writers, you are saying a word or two about each thing you see on your hand. Will you go back and look at your hand again, and this time say a lot of sentences about whatever you notice?"

After about a minute, I said, "Look at your writing now—the writing you started today—and think, 'How can I make this even better?' Use your writer's eyes to see more and notice more!" I gave them a minute to think, then called on some kids to say suggestions. "So, writers—you have fifteen more minutes! Get to it!"

STUDENT WORK ✦ Learning from Maya's Exemplar Book

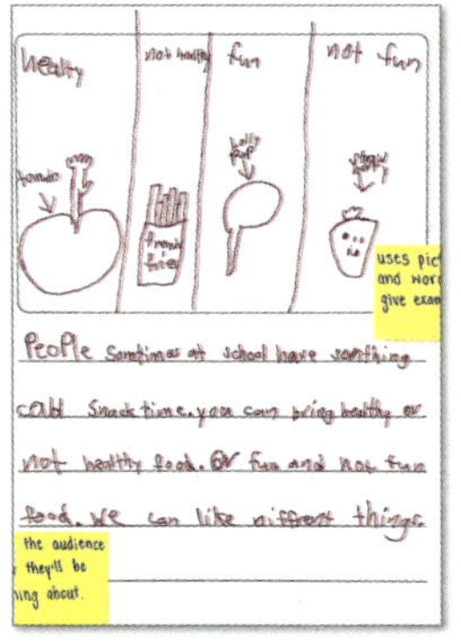

BEND I FIG. 4–1 Maya's piece, "We Eat Snack"

Part of the Text	Moves to Learn From
"People sometimes at school have something called snack time."	The writer tells her audience what this book will teach.
"You can bring healthy or not healthy food. Or fun and not fun food."	The writer splits the picture box to show different choices and examples. Her picture enhances her words.
". . . When you really really really really need it."	The writer uses repeated words to emphasize an important point or fact. You can hear her voice in her words.
The writer describes a process within the topic—what a student does when someone doesn't have a snack.	As students write about things within their classroom, they can write pages that teach how to use something or how to do something.
The writer concludes with an opinion and provides several reasons for that opinion.	This can be a powerful way to end an information book, and it provides a sense of closure to the reader.
The writer uses domain-specific vocabulary throughout: *allergies, sour, salty, sweet, spicy, focused, energized*.	The author is brave in spelling these words. The author knows that teaching readers the language of a topic helps.

 Details Matter in Writing

Tell a silly story about a child who misunderstood the word *details* to be a *D* with tails on it. Encourage kids to find a detail (without the tail) that helps their book.

"Writers, I want to tell you a story. Once upon a time there was a writer, just about your age, who heard his teacher talking on and on about how special it is to include details in books. He wasn't sure what his teacher meant by the word *details*, so in his book, he added this." I drew a capital letter *D* with a tail on it. "He thought she meant that it is important to write the letter *D* and to add tails onto that letter. D-tails." The students laughed and I chuckled along with them.

"You laugh because you know details are important, but that doesn't mean you should put *D*s with tails on them in your books. But writers, I want to be sure you understand why it *is* important to write with details. Details help your reader really understand what you are trying to teach. Details can make your readers say, 'Wow!' and help you teach more. Will you look over your book and find a detail that makes your writing better and show it to your partner? Talk about why that bit of writing helps your book."

BEND I FIG. 4–2 Collin looks closely to add details in his piece about the classroom library. 

PHONOLOGICAL AWARENESS AND PHONICS EXTENSION ✦ "The Add and Change Song"

For this extension, you'll need a copy of "The Add and Change Song" lyrics.

Sing "The Add and Change Song" with your students to reinforce phoneme manipulation.

"Writers, one of the reasons to get really good at working with sounds is because it makes you better at reading and writing. Today we're going to sing another song that will help us switch sounds around in a word."

I began singing and gestured for students to join me.

> If you add /b/ to /ake/ the word is *bake,*
> If you add /b/ to /ake/ the word is *bake,*
> If you add /b/ to /ake/ the word we made is *bake,*
> If you add /b/ to /ake/ the word is *bake.*

As I started off each following verse, I allowed students to call out the new words that we were forming.

> If you change /b/ to /sh/ the word is *shake,*
> If you change /b/ to /sh/ the word is *shake,*
> If you change /b/ to /sh/ the word we made is *shake,*
> If you change /b/ to /sh/ the word is *shake.*

We sang a few more verses, changing the beginning sound to *fl*, *sn*, *br*, and, finally, *c*. We also repeated the song on future days to practice a few other long-vowel patterns.

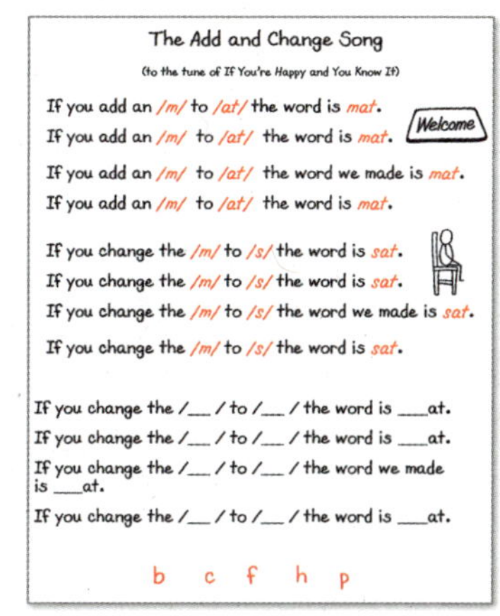

The Add and Change Song

(to the tune of If You're Happy and You Know It)

If you add an /m/ to /at/ the word is *mat*.
If you add an /m/ to /at/ the word is *mat*. *Welcome*

If you add an /m/ to /at/ the word we made is *mat*.
If you add an /m/ to /at/ the word is *mat*.

If you change the /m/ to /s/ the word is *sat*.
If you change the /m/ to /s/ the word is *sat*.
If you change the /m/ to /s/ the word we made is *sat*.

If you change the /m/ to /s/ the word is *sat*.

If you change the /___/ to /___/ the word is ___at.
If you change the /___/ to /___/ the word is ___at.
If you change the /___/ to /___/ the word we made is ___at.
If you change the /___/ to /___/ the word is ___at.

b   c   f   h   p

Researchers Study (and Write about) How Things Look

TODAY YOU will build on the work students did in the previous session, looking closely at their objects, with a focus on studying how things look on the outside and on the inside. You'll demonstrate looking closely at something you're writing about and recording what you see on the outside on a special kind of paper for this bend. In the mid-workshop teaching, you'll ask students to look at and write about the inside of their objects, using magnifying glasses to examine them closely. During the share, you'll teach students that their partners can help them see even more. You'll also invite them to bring an object from home to study in the next session.

TODAY YOUR STUDENTS will choose a book they want to add more to and begin the workshop by research-ing to get more information for that book. To research, students will look closely at the outside of the object they are writing about, and then write about what they noticed. After the mid-workshop teaching, writers will transition to looking and writing about what they noticed on the inside. Expect that students will write both an "On the Outside" and an "On the Inside" page during today's work time. If time permits, they might do the same work for a second book. The addition of magnifying glasses will help writers see more.

Getting Ready

YOU WILL NEED . . .

- a clipboard with the new "How _______ Looks: On the Outside" and "How _______ Looks: On the Inside" paper. Place the "On the Outside" paper on top, so that the "On the Inside" paper is underneath.

- your "Stapler" demonstration text from Session 1, with the cover prepared. An example of today's demonstration writing can be found in the online resources.

- to prepare clipboards as described above for students.

- to plan ahead where in the classroom students will store their objects from home for the next session (see Share).

- Rasheed, the first-grade phonics mascot (see Share).

STUDENTS WILL NEED . . .

- to bring their folders to the minilesson.

- clipboards and the "How _______ Looks: On the Outside" and "How _______ Looks: On the Inside" writing paper.

- magnifying glasses (see Mid-Workshop Teaching).

- a copy of "Research Objects from Home" letter to parents or caregivers to bring home (see Share).

Ensuring Access

YOUR ULTIMATE GOAL TODAY is for kids to return to a book they've been writing, this time studying the topic closely to describe what the object looks like on the outside and inside.

- Support for all students is woven into today's lesson. By first watching you model how to describe an object, then studying their own topic and describing it in more detail, students will be set up to succeed.

- Notice which students struggle to describe the stapler in detail during the active engagement. Coach them to see that there is always more to say when describing how objects look—even the smallest details.

- Keep in mind that MLLs' English language input (the amount of English they can understand) is higher than their language output (the amount of English they can produce in speech or writing). Though they may understand the concepts you are teaching, they may not yet have the English vocabulary to show it. Invite them to describe their objects in a different language, enabling them to practice the important work of noticing deeply and elaborating to teach more. When conferring, focus on extending their English vocabulary—especially for those in the early to intermediate stages of English acquisition. You might slip in the specific word for something a child is pointing to. Celebrate their risks!

Researchers Study (and Write about) How Things Look

CONNECTION

Tell students that they'll continue researching today, this time studying how their objects look.

"Writers, I was thinking about how carefully you looked at your topics yesterday. You noticed so many tiny, interesting details and added them to your writing. We're going to keep researching today, and I'm thinking that we could have some special paper where we could teach exactly how things look. What do you think?"

✦ **Name the teaching point.**

"Today I want to teach you that researchers ask themselves, 'How does this thing look?' To answer that question, they turn things over, look carefully, and peer into the cracks of things. Then, they teach their reader how the thing looks."

TEACHING

Introduce the new "How _____ Looks: On the Outside" paper and demonstrate its use to students.

"Yesterday you started gathering up your research kit. Well, today you're also going to need a special research clipboard." I held up my makeshift clipboard with a page attached to it titled "How _______ Looks," with the subtitle, "On the Outside."

"Let me show you how I can really research something that I'm writing about." Returning to my collection of covers that I'd made earlier, I chose my stapler cover and said, "I think that my book about the stapler really needs more information, so I need to do some research. And if I'm going to research something, I need to be right next to it!"

I walked over to the writing center and picked up the stapler, holding it in my hand. "I know that I want to study how this thing looks on the outside." I took a cursory glance at it, then said in a dull, robot voice: "'The stapler is black. . . .' So, how'd I do as a researcher? Thumbs up? Down? Did I look closely and carefully, noticing all of the important things, telling my readers everything that's special about the stapler?

"So many thumbs down! I guess I have to look closer and say even more." I took a deep breath and again held the stapler up to my eye, examining it closely.

"Oh! I thought the stapler was all black, but I should add that it is a shiny, glossy black. And other parts of the stapler are shiny and silver! Look at this part!" I held the stapler up.

You haven't worked on this book yet in front of your kids, although you mentioned the topic in Session 1. If any of them ask, you might just say something like, "I've been working on my book about the stapler at another time of the day!"

This type of counterexample can be fun and silly but remember that it serves an important purpose. Cognitive scientists have shown that students benefit from seeing both examples and nonexamples. As you show an example and a nonexample, students build up their understanding of what it means to be a researcher.

Debrief, emphasizing the close-in work that you just did.

"I think that was a little bit better, don't you? This time, I looked closely and I noticed different parts of the stapler. This is the kind of work that researchers do. Now that I've studied how the outside of the stapler looks, let me do a quick sketch and then write."

I quickly sketched a stapler in my blank booklet, added labels for "black part" and "silver part," and quickly wrote the first two sentences on my paper.

ACTIVE ENGAGEMENT

Recruit students to help you add more to your "How _____ Looks: On the Outside" page by looking closely.

"Will you help me research more? I'll put the stapler under the document camera so you can get a good look at it. We talked about its color, but to describe how something looks on the outside, we should be able to talk about other things too. Hmm, . . . what about its shape? Its size? Its feel? Its weight?

"With your partner, look and think about other things we can say on the 'How _____ Looks: On the Outside' page. Turn and talk. Remember, you can talk first in another language if it helps you."

As the kids talked, I recorded some of what they said, adding on to my sketch and words. Then I called the class back, saying, "You used your brainpower to see so much more." I showed them what I'd added.

LINK

Set students up to add a "How _____ Looks: On the Outside" page to their book.

"Writers, our writing workshop is going to look a little more like a researching workshop today. Let's get started by doing some research in our own folders! Flip through the books you've written so far, or the books that you still want to write, and ask yourself: 'Did I teach enough about this? Do I need to do a bit of research, get some information, so I can teach even more?' If the answer is 'no,' you'll probably want to add a page to teach how your object looks!" I set up clipboards with our new 'How _____ Looks' paper.

I gave students a moment to look through their folders and decide which book they'd work on. Then I said, "Okay, researchers. Get a clipboard and go right to that thing you're writing about. Study how things look on the outside and see what you can teach, and then . . . start writing! I can't wait to see what you learn today, and what you teach others too."

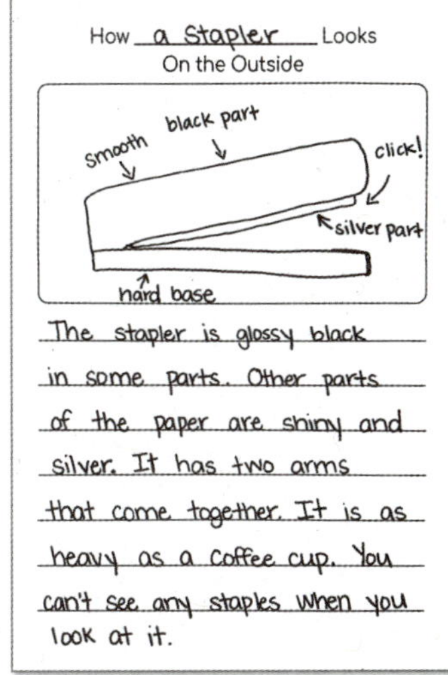

Using realia (objects) to scaffold learning is an excellent way to support MLLs!

BEND I

Conferring Supports ✦ Predictable Problems Can Prompt Reteaching

If you notice . . .	Then you might . . .
Writers with sparse drawing and writing	Remind them not to write **too-short books**: "Do you remember when our principal sent us that book about the playground that just said, 'Playgrounds are great. You play on the playground.' and we felt a little bummed reading it? We couldn't wait to learn a lot of information, but the book didn't teach us very much. We decided that we never ever wanted our books to be sort of empty. I'm reminding you of this because you went so fast today that you actually, by mistake, have some pages that are nearly empty. I just *know* you can go back and add so so much more to those pages. You're willing to do that, right?"
Writers want to move to a new piece without rereading	Invite them to use their **power pens**: "You're ready to take a next big step with your writing—rereading! To do this, take out your power pen! Remember, you can flip your pen upside down as you reread your writing, and point with the nonwriting side. If you find places that make you say, 'Huh?,' 'Tell me more,' or 'That needs fixing,' turn your pen right side up and use it to fix those places up! Ready to give it a go?"
Writers who would benefit from additional oral rehearsal to add more detail	Remind them to talk to their **imaginary friend** (hand): If the child is an MLL, use sentence stems and teach specific detail vocabulary. Remind them that they can also use words in another language to describe the object.

Mid-Workshop Teaching ✦ Looking Closely at the Inside

"Well, writers, you guessed it. I can't hide anything from you!" I held up my clipboard and lifted my "On the Outside" paper. "Underneath the 'On the Outside' paper, there's another special paper for you to write about what your object looks like on the *inside*! Whoa! I am so curious to know what's inside a pen, right? Or, what's inside the cereal box? That will be fascinating.

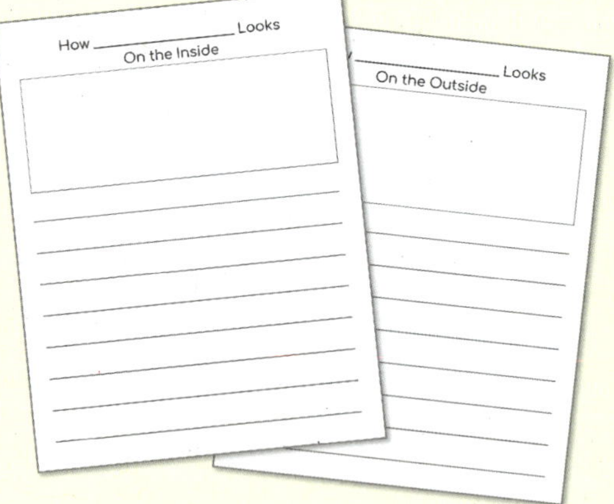

"I'm going to give you a special tool that can help you investigate what's on the inside of your object: a magnifying glass! I'll give a few to each group. These will help you see all the teeny, tiny details of your object. Remember to look closely and to write everything you notice."

Once students started looking inside their objects, I walked through the classroom, occasionally helping them open their objects safely, but mostly reminding them to write. "Now that you've noticed that important detail, make sure it gets on your 'How ______ Looks: On the Inside' paper."

CONFERENCE ◆ Looking Closely and Writing a Lot (MLLs in Intermediate Stages of Language Development)

■ RESEARCH/DECIDE

As you join a student, spend a moment asking questions. Support vocabulary as you elicit oral language.

I sat down next to Nadia, who was examining a tape dispenser.

"You're looking really carefully. What do you notice?"

Nadia said, "This tape thing . . ."

I told her, "Yes, the fancy, grown-up word for this is *dispenser*. You'd say, 'The tape dispenser. . . .'"

Nadia took a deep breath and began to speak again. "I see the cutting part and a different part and I don't see the sticky part." As she spoke, Nadia pointed to the different parts of the dispenser.

■ COMPLIMENT

Celebrate how closely the student is looking at the object, and name that you want the student to look closely and talk a lot.

"Nadia, can I tell you what I notice you doing? You are looking at the tape dispenser," I touched it, "so carefully, seeing all the details and the parts. That's important work for you to do." I gave a thumbs up, "It'll help you to write a really interesting book!"

■ TEACH

Be explicit, and use language that is transferable to another day. Then scaffold the learner's work.

"One thing that'll help you is not only *looking* closely," I pointed to my eye, "but also *talking*." I held up my hand in a sort of mouth-moving gesture. "Try talking a lot about what you notice. You were talking about how the tape dispenser doesn't have the sticky part. What does it have?"

"I see the round thing with parts sticking out . . . where you put the tape."

I pushed her to add more language. "Say more! What else do you see?"

Nadia answered, "It's not big, so it rattles. And also this part is for cutting."

"Great! Let's look really closely and research the cutting part. Say exactly what you see."

"It has a few spiky things on it, and don't touch it 'cause you could hurt your finger on it!" Nadia explained.

■ LINK

Connect the child's work with oral language to the child's writing.

"Nadia, do you see what you have done? You went to one part, the round part, and you researched and said a lot about it. Then you went to the next part, the cutting part, and you looked carefully and said a lot about that. You could go back now and use the special paper to teach your reader about exactly what you saw. Keep doing this: Say a lot, and then make sure you get it down on the page."

BEND I FIG. 5–1 Nadia's page about the tape dispenser

STUDENT WORK ✦ Analyzing Phonics Patterns in Abigail's Writing

To assess what a student understands about phonics, look across a few pieces of writing, noticing patterns, as we've done with Abigail's writing.

Words from the Text	What the Writer Is Doing Well	Phonics Concepts You Might Teach
conoctid	The writer is hearing sounds all across words and is doing her best to approximate the sounds she hears at the end of a word.	Inflected endings—ways to spell the *-ed* sound at the ends of words, and the fact that the same *-ed* can sound differently as in *wanted* and *walked*.
tak *cape* *make* *inside*	The writer hears and represents short and long vowels. She often (but not always) signals the presence of a long vowel with a final *e*.	The writer can be encouraged to reread to notice if she's signaled a long vowel correctly or not (*cap/cape, tack/take*).
sonde *ot*	The writer knows to use a vowel, even when the medial sounds in words are not the long- or short-vowel sounds.	The diphthong *ou*.
ol *does* *on* *not*	The writer writes the sounds she hears for words.	High-frequency words, especially ones she uses often (e.g. *because*, *all*, *what*).

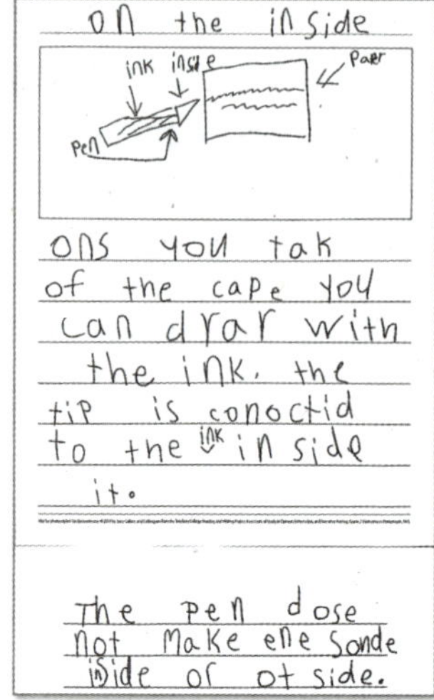

BEND I FIG. 5–2 Abigail's writing

GRADE 1 ✦ TOPIC BOOKS

 Helping Your Partner See More

Set partnerships up to share the pages they created.

"Writers, you have done a lot of work today! Will you show your partner what you noticed about your object? Share what you wrote and what you drew. Think about what else your partner could add to his or her 'How It Looks' page. You might even become a researcher of your partner's object. Turn and share."

The room buzzed. "Wow, writers, I mean *researchers*. You found some interesting things. Who knew that a pen had all those parts in it, for example? And same with a clock. You all have such fascinating objects."

Invite students to bring an object from home to study.

I turned from the meeting area, then stopped as if I'd heard something. "Wait, wait, Rasheed wants to tell me something," I said, gesturing to the stuffed lion. I put my ear close to Rasheed. "What a cool idea!" I said to the lion. Turning to the class, I said, "Rasheed wants to join us. He wants to bring in something from home to study. And, I'm getting an even better idea. How about if *all* of us find something at home that we want to study— something most people might think is ordinary, but we actually think is interesting? Then we all can study and write books about our own objects. You game?" The kids agreed. I passed out copies of the "Research Objects from Home" letter to parents or caregivers for them to bring home.

PHONOLOGICAL AWARENESS AND PHONICS EXTENSION ✦

For this extension, show a phonological awareness video. 

This video begins with an onset-rime word-building activity. Students will read the rime *-ang*, and will be presented with a collection of initial consonants and blends to build words. The video then moves on to dictation. Students will segment words ending in blends, then write those words.

Researchers Study (and Write about) How to Use Things

In This Session

TODAY YOU will teach your students that researchers also study how things work and teach their readers how to use those things. You'll show a mentor text that does this, and then make a "How to Use" page for your own object, demonstrating that to write the page, you'll make your object work and note the steps you took to do that. During the mid-workshop teaching, you'll set up a quick gallery tour so that your students can learn from one another. The day will end with a quick celebration of the work students have done so far and a reminder to students that they will write about objects from home in the next session.

TODAY YOUR STUDENTS will start by writing a "How to Use" page, and then progress to making other pages, all about the object they have been studying. They will probably write only one book today, though each student should be able to write several of these pages today. During the mid-workshop teaching, kids will move about the room, studying what others have done so as to get ideas for their own work. Then, during the share, they will celebrate the work they've done so far.

Getting Ready

YOU WILL NEED . . .

- a copy of *Now You Know How It Works* by Valorie Fisher.

- the new "How to Use" paper option on your clipboard and a pen. An example of the "How to Use a Stapler" page of the demonstration text, "The Stapler," can be found in the online resources.

- a stapler and several sheets of normal picture box pages as well as blank pages.

- to play a song for two minutes (see Mid-Workshop Teaching).

STUDENTS WILL NEED . . .

- their object from home. You'll give them another day to remember to bring these in.

- the new "How to Use" paper option. You'll want to stock this in the writing center as well.

- to move throughout the room to sit next to and research the things they are writing about.

Ensuring Access

YOUR ULTIMATE GOAL TODAY is for children to write several more pages in their books about their object. For starters, you'll set them up to write a page on how their object is used.

- Children will benefit from help thinking and writing sequentially and using transitional phrases to do so. For example, when describing how a pencil sharpener works, you can coach the child to think about that bit by bit, to progress from start to finish. You can also remind children to draw on high-frequency words such as *first*, *then*, *next*, and *also* to show the sequence.

- Writing about how to use certain objects is a perfect time to do a lot of acting. You might coach writers to work with a partner, first pretending to use an object and then breaking it down step by step. Especially for MLLs, this kind of concrete example, using the actual object, helps them build language—they can speak and write about something they *see* rather than using their mental energy to first imagine something and then write about it.

- There are so many possibilities online for showing kids how certain objects work. Consider locating kid-friendly demonstrations on a site like YouTube. Kids could watch, and rewatch, those videos, before they begin writing. You might even add the videos to a Padlet for easy access for your students.

- If you teach writing workshop in Spanish, or if you have students who speak and write in Spanish, today you might use a Spanish mentor text. See the online resources for a list of recommended texts.

Minilesson

Researchers Study (and Write about) How to Use Things

CONNECTION

Build enthusiasm by explaining that you told everyone about the kids' research. Share an idea your sister had—creating How to Use pages.

After kids convened, I said, "Last night I called my sister and told her about the work you did yesterday. Then I called my mom and dad and told *them*. Did you do the same? Did you tell lots of people about your investigation and how carefully you were studying the thing you are writing about? That's how it goes when you do research. You start out studying something on your own, or maybe with a partner, and then you end up with a whole crowd of people pulling in to study with you. And everyone has thoughts and ideas!

"My sister was full of ideas for things we might try next. She's a researcher too—she actually works in a lab building robots that help people. She said that whenever she is researching something, people always ask, 'How do you use it?' And I thought, 'What a cool idea!' We could add pages like that to *our* books."

◆ **Name the teaching point.**

"Today I want to teach you that when you study an object, it helps to ask not only, 'How does it look?' but also, 'How do you use it?' To answer that question, use your object, slowing the steps down. Then write the steps like you might write a recipe, saying a lot about each step."

TEACHING

Set students up to investigate the way a mentor author writes How to Use pages. Debrief the author's specific writing moves.

"Before we make our own How to Use pages, I want to show you a page from a book, *Now You Know How It Works*, where the author, Valorie Fisher, told us how a pencil sharpener works. Will you notice what the author has done to teach us how to use a pencil sharpener?" I displayed page 18, titled "Pencil Sharpener," and read it aloud.

As you turn the pencil, the blade shaves off a thin layer of wood and lead, making a sharp point.

I displayed the accompanying pictures, which show a pencil in the pencil sharpener, the pencil being turned, indicated with arrows, and the layer of wood being shaved off.

"What has the author done in her writing that you could do in your writing about tape dispensers and pens and clocks?" I reread the passage, this time using my voice to emphasize the step-by-step nature of the explanation and pointing to the author's moves. "Do you agree with me that it's almost like she slowed down the pencil being sharpened so she could draw and say the steps? Step 1, put the pencil in the pencil sharpener. Then step 2, spin the pencil in the pencil sharpener. You can see how she showed that with these curly arrows. And then, step 3, when you turn the pencil, the pencil sharpener shaves off the wood to make it sharp again. Do you see that the author has slowed down what actually happens super-fast, and come up with the steps? And she has a picture to go with this, a picture that shows the three steps."

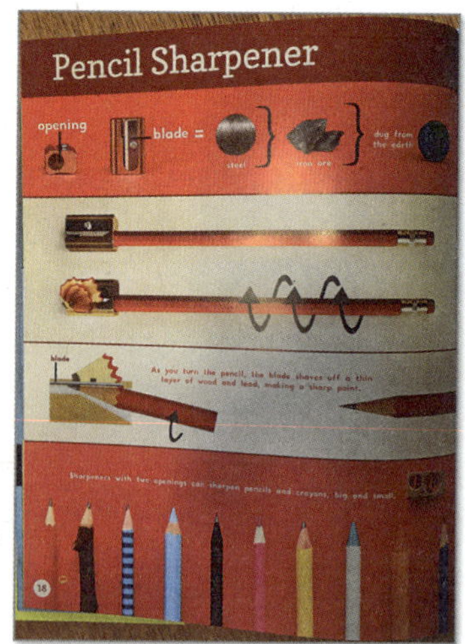

You might provide labeled bags for students to store their home objects in and secure them somewhere so that the objects aren't a distraction for students. They'll have the opportunity to write about the objects in Session 7.

You will, of course, alter this so that you refer to the people in your circle. The point is simply to convey your enthusiasm for the work the class has been doing and to bring your students along toward the suggestion of the day.

ACTIVE ENGAGEMENT

Recruit kids to describe how to use your object, the stapler. Channel them to first name each step, then elaborate on each step.

"I'm going to add another page to my book about staplers. Will you help me write about how to use the stapler?" I displayed a "How to Use" page on my clipboard. "I'll make it work while you study it with me, okay?"

I picked up the stapler and a few sheets of paper and demonstrated how to use the stapler to staple the pages together into a booklet. "Did you notice the steps I followed? Name them across your fingers with your partner. Then tell each other what you'd sketch in the boxes on this paper."

The children talked, and after a very short interval, I convened the class, saying, "Okay, so I need to remember the steps of how to use a stapler." I reenacted stapling, then said, "Let me see if I heard you: 'First you put some paper under the front of the stapler.'" I muttered that I didn't know what the front part is called, and then said, "Hmm, . . . it's almost like I put it under the stapler's *nose*." I added that into the sketch and continued quickly sketching each step into each of the boxes, as I thought aloud.

"Now, help me write the steps. Pretend to touch the first box, and say to your partner what I should write first." Kids touched and said what I should write in the first box while I wrote. I pointed to the second box. "Then . . ." I let my voice trail off so the class could fill in the second step. I collected their ideas and wrote them down. Soon the page looked like this.

"I'm going to stop there, so that you have time to work on your own objects," I said. "You can already see that this page will definitely help answer that question: 'How do you use it?'"

LINK

Invite kids to write a "How to Use" page for their books. Explain that there are other kinds of pages they could create as well. Get them started.

"Writers, as you head off to research today, I have 'How to Use' pages. You're going to continue adding to your book about something in the classroom, and, today, will you try writing at least one new kind of page?

"In addition to a 'How to Use' page, you can add any other kinds of pages you want." I held up each kind of paper as I mentioned it. "I've got more 'How ______ Looks' pages if you want to work on another book about something else in the classroom. I've got regular picture box pages if you want to write more about your object. And, I've got blank pages if you want to design your own page."

As your concrete model can be helpful for MLLs, you might encourage them to also start with a "How to Use" page and follow a similar structure, voicing over sentence stems, like "First, you . . ." "Then, you . . ."

SMALL GROUP ✦ Adding Tips and Warnings

For this small group, you'll need copies of the picture cards for each partnership and the "How to Use a Stapler" page from your demonstration text.

▪ RALLY

Let students know that tips are another way to teach. Give them picture cards and channel them to come up with tips to accompany each.

"Writers, another way people can teach their readers how to use something is by giving tips and warnings to people who are learning. They might start, 'Remember to . . . ,' or 'Watch out . . . ,' or 'Be careful . . . ,' or 'Make sure . . .'

"I'll give you and your partner picture cards of people using certain things. Will you two look at each of them and think, 'What tips or warnings would someone learning how to use these things need?' See how many tips and warnings you can think of!"

The kids listed tips such as: "Slow down." "Be sure you get everything!" "Look at all the letters in the words." "Watch while you do it." "Check it!" "Careful."

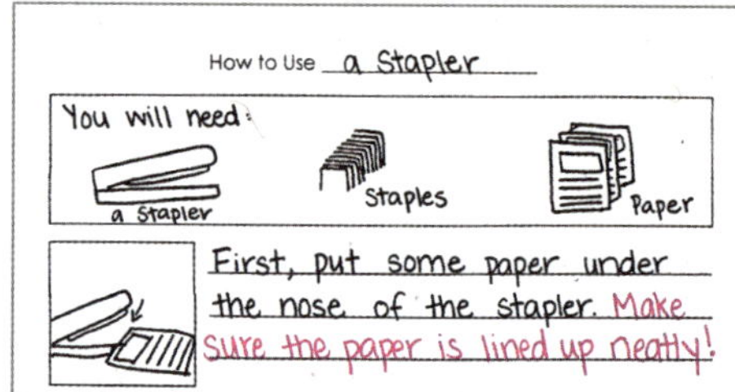

▪ TRY IT #1

Channel students to come up with tips and warnings that can be added to your demonstration text.

"Will you help me come up with a tip or warning for each step on my 'How to Use a Stapler' page?" I read Step 1 out loud.

"Hmm, . . . what tips or warnings could I give about this step? Think about what the hard parts of the step are and then think of a tip or warning that could help. Turn and share with your partner." I listened in while students talk, and then added some of their suggestions to the demonstration writing.

▪ TRY IT #2/LINK

Have students add tips and warnings to their books.

"I think you're ready to do this for your own readers in your own books. Read a step or a part and think, 'Are there any tips or warnings my reader would need?' Once you've thought of one, add it! Then, add another."

> **Possible Coaching Moves:**
> ▸ "Read a step. What advice could you give to help your reader?"
> ▸ "What's the hard part of that step? What would help?"
> ▸ "Try starting with 'Be careful to . . .' or 'Remember to . . .'"

MID-WORKSHOP TEACHING ✦ A Quick Gallery Tour to Learn from Your Classmates' Pages

"Writers, can I stop you? Your classmates are creating the coolest pages for their books. Before you do anything else, will you all lay out just the pages you've written today, and your object, as if they are murals in your neighborhood? I'm going to play a song for two minutes. While it's playing, will you study—super-closely—the pages the writers in this class made? You might get some ideas for pages you want to add to *your* book too! When the music stops, head back to your writing spot."

When the music stopped and kids settled back in their writing spots, I said, "I bet you have so many new ideas! Keep working!"

TOOLKIT ◆ Using the "Questions to Ask One Another" Chart to Say More

Encourage writers to say and then write twin sentences in response to questions on the chart (a twin sentence is when the first sentence is followed up with a second, clarifying sentence). They might write, "We decorate the apartment with calaveras to celebrate Día de los Muertos. Día de los Muertos is a big celebration that lasts for two days!"

As writers ask and answer questions in their topic books, push them to think logically about the sequence of information they are teaching. They might ask themselves, "Which of these questions would be important to answer next?"

Invite writing partners to use the chart to ask each other questions about their objects. Prompt writers to add the information they rehearse onto the pages of their book.

Teach writers that they don't need to know the answer to every question on the chart. They can wonder about a question and then share those musings in their books. They might say, "Maybe it . . ." or "Perhaps it . . ." They might support their thinking by saying "I think this because . . ."

The "Questions to Ask One Another" chart can be found in the online resources.

Encourage writers to read over all of the questions on the chart, selecting a few that feel especially important to ask about their object. Then, students can work to answer just those questions in their teaching books, saying as much as they can about each question.

Invite students to think about which of these questions they usually answer in their teaching books without anyone reminding them of that question. Push writers to think about the questions they can begin to try to answer more often.

Teach writers that one way to say more in their teaching books is to include questions in their actual writing. Students may write, "You might be wondering where the object is from . . ." or "You might ask, 'Where is it from?'" and then try to answer those questions in their writing.

 A Quick Celebration of a Strong Start

Celebrate the books that students have written thus far. Remind them that they will begin new work tomorrow—writing about objects they bring from home.

"Writers, have you ever seen teams celebrate after they've won a big game? Have you noticed how teammates often high-five each other, pat each other on the back, say, 'Go team!'? I think you deserve a celebration like that! Go ahead and celebrate with your writing partner. You've learned a ton!" I gave kids thirty seconds to celebrate.

"Tomorrow, we'll study the objects we bring from home. So, if you haven't yet found an object at home that you think is worth studying, find one tonight and bring it in. I can't wait to learn about your special objects!"

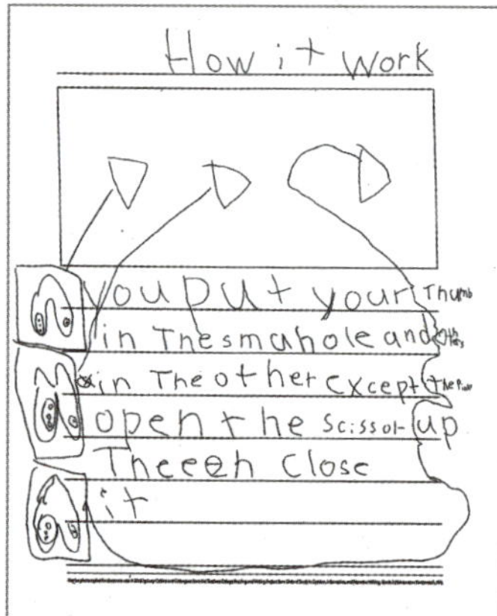

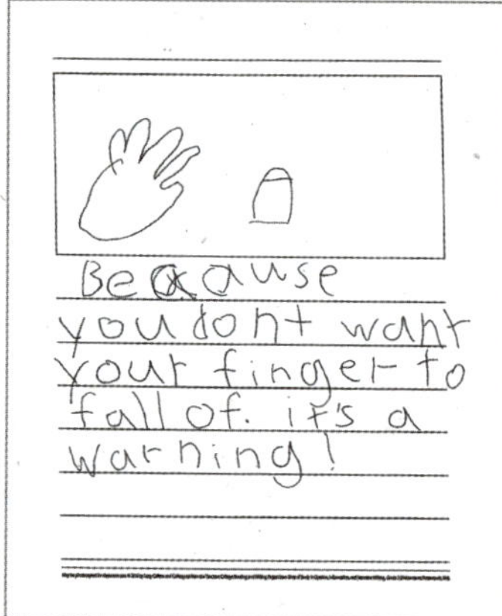

BEND I FIG. 6–1 Zach's story about how to use scissors 

PHONOLOGICAL AWARENESS AND PHONICS EXTENSION ✦

For this extension, show a phonological awareness video. 

This video begins with an onset-rime word-building activity. Students will read the rime *-ast*, and will be presented with a collection of initial consonants and blends to build words. The last activity in the video is writing by analogy. Beginning by reading the familiar high-frequency words *see, out,* and, *and,* students then write each new word the instructor says, using part of a familiar word to write the new word.

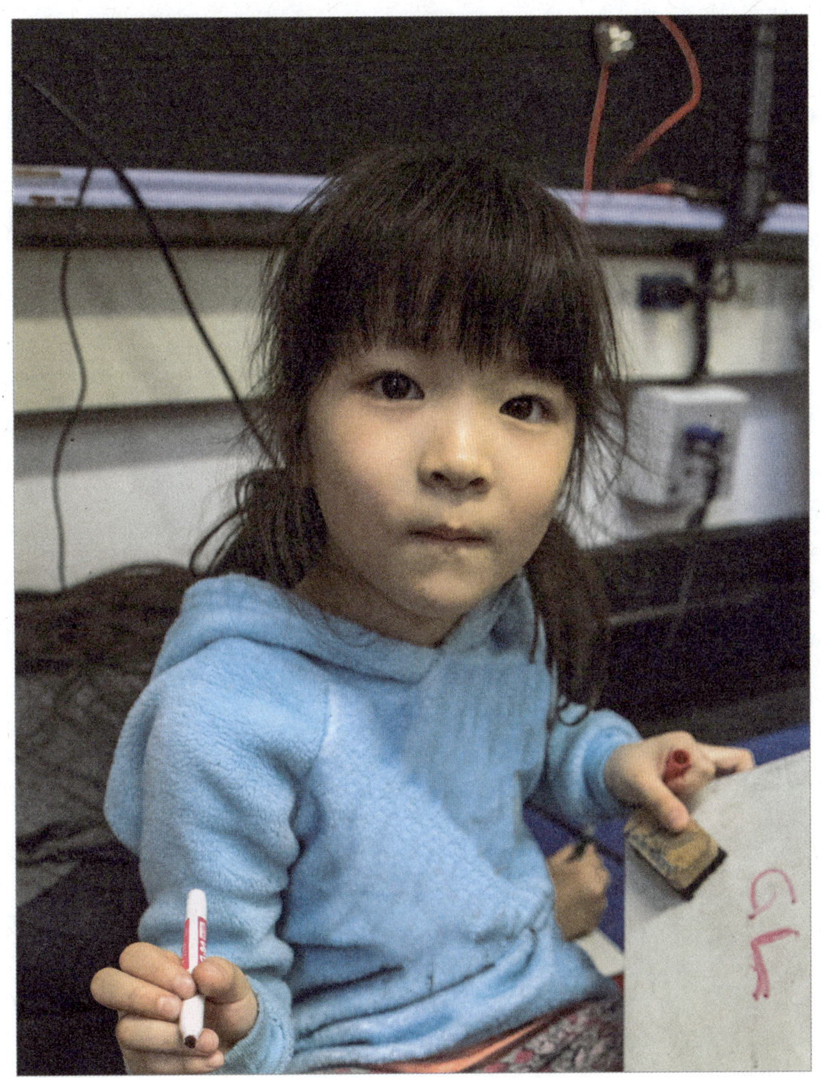

Session 7

Using Sensory Details to Add Describing Words

In This Session

TODAY YOU will teach students to use "just-right words" (sensory descriptive words) to describe the objects they brought from home as they start a new book. You'll first work as a class to create a chart that describes Rasheed using specific, descriptive words. You'll then begin writing your book about the object you brought from home; we use a key ring. You'll show students how you gather pages for your new book from the writing center and then quickly sketch the object and write a detailed description with sensory words. In the mid-workshop teaching, you'll ask students to review the words they have already used to see if they can be even more accurate and specific. In the share, you'll teach writers about commas by revisiting *Now You Know How It Works*.

TODAY YOUR STUDENTS will use the object they brought in—or one they borrow from Rasheed—and begin their new topic book. They'll pick page options from those in the writing center (and from a chart of options), and then, as they begin each page, writers will touch and teach, sketch and write. They'll begin this book today, but will most likely finish in the next session. They will work to include specific details that relate to the senses as they write. They will also learn about commas, and how to use them to separate items in a list.

Getting Ready

YOU WILL NEED . . .

- Rasheed, or another interesting object that can be passed around, to study during the connection.

- chart paper and sticky notes to create the "Words that Describe" chart as a frame to fill in. You'll need additional sticky notes to fill in the chart with students' help. You'll find an example of this chart in the online resources.

- the "To Describe, Writers Tell About" chart.

- an object from home that you'll use as the subject of your own topic book. We use a key ring.

- a copy of each new type of writing paper, specifically the "Different Types" paper, which you will use to start a new demonstration text, "The Key Ring."

- a copy of *Now You Know How It Works*, by Valorie Fisher (see Share).

- a copy of the "How _______ Looks: On the Outside" paper to draft another demonstration page (see Share).

STUDENTS WILL NEED . . .

- an object from home to study, or one of Rasheed's to borrow.

- a fully stocked writing center, including all the new paper options. We also suggest putting small stacks of each option on each table for today only.

Ensuring Access

YOUR ULTIMATE GOAL TODAY is to help writers use describing words in their writing as they start a new book.

- You already know which students will have trouble with this skill; be sure to call on them and encourage their suggestions during the beginning of the minilesson if they don't volunteer ideas to fill in the "Words that Describe" chart. Use gestures yourself to communicate details, and welcome students' physical interpretations of concepts such as squishy, soft, rattly, and so on. You'll find that this type of gesturing will be supportive not only to your MLLs, but to all of your students. When you use gestures, and exaggerate them as much as possible, you make this type of writing a physical, kinesthetic experience.

- If a writer writes a word like *silver*, it might be tempting to encourage them to think of and write a word like *sparkly*. Remember that today's lesson is far more about the process than about coming up with the best, most specific, sensory words, and honor and celebrate the words that students do come up with and use.

- Anticipate that many of your students will approximate the use of commas in a list, since the share today may be the first time your students are introduced to this concept. Rather than working toward mastery today, value all the ways in which your students try out the use of commas in their writing.

- If you teach writing workshop in Spanish, or if you have students who speak and write in Spanish, today you might use a Spanish mentor text. See the online resources for a list of recommended texts.

Minilesson

Using Sensory Details to Add Describing Words

CONNECTION

Reveal a particularly interesting object. Pass it around, inviting students to generate descriptors. Chart them on sticky notes and sort those by senses.

"Writers, come quickly! I can't wait to show you what I brought in to study." I held an object behind my back, making sure it was hidden from the students' sight. Once students had gathered, I said, "Are you ready to see? Drumroll, please!" Once students were tapping a drumroll on their legs, I revealed what I'd been hiding.

Students exclaimed, "*Rasheed*!" as I held him up for everyone to see.

"I thought Rasheed could be the special object we study to start today! I'll pass him around," I went to the back row of the meeting area, "and when you get him, look at him, feel him, smell him . . . and tell us a word that comes to mind!" Rasheed made his way down that row of writers, and the row in front of it, and kids called out describing words, which I jotted on sticky notes. I added several of my own, too, then stuck each sticky note on a blank sheet of chart paper.

Soon, I had a "Words that Describe" chart. "Hmm, . . . take a look at these words with me." I paused and looked at the chart. "Are you noticing that some of these words tell what Rasheed looks like, some of them tell what he feels like, some tell how he sounds, and there are even words that tell how he smells!" As I named each category, I added headings to the chart and sorted the words.

"I bet we could use those kinds of words inside of our object books too!"

We chose Rasheed, the mascot for the Grade 1 Units of Study in Phonics, for this connection because he fascinates first-graders, and because we imagine many of you will have him in your classrooms. You can choose any interesting object that you think your students will be able to use different words to describe—even slime!

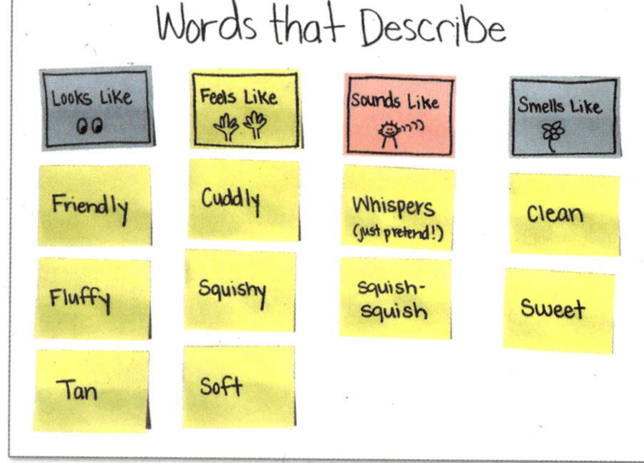

✦ Name the teaching point.

"Today I want to teach you that when a researcher tries to describe something carefully, the researcher describes what the thing looks like, feels like, sounds like, and maybe even what it smells like. Researchers use lots of descriptive words to teach readers all about the object."

I displayed the new "To Describe, Writers Tell About" chart.

TEACHING AND ACTIVE ENGAGEMENT

Reveal your object. Model the process of choosing pages for your new book.

"Before I try to use descriptive words in the book I'm going to write today, let me show you the object I brought from home!" I reached into my pocket and took out a key ring with several different keys and my library card.

I jangled my keys. "Now that I have my special object all picked out, I need to think, 'What do I want to teach about this topic? What pages should I include in my book?' Hmm, . . .

"Wait, I bet it would help to look at all the kinds of paper to help me think about the different things I could teach about my object." I went to the writing center and dramatically examined the new paper choices. "You gotta see this!" I said. "Whoa, great!" I collected several different pages, stapled them together, and returned to the meeting area.

We model with a key ring, aware that teachers tend to have a lot of keys. You could instead reference an object that's special and unique to you. If you plan to change the object, look through the remaining sessions to see how your demonstration writing will need to build.

I then displayed the "Different Types" page under the document camera. "You know, there are some pages I've never seen before, like this 'Different Types' page. See—it has boxes for all the different types of something. I know one of you has a stack of playing cards and you can definitely use this paper, for the black cards, the red ones . . . I can use this too—for different types of things on my key ring."

Recruit the kids to help you write a page in your new book.

"Now, I need to think, 'How can I use what I just learned about describing words—ones that use different senses—on the pages I'll write today about my keychain?' Hmm, . . . will you help me try this work on my 'Different Types' page? My page can be different types of things on my keychain!"

I held up my key ring. "I could just write *key*, *library card*. But that wouldn't be teaching much, would it? So, I want to use some describing words." I gestured toward the "Words that Describe" chart.

I removed the library card from the ring and passed it to the kids in the front row, saying to them, "Will you help me think of more descriptive words, not just *library card?* What does it *look* like?"

Kids called out, "White and blue!" "Shiny!" "Rectangle shaped!" One said it was "Flat like a piece of paper." Another pointed to the chain and said "Silver!"

"What powerful words, writers! Now I need to add them to my writing. I want to teach that the library card is flat like a piece of paper. It's also white and blue with a silver chain on it. Oh, and it's smooth. I bet I can put those all together." I touched the page and taught: "The library card key ring is smooth and blue and white with a silver chain. It's flat like a piece of paper."

After I rehearsed, I picked up a pen, sketched a quick picture of the library card, and added a few sentences.

Debrief, emphasizing the process of choosing descriptive words, then using those words to draft.

"Did you see how we thought really carefully about how this library card key ring looks and feels?" I gestured back to the chart. "Then, we used those descriptive words to write that page!"

LINK

Channel students to use descriptive words as they write.

"Writers, are you ready to try this same work in *your* new object books? As you head off to your writing spots, get the object you brought from home and put it on the table next to you. (If you don't have one, don't worry! Rasheed brought some for you to borrow.) You'll also notice that I've put little stacks of the different paper choices at each table. Look carefully at the options and choose the different types of pages you'll need. Add a staple to turn it into a booklet and then you're ready to touch and teach, sketch and write!

"And remember to make sure your writing is full of those descriptive words and phrases. That will help you teach your readers a ton." I pointed to the chart we made during the connection. "Off you go to write! If you need to borrow an object, stay here for a moment."

Different Types

Library Card

The library card is flat like a piece of paper. It is smooth, white, blue, and has a silver chain.

For students who are new to English, you could ask questions: "Is it big? Is it small? Is it hard? Is it soft?" Then, coach children to repeat the full sentence (for example, "Yes, it is big").

Work Time

CONFERRING SUPPORTS ✦ Getting All Kids Writing about Their Chosen Objects

If . . .	You might . . .
A child's object seems plain or generic (e.g., a rock or a broken crayon)	• Remember that objects do not need to be fancy, unique, or significant to generate powerful descriptive writing. Indeed, much of the rigor in this bend comes from looking closely, finding the smallest details, and carefully describing even the most ordinary of objects. • Talk about these ordinary, generic objects as if they were gold. You might say things like, "Look at that fascinating rock. You'll be able to fill up pages with all of the things you see when you look closely at it!" • Ask the child to tell you *why* they chose the object. A seemingly simple item may have great meaning or hold real interest for that child. Be careful not to make assumptions; instead, offer the benefit of the doubt.
A child doesn't bring in an object	• Say, "Let's look at your school bag. Wow—there's so much here you could write about. Your soccer key ring or even your awesome backpack." • Spend time helping the child find an object at school that is meaningful to them. "You love PE. Let's ask Ms. Riel if you can borrow one of the PE scooters to write about."
A child says, "I don't know what to write" or "There's nothing to write about this!"	• Invite them to talk with a friend. "How about meeting with your partner? I'm sure Kyla has lots of questions about your baseball cap to help you get started." • Provide encouragement and enthusiasm, and remind the child of what they've learned already about this type of writing. You might say, "Remember, even ordinary things, like the trash can, can be so interesting if we look carefully. Look closely and really research. What could you teach someone?" • Offer other options: "If you aren't sure you want to write about what you brought, you can always write about this another day when you are ready. Is there something else in the classroom you'd like to write about?"
A child is interested in writing about a friend's object instead of their own	• React with enthusiasm. You might say, "I'm so curious to learn more about what *you* brought. I'm sure there are things only *you* can teach about this item." Or, "Wow! Is that a diya? For diwali? Tell me what you know about that!" • Kids may simply be excited about each other's objects. You might offer them the chance to investigate the friend's object as part of a Choice Time observation station, or you might suggest that they borrow the object to write another book on a future day. Or, if the other child doesn't mind, you could suggest that the friends share the object, making sure they write about it separately.
A child begins to tell or write a story about their item, instead of authoring an information book	• Remind the child of the purpose of the paper they chose: "Hmm, . . . this page says, 'How It Looks.' Does what you wrote teach somebody about how your object looks? Reread it and check." • Say, "Wow, your notebook must be so important to you—you wrote all about the time you got it. What can you *teach* us about your object? Make sure you write that in your book too."

SMALL GROUP ✦ Starting an Information Book

For this small group, you'll need the "Ways to Start an Information Book" chart. 

■ **RALLY**

Explain that there are many ways to start an information book.

"Writers, you're all starting new books today. Congratulations! Can I give you a tip? There isn't just one way to start an information book. There are *many* ways to start them! Let's look at this list of beginnings that writers use for information books." I read aloud the chart to kids.

■ **TRY IT #1**

Ask students to help you rehearse different ways you could start your book.

"I already created my cover for the next book I'm going to write, 'All about Staplers.' I'm ready to rehearse how the beginning could go. Let me look at this chart for ideas. I could say, 'Did you want to know all about staplers? I can teach you!' or I could say, 'Did you know that we have three staplers in the classroom?' Or I could say . . . Can you help me out? What other ways could I start my information book about staplers?" I gave students a quick moment to say how my book could start.

■ **TRY IT #2**

Recruit students to rehearse the beginning for their own books.

"Now it's your turn. Grab the cover for the book you're going to write next. Then, tell your partner how you might start that book. Try a few different ways to see what sounds best. Use the chart to help you."

■ **LINK**

Send students off to write their books, reminding them to keep this chart in mind as they start new books.

"Wow, writers! You've rehearsed so many different ways to start your next information book. Decide on one and then get writing! And remember, any time you start a new book, you can use this chart to help you."

MID-WORKSHOP TEACHING ✦ Choosing the Just-Right Word

"Writers, do you remember the story of Goldilocks? Do you remember how she tried a few different bowls of porridge? One was too hot, one was too cold, and one was just right! And she did the same thing with chairs and with beds. I bet that if Goldilocks were here writing with us, she'd spend lots of time choosing the just-right word. You can do that in your writing too.

"Let me explain what I mean. Greyson is writing about his medical ID bracelet. First, he said that the bracelet was shiny. Then he thought, 'Is *shiny* the just-right word?' And he realized, no way! Greyson's bracelet has these little pieces of silver, so he decided it is *sparkly*. *Sparkly* was his just-right word.

"Do you want to try out some of this Goldilocks work right here, right now? Go ahead and find a place in your book where you used a descriptive word." I gave students a moment to hunt through their books. "Now think to yourself, 'Is this the just-right word?' If it is, keep writing. If it's not, think for a moment, find the just-right word, then add it in."

As students got started, I added, "If you don't have any descriptive words that you can work with, though, you know what to do. Reread, find a place where they might go, and then add them in!"

SMALL GROUP ✦ Writing with Sensory Details

For this small group, you will need copies of the "Writers Include Lots of Different Details!" chart. You will also need your demonstration text, "All About the Trash Can."

■ RALLY

Explain that one way to elaborate is by adding in lots of sensory details.

"Writers, all of you who are sitting here have already done a lot to incorporate really tiny details in your books. Congratulations!

"I'd like to give you a tip. Great writers don't just add in more and more and more details. They add in different *kinds* of details such as sensory details. Sensory details show what you hear . . ." Touch your ear. "And details that show what you feel . . ." I touched my hands. "And there are also details that show . . ." I touched my nose and my lips, letting kids chime in to name the other senses.

■ TRY IT #1

Return to your book about the classroom trash can, this time channeling students to help you add other sensory details.

I opened my book about the trash can to the third page, about what to do when the trash can gets really full. "I know that I have details about what I *see* when the trash can is really full, but I don't have anything about what I *feel*. Or what I *smell*."

When the trash can gets really full, you can squish things down and fit more in it. Be careful! If your trash can has food in it, like banana peels and apple cores, you want to try not to touch those when you are squishing the garbage down. Yuck! A full trash can is very smelly. It smells like apples and stinky bananas.

I stood over the trash can and took a big, dramatic sniff. "Hmm, . . . the trash can sort of smells like apples, and I smell old papers, but mostly . . . apples." I picked up a pen and quickly added this to my book. "Can you all help me out? Don't get too close but take a sniff. What do you smell? What should I add to my book?"

I gave students a quick moment to smell the trash can and come up with a new sentence.

■ TRY IT #2

Recruit students to add sensory details to their own books.

"Now it's your turn. Carefully study your subject to find more kinds of sensory details to add to your writing. Pay attention not only to what you *see*, but also to what you *smell*, *hear*, *feel*, maybe even what you'd *taste*!

"Take this chart with you, since these sentence starters might help you get started."

■ LINK

Remind students to continue this work as they write independently.

"Wow, writers! After this, as you work in this book, and on your next books, make sure you remember that you can add not only more *details*, but also more *kinds* of details. You can add what you . . ." and I touched my eyes, my ears, my hands, as the kids joined into a recitation of the senses.

 # Commas Can Help Punctuate a List

Tell students that writers use commas to separate the words in lists. Emphasize this by using gestures, and invite students to gesture with you.

I gathered students back at the carpet and pointed to the chart with descriptive words for Rasheed. "I bet, once you started writing, you came up with so many descriptive words to include in your book—maybe even as many as are on our chart!

"When you come up with that many words, though, writing them down can get really tricky." I took out a blank piece of "On the Outside" paper. "Now, let's say that I wanted to write about how Rasheed looks." I quickly jotted *Rasheed is*, then began moving the sticky notes from the chart onto my page, placing the sticky notes next to each other. Soon, it read *Rasheed is friendly fluffy tan*.

"Now, listen to how it sounds." I read the sentence, exaggerating the speed and closeness of the words. "Yikes!" I said, wiping my brow. "So many words, all squished together! Let's see if Valorie Fisher can help us solve this problem and make it sound smoother."

I took out *Now You Know How It Works* and opened to page 15, that is all about garbage. I read:

Glass, metals, and plastics are crushed, chopped, and melted.

"Do you all see those marks that the author put in between each of these words?" I pointed to the commas in the first series of words. "These are called commas, and they separate words in a list. See how there are lots of words here in a list: *Glass*, *metals*, and *plastics*? And she does it again with another list." I pointed to the second series in that same sentence and again read it aloud. "'Crushed, chopped, melted.' Listen to how it sounds when I read this page with the commas." I modeled reading the words, making a big dramatic comma hand gesture in the air as I encountered each one. Then, I invited kids to make comma gestures with me as I reread the sentence.

Channel students to check if they have written lists of words that require commas.

"I bet there are places in your books where you have lists like Valorie. You're going to need to add commas to those lists. Go ahead and take out the book you worked on today. Look for a list, and, if you find one, read it out loud, add the commas with your hand, then add the commas with a pen! If you don't have a list, add one!"

PHONOLOGICAL AWARENESS AND PHONICS EXTENSION ◆

For this extension, show a phonological awareness video. 

This video begins with a poem containing many blends and digraphs. While reading the poem with the instructor, students listen for the blends and digraphs. The video moves on to reading by analogy. The instructor shows a snap word, followed by a few words that have similar endings; for example, *went*, *spent*, and *tent*. Students will find that the sounds in the snap words they've just read will help them read the vowels and the word endings of the new words. Finally, the video moves on to dictation. Students first orally segment words starting and ending in blends, then write the word.

Writing More Quickly, Using Words You Know in a Snap

TODAY YOU will teach kids that to teach lots, writers need to write quickly. You'll provide your students with a concrete way to do this—by spelling word wall words and other words they've memorized "in a snap," not stopping to think about those spellings. You'll demonstrate this, channeling kids to participate by snapping as you write snap words. You'll want to keep the momentum high as kids go off to write; you'll coach them on spelling quickly so they can write lots. During the mid-workshop, you'll give kids a way to troubleshoot, telling them that if they slow down, they can go back and reread to get some momentum. In the share, you'll rally kids to use "I did it!" stickers to mark words they worked hard to spell before they show those words to a partner.

TODAY YOUR STUDENTS will continue writing information books about their special objects from home. They'll begin this process during the minilesson, rehearsing a page in their booklet, figuring out what words they can spell quickly, and then beginning to write the words on the page. Students will head off to write fast and furious, working to write without stopping after each word. As the session wraps up, students will use "I did it!" stickers to mark words they worked hard to spell correctly, and they'll celebrate those words with a partner.

Getting Ready

YOU WILL NEED . . .

- the "Our Spelling Toolbox" chart, the version with two strategies displayed.

- a blank "Question and Answer" paper to continue writing your demonstration text, "The Key Ring." An example of the revised demonstration text for this session can be found in the online resources.

- the class word wall displayed.

- Rasheed, the phonics mascot, close at hand. If you do not use Units of Study in Phonics, you can simply skip that part of the link.

- to coordinate with a kindergarten class to have them visit during the share of the next writing workshop.

STUDENTS WILL NEED . . .

- their booklets from the previous session.

- three "I did it!" stickers (see Share). You may decide to print these templates on adhesive paper so students can stick them directly on their writing, or print the them on blank paper and provide students with tape.

Ensuring Access

YOUR ULTIMATE GOAL TODAY is to boost students' writing fluency, so that rather than pausing after every word, they write longer before taking a break.

- For some children, the self-directed nature of the workshop can make writing fluently difficult, because it can be hard to plan and anticipate where to take breaks within this time, making it feel unending. This is particularly true for children who have difficulty with executive functioning. If you notice kids who become frustrated or fatigued, help them to design an individualized checklist or personal schedule for writing time to encourage them to work for longer and longer stretches, interspersed with movement breaks.

- If you have students who are still working to spell the snap words correctly, consider different ways you can provide practice. Give pointers to a few kids who need to practice their snap words, and invite them to stand by the word wall, pointing to the words on the word wall as you say them. Or, you could invite those students to pull out their own personal word walls, referencing those as they write. They might write a word, check their personal word wall for the spelling, and then rewrite the word correctly if needed.

- There's a risk with any spelling session that kids will get nervous to take spelling risks, deciding to spell only the words they can spell with 100% accuracy. Even though you're pushing for correct spelling of known words, make sure you also cheerlead risk taking today. Encourage kids to use big domain-specific words as they write, and to do their very best to stretch out those words. Coach students as they write these words, pushing them to listen for more sounds in each word and to make sure each syllable has a vowel.

- For beginning writers who are comfortable labeling and are ready to write simple sentences, you could give each a few key snap word cards, such as *this*, *is*, and *a*, and have them say the sentence as they form the cards into a personal sentence starter to use. Try to stay away from providing students written lists of sentence starters at their desks, as it is more important that they orally practice sentences and then write what they say.

Minilesson

Writing More Quickly, Using Words You Know in a Snap

CONNECTION

Act out a hike in which you stop every few steps to rest. Use that to rally students toward the work of writing without constant stopping.

"Writers, let's do some pretending. Let's pretend that I'm going to hike from our school to a school that is in a whole other town." I stood up and pretended to gather my things. "I've got my hiking stick and my knapsack. Here I go!"

I put the heel of one foot against the toe of the other, making tiny steps. I took two baby steps and said, "I better stop and rest!" I sat down, took a deep breath, and stood back up. Then I took one more tiny step, and again took a seat.

"How's my hike going? Turn and talk."

The kids agreed that I wasn't making much progress. "So writers, to travel a distance, to make a lot of progress, people can't walk two baby steps and then take a break, then walk one more baby step and take another break. People can't move in a stop-and-go way.

"But that's exactly how some people write! Some people write like this . . ." I pretended to write a word, then shook my hand out, stretched, and then wrote one more word. "If you want readers to learn a lot from your writing, you need to write a lot, and that means writing a whole bunch of sentences before you take a break."

◆ **Name the teaching point.**

"So today I want to teach you that writers write a whole sentence or even a few sentences before taking a break. One way they can do this is by writing words they know how to spell quickly in a snap. If it's not a snap word, they quickly stretch it out."

I displayed the "Our Spelling Toolbox" chart with the first two strategies.

TEACHING

Continue writing the key ring book. Emphasize that using words you know can help you write more quickly. Invite kids to snap when you get to a word-wall word.

"Let me show you how I do this. I'm working on a question and answer page for my book about my key ring." I displayed a blank question-and-answer page to the class. "If a word is one that is on our word wall, remind me by snapping your fingers like this." I snapped, and the kids followed suit, snapping as best they could.

"Okay, I want to write 'Why does the key ring have a library card?'" I picked up my pen. "*Why* . . . nope! Not a snap word, but I bet I can still write it pretty quickly." I wrote *why* on the page and continued. *Does.* That's also not a snap word, but I'm going to stretch it out quickly." I modeled writing the word *does*, stretching out the sounds I knew. *The!* I glanced at the word wall as a chorus of snapping fingers interrupted me. "That's right! *The* is a word I know. I can write it in a snap. *T-H-E.*" I quickly wrote the word.

I continued writing the question, modeling how I stretched out the words *key* and *ring*, and used the word wall to quickly write *have* and *a*. I also quickly stretched out *library* and *card*.

I moved through the rest of the sentence, pointing out the snap words and the stretch words. I wrote down the snap words as quickly as possible, using the word wall as a reference.

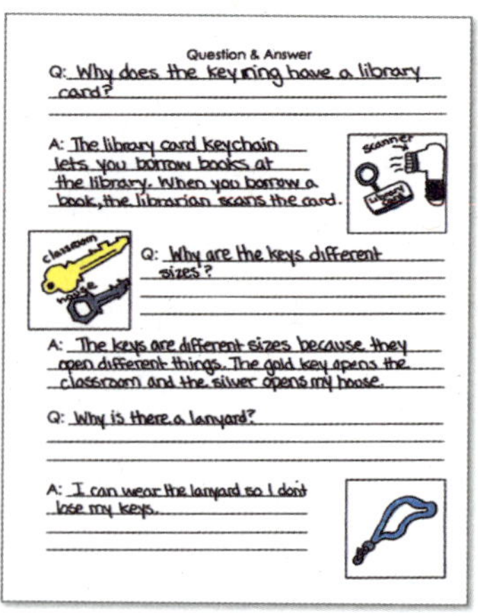

When I reached the end of the sentence I continued. "Did you see how I wrote a whole sentence without taking a break? I didn't need to rest at all. I said each word and thought, 'Is it on the word wall?' If it was, I wrote it in a snap." I snapped my fingers to punctuate the point. "Any words that weren't on the word wall I did my best to stretch quickly so I could get my whole question on the page."

ACTIVE ENGAGEMENT

Channel students to rehearse and then quickly write their next sentences. Tell them to do this by writing high-frequency words in a snap, only stretching out some.

"Writers, I know you all are trying to write loooong books with a lot of information. So, you will want to use our word wall which helps us speed up our writing!" I gestured toward the word wall. "Search through your folders and pull out the book you'll write today. You'll probably be writing more about your object from home, but you might decide to start a new book about another object in the classroom.

"Once you have your book, open it to the page you are going to write first. I'll give you a minute to think, think, think about what you'll write on that page."

"Touch the page and quietly say what you'll write on it.

"Now do it again. Whisper what you're going to write on your page, and this time, and as you do so, snap for every snap word. Watch me do it first so you know what to do." I said my next sentence, "The library card keychain lets you borrow books at the library.

"Are you ready to write? Let's see how fast you can go. You are going to try to write everything without stopping, no breaks. And remember when you come to snap words—don't stretch them out. Just think, 'I know this word' and spell it from your memory, or from the word wall, in a snap!" I snapped my finger when I said "snap." "Grab your pens, ready, write!" I gave students just a minute to get started and coached in as needed, snapping when I saw kids writing snap words.

LINK

Remind writers of the tools they have in their writing folders and throughout the room to help them write their sentences quickly.

"Writers, it's time to head back to your spots to keep working on your writing, but I want to remind you that there are tools all over our classroom that can help you! Look around! Point to something that might be useful when you're stuck on a word."

Kids pointed to word walls and charts around the room. "Yes! The word wall. The ABC chart! Look, Rasheed popped in to point out our blends and digraphs chart!" I held up the class phonics mascot. "And he said to remember the copy of the word wall that is in your writing folder! Thanks, Rasheed! Don't forget to use the tools around you, and don't slow down! Off you go!"

You may want to finish this page later on, so that you have a completed book by the end of this bend.

If kids are out of booklets with sketched covers, quickly offer a few suggestions for new writing topics.

If you have students in the earliest stages of language development— new to speaking English, or still in a silent stage of acquisition—they may be mostly working to label pictures. You might encourage them to add snap words to their labels. For example, instead of just hook, they might write "the hook" or "a hook." Encourage them to orally use simple sentences (using lots of snap words!) as they point to pictures, even if this is not yet what they are comfortably writing. Also, remember the importance of having students perhaps write or speak in their own language, since their understanding of concepts and ability to teach about an object may far outstrip their learning of English.

Digital Writing Tip

Charts can quickly turn into wall clutter, and writing folders can become overstuffed. You can use digital tools to help solve these problems. If you work in a classroom with one-to-one devices, students might keep copies of their own collection of charts, including the word wall, on their device to access during writing time. If students learn remotely, add the relevant charts to your learning management software.

Work Time

SMALL GROUP ✦ Using Syllables to Spell Multisyllabic Words

For this small group, you'll need a few classroom objects that represent multisyllabic words (we use a stapler, scissors, pencil sharpener, eraser, ruler, and highlighter), as well as numbered sticky notes. Each partnership will need whiteboards and dry erase markers. You will also need copies of the "Writing Longer Words" chart.

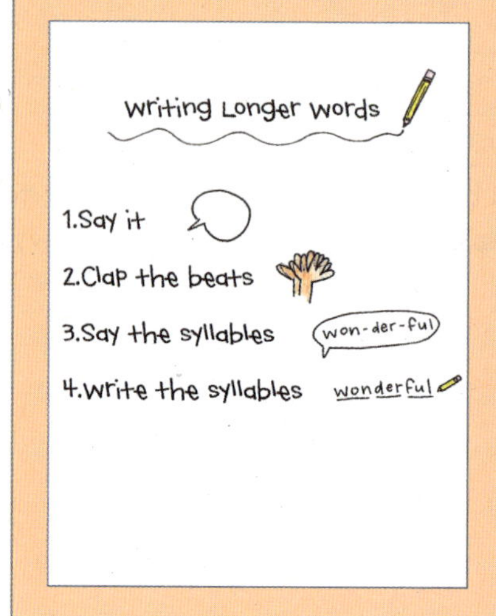

■ RALLY/ACTIVATE

Activate what students already know about syllables.

"Writers, I brought you here because all of you are making brave choices in your writing. You are writing big huge words. Sam wrote *stapler*; Gabe wrote *bulletin*. I want to help you write those looooong words.

"Remember that it helps to break those words into syllables, parts, like this: syl/la/ble. I have some school supplies here." I laid out a stapler, scissors, sharpener, eraser, ruler, and highlighter. "With your partner, touch each object, say what it is, and then clap the beats. Make sure you can hear the syllables.

"Now remember, if you are writing one of those big long words, you write it part by part, and when you go to write a part, think, 'Are there other words I know that have that same part?'"

■ TRY IT

Invite students to help you write some big words by clapping the beats, saying the syllables, and then writing on a whiteboard.

"What if I was writing about school supplies and needed to write all of these words? Can you and your partner help me figure out how to spell each of these things?" I gestured to the pile of objects. "Work with your partner to write the name of each object, thinking carefully about the word parts you know that could help you spell these longer words." I distributed a whiteboard and marker to each partnership.

■ LINK

Set students up to continue spelling multisyllabic words syllable by syllable as they write.

"I know you are so excited to get back to your own writing. Do that—and when you come to a big long word, remember to spell it syllable by syllable."

Possible Coaching Moves:

▸ *"Clap it. What's the first syllable? Write the sounds. What's the next syllable? Write the sounds."*

▸ *"How many syllables did you hear? Draw a line for each syllable. Now write each syllable!"*

▸ *"Sharpener . . . break it into parts. Are there other words you know that have some of the same parts?"*

▸ *"Make sure each syllable has a vowel!"*

▸ *"Check it! Slide your finger under the parts and read the word you wrote."*

MID-WORKSHOP TEACHING ✦ **Writers Gain Momentum by Backing Up and Rereading**

"Writers, many of you are writing up a storm; that's great! I've also noticed that some of you are coming to hard words and getting stuck. Thumbs up if that has ever happened to you." I nodded and stuck my own thumb up. "It definitely happens to me," I said.

"My suggestion is to think about writing kind of like riding a bike. If you're on your bike and you come to a bump in the road, you don't just sit there, do you? No way! Maybe you decide to back your bike up a little, and then go at it again. Backing up can help you get over the bump and keep going; backing up helps build momentum.

"So remember, if you come to a bump in the road when you are writing, back up. Reread your writing, get some momentum, and whew! You'll be over it and racing along, writing, writing, writing."

VOICEOVERS ✦ Writing with Volume, Stamina, and Independence

Voiceovers to Support Volume

- "Turn the page and teach some more!"
- "What will you teach next? Write it fast and furious. Don't stop. Just keep writing!"
- "Touch the page you want to write next. Ready, set, write!"
- "Study your picture, and then add what you notice to your book."
- "There are just five more minutes of writing workshop. Touch the line you will write to and keep going."
- "__________ just added another page to her book! Who else plans to add another page today?"
- "If you're not sure of a word you want to write in English, you can write it in another language or skip it and come back later. Keep writing!"

Voiceovers to Support Stamina

- "Try not to stop after you write each word. Write the whole sentence."
- "That's a snap word. Write it in a snap."
- "Try to write, write, write to the end of the page before you take a break."

Voiceovers to Support Independence

- "Don't forget that you are brave spellers! Say the word, stretch it, and write all the sounds you hear."
- "Use the word wall to help you spell your snap words."
- "Remember, when you are done, you can add more to your pictures, add more words, or start a new book."

CONFERENCE ✦ Returning to Unfinished Books to Teach Even More

■ RESEARCH/DECIDE

Show fascination with the writer's topics. Convey your desire to learn more.

I pulled up next to Lucas and noticed that he had a folder with many books on the red "completed" side of his folder. "Look at all of your books! You've been hard at work for the past few days, haven't you? Can you take me on a tour through your folder?"

Lucas showed me a few books, saying, "I wrote here about my cubby, and in here about the block center, and here is something I taught people about the lunch bin." As Lucas showed me his books, I noticed a pattern: each book only had a sentence of writing on the first page or two, and the remaining pages were blank.

Compliment the writer's work and affirm that he still has more to teach.

"Lucas, you're the kind of writer who is really thoughtful about what you want to teach your readers. You've got all of these topics planned, and you are just overflowing with things to write!"

State the teaching point.

"I'm noticing that there are lots of books that you didn't finish." As I spoke, I pointed out the pages that were still blank. "I bet that if you filled up these pages you could teach your readers even more!"

■ TEACH

Channel the writer to sort their books into two piles—one for completed books, and one for books that are still not finished.

"Let's take out the books that you thought were done, and see if there's still more that you could teach."

Lucas picked up his block book and flipped through it. "I was thinking that the block book was done, but I didn't write anything here or here." He showed the last two pages.

"Okay," I said. "Let's move it to the green side. You've got more work to do on it!"

Lucas and I repeated the process with the rest of the books on the red-dot side. "Whoa, I don't have *any* finished books!" said Lucas.

Help the writer plan for completing these books.

"Lucas," I said, "you have important work to do! Let's make a plan to finish some of these books! You know how during reading workshop you make a reading stack, so you can read your books in order? Today, you can make a *writing* stack so you have a plan to finish one book, then the next, then the next. As you write, think, 'What else would my reader want to know?' This will help you to both write an entire book and teach tons inside of that book!"

BEND I FIG. 8–1 Lucas's book about the block area has many empty lines.

When you research looking for a teaching point, keep your eyes peeled for patterns that show up across many pieces. One unfinished book isn't something to fret over, but Lucas had several unfinished books across the week.

Make your compliment as far-reaching as possible. Avoid complimenting the minutiae—use your compliments to teach about big ideas of the genre.

State the "why" as you give the teaching point. Having a real, authentic purpose makes it more likely that the child will engage in the work.

Embedded here are some big messages about process. As Lucas sorts his books, he learns that writing is never finished, that adding more and revising are always options.

I make this part of the teaching quick, and I don't belabor elaboration strategies. After all, Lucas has already been taught something. I make a note to check how his work is coming later in the workshop.

Tackling *Humongous* Words and Familiar Words with Courage and Confidence

Channel kids to prepare for partners by finding spelling accomplishments to share. Then, invite them to share and celebrate.

"Writers, in a minute or two, you'll have some time to share your writing with your partner. But first you need to get ready by rereading your writing and thinking about spelling. I'm going to give you three 'I did it!' stickers. Will you reread your writing and find hard words that you tackled? Places where you are proud of yourself? Put your 'I did it!' stickers on those parts and get ready to tell your partner all about it!" I roamed the room as kids worked.

After a moment, I called students back together and said, "Writers, so many of you tackled those *humongous* words with courage! You didn't let the length of those words stop you. And others of you wrote snap words " (I snapped), "in a flash, quick as a wink!

"Okey dokey. Go for it! Share and celebrate!"

Explain that kids will share their books with a different audience tomorrow—a class of kindergartners.

After a bit of time for sharing, I called the group back together. "Wow! These books are so fantastic that other people just *have* to read them. I invited a class of kindergartners to visit at the end of writing workshop tomorrow. You'll get to share your books with them. They will learn *so* much from you!"

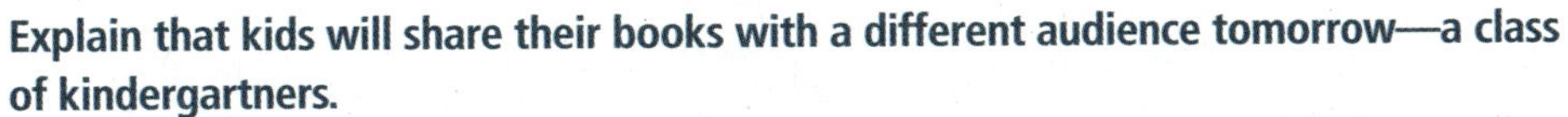

PHONOLOGICAL AWARENESS AND PHONICS EXTENSION ✦ Listening for Blends and Digraphs

For this extension, you'll need a copy of the "Blends and Digraphs" chart. 

Say a series of words that have blends or digraphs at the beginning or end. Have students point to the blends and digraphs chart to indicate which sound they hear.

I asked students to gather on the carpet with their individual copies of the blends and digraphs chart. "Friends, we're going to play a listening game. I'm going to say a word, and the word is going to have a blend or a digraph. You're going to listen to the words that I say, figure out which blend or digraph you hear, and point on your chart to show which one you hear."

I initially said a few words out loud that had blends or digraphs at the beginning. When students had difficulty, I coached and said, "*Frog, friend*. Do those two words sound the same at the beginning?" After we did a few words with blends and digraphs at the beginning of words, we worked on a few words with blends and digraphs at the end.

Words with Beginning Blends and Digraphs: *shower, thunder, cheese, friend, skirt, green, stop, clap, plant, flute, sleep*

Words with Ending Blends and Digraphs: *best, crash, mask, munch, fifth*

Getting Our Books Ready for Readers

TODAY YOU will remind students that this is the final work session they'll have to get their writing ready for the kindergarten visitors, who will arrive for the share. You'll set this up by explaining to students that they need to be responsible for their writing and make sure that it makes sense for readers. Rasheed will leave a book for your class, and you'll help him by finding confusing places that could be fixed up. As students write, you'll remind them of the tools around the room that can help them spell words quickly. During the share, you'll welcome visitors to your room, and invite students to share their writing.

TODAY YOUR STUDENTS will publish their topic books by sharing them with kindergarten visitors. Before that, they will choose a book they've already written, and then reread and fix their writing, using a *power pen* (a familiar tool from kindergarten). Students may fix up their writing in different ways: by practicing spelling longer words, revising parts that don't make sense, or editing for punctuation. Regardless of what they work on, all students will use the word wall, charts, and other tools around the room.

Getting Ready

YOU WILL NEED . . .

- Rasheed, the first-grade phonics mascot. If you are not using the Units of Study in Phonics, you will need to alter the teaching.

- a copy of Rasheed's book, "The Block Area." 

- a few star stickers, to mark up Rasheed's writing.

- to arrange for kindergartners to visit your classroom during the share, if you have not yet done so.

STUDENTS WILL NEED . . .

- a colored pen (referred to as a power pen) for editing, one per student.

- their published book to share with the kindergarten visitors (see Share).

Ensuring Access

YOUR ULTIMATE GOAL TODAY is twofold. First, you'll teach students that writers spend time fixing up their writing before they share it with readers, to make sure that their readers will be able to read their work as easily as possible. And second, you'll help drive home the concept of writing for an authentic audience. Writing becomes more real and more powerful when it's shared with others; this concept can be incredibly motivating to young writers.

- If you have students who normally need support when they work in partnerships, be ready to offer reminders of the ways partners work together when they are meeting with their kindergarten visitors. Reference partner charts you have in your room to support this work. You could even join a partnership as a "proficient partner," modeling the partner behaviors you hope to see your first-graders take on.

- MLLs in the early stages of English language acquisition can sometimes feel put on the spot when asked to read their writing with others. Give students a chance to prepare for the share by inviting them to read their writing a few times to prepare. If students are not yet producing oral language in English, pair them in a triad with two other first-graders and invite the three students to study the book together, discussing what they see. You'll want to make sure all students get a chance to share their books, even if they don't share orally.

Getting Our Books Ready for Readers

CONNECTION

Speaking quickly and with urgency, remind students that visitors are coming today. Tell students that they need to get ready to show off their writing.

"Writers, hurry, hurry. The visitors are coming, the visitors are coming! The kindergarten kids are coming *today*, and they are getting excited to read your books. You just have today's writing workshop to get ready to show off the information writing you have done. Let's have a super-quick minilesson because we have a *lot* to do."

✦ **Name the teaching point.**

"Today I want to teach you that before you share your writing, you need to reread it, checking that your readers will be able to read it easily. You can check your writing by pretending to be the reader and finding places you need to fix up."

TEACHING

Tell a quick story that illustrates the importance of being responsible and checking on yourself.

"I've been remembering how, when I was your age, my mom used to ask me to open my backpack and show her my homework so she could check that I'd remember to bring it. Then she'd look at my shoes and check that I'd tied them. After that, I'd grab my lunch and head out to the bus.

"But one day, as I was getting ready to head out to the bus, I approached my mom in the kitchen and opened my backpack. She said, 'Zip it up. I don't need to see your homework.' I was a little confused because I was so used to her checking for my homework; she did it every morning! 'You mean I don't have to bring my homework to school anymore?' I asked her. 'Or tie my shoes?' She laughed and said, 'Of course you need to bring your homework and tie your shoes! But you are becoming a big kid now, and you don't need me to check on you.'

"I'm telling you this because this morning Rasheed brought me this book and asked me if it was okay. This is what I said to him."

I picked up Rasheed and looked him in the eye. "Rasheed, you want me to give your writing a thumbs up. But *you* are the writer, so that means *you* need to be the one who checks your writing. And to know if your writing is okay, you need to read it over. You read it over, fix it up, and then *you* give it the thumbs up."

This story has a lot of language. Don't worry if it is confusing for some students—the point will become clear as you model.

Rasheed's writing

With Rasheed on my lap, I projected the first page of his book, and said, "Let's pretend we are Rasheed, checking his writing." We read: "Her iz." Here I changed my voice and said, "'Her iz . . .' What does that mean?"

I continued reading: "the blocks place." I shook my head exaggeratedly.

Playing up the drama and the playfulness, I read the last sentence: "You play it here." I then wondered aloud, "What do they play here? And who is *you*? Who plays here?"

I pretended to wipe my brow. "Wow, that was confusing. Rasheed, I think you have some work cut out for you! You've got lots of fixing up to do!" I placed a few star stickers in the margin of his writing, where I'd stopped and noticed confusing parts. "Rasheed, these little stars will remind you of where you need to fix up your spelling, or tell the reader more about what you're trying to teach them." I added as an aside, "Writers, you won't need those star stickers, because you'll work with a different tool. I'm just doing this so Rasheed doesn't forget!"

Debrief, emphasizing the urgency and self-directed nature of this work.

"Writers, the kindergartners are coming today to learn from us. You need to get your books ready, so the kindergartners can read them. While Rasheed rereads and fixes up his book, will you do the same work with your book?"

ACTIVE ENGAGEMENT

Remind students of the "power pens" they used in kindergarten. Channel them to reread their own books to find places that need fixing up.

"Let's get started! First, sit up tall. To do this work today, you're going to need one of the tools that you might remember from last year: a power pen!" I held up a pen to the students.

I explained as I distributed the pens. "Do you remember how these pens work? No? Let me remind you, then. You'll turn this pen upside down, to the 'not-writing' side, to reread your writing and—here's why it's so handy—if you find that you need to fix something, you can turn it rightside up and use it to edit and write!

"Now that you're ready, get out the book you most want to share with our visitors. Start rereading it. When you see something that needs fixing, turn your pen the other way and fix it!"

I gave students a moment to reread and fix up their writing. As they worked, I gave a reminder. "Remember that you are responsible for your book. It's your job to make sure our visitors can read it easily."

LINK

Send students off to their seats with their books and pens so that they can fix up their writing for a celebration during the share.

"Writers, eyes up here, just for a second. You're off to such a good start, finding parts that need fixing, and even being super responsible and just fixing them here and now. Give a thumbs up if you've already fixed something." I paused, then added, "And give a thumbs up if you know what you're going to fix next."

I saw the rug fill with thumbs-up signals, with students nodding or holding up pages they'd marked to be fixed. "Okay then, off you go! Head to your seats and get your pieces ready for our visitors. They're coming in twenty minutes!"

Q&A ✦ Editing and Preparing to Celebrate

Q **Why celebrate at the end of the bend? Why not wait until the end of the unit?**

A Your celebration here is small—just a share—but we urge you not to skip it. It's important to give students a purpose for writing, to celebrate what they've tried, and to fuel their enthusaism for the remainder of the unit. Your students have accomplished a lot in a short amount of time; celebrate all of their early approximations in this new genre.

Q **What if my students make little to no changes to their writing? Or too many changes?**

A You might form small groups today based on students' approaches to editing. For example: students who aren't eager to make changes to their writing, students who add random information to a page, and students who are great at finding places in their writing to fix but aren't sure how to follow through with changes. Consider tools that might help each group.

Q **What if my students don't fix all of their spelling mistakes?**

A They likely won't! It isn't necessary to correct all spelling mistakes, since this is discouraging for most and has little transference to future pieces. Instead, invite students to look for words that don't look right and see if they can use their phonics knowledge to fix them up. Hold students accountable for using the word wall as they fix up snap words and add any frequently used words to their own personal word walls. What's most important is to teach students the hard work of editing and fixing their writing; that is work that real authors do, and it comes with the reward of others being able to read your writing.

Q **What do I do if kids' writing doesn't make sense?**

A Consider pulling students in a small group or having them work with their writing partner to read their writing aloud. As they hear their writing read aloud, they can listen for where words are missing or where they've added extra words and get feedback. Rereading their own writing can sometimes be tricky. Have writing partners trade their writing, read it aloud, and ask themselves, "Does this part sound like how a book would go?"

Q **What if students have written some of their piece in another language?**

A First, celebrate! This means your writers feel comfortable expressing themselves and their stories using their full linguistic repertoire, which is called *translanguaging*. Encourage students to proudly share their writing, whatever the language.

SMALL GROUP ✦ Finding Fix-Up Spots, and Fixing Them Up!

For this small group, you'll need copies of Gerty's writing, "The Writing Center," one per partnership.

■ **RALLY**

Suggest that writers look closely and find more things to fix. Brainstorm and list things they can look for when editing.

"Writers, some of you are finding just one thing to fix up on each page of your writing. We've been looking closely at lots of different things in this unit. I think we can do the same in our writing, and find lots of things to fix up.

"Let's make a list of things to check for. You say them, and I'll write them on this white-board!" Students' list included: capitals, periods, exclamation points, question marks, snap words, missing words.

■ **TRY IT #1**

Ask students to help you do this work on your neighbor Gerty's writing.

"My neighbor, Gerty, brought me her writing. She wants your help fixing it up! Read her writing, and if you notice anything that needs fixing, jump in and help her."

■ **TRY IT #2**

Ask students to switch pieces and count the number of fix-its needed. Then have them switch back and try to fix up those places.

"Sometimes it's easier to see fix-ups in another writer's writing, just like we did with Gerty's writing. Gerty doesn't have her own writing partner, but you do! Swap your writing with your partner and read. If you see a fix-up that is needed, leave a tiny pencil dot in that place. Remember, look for things like snap words that need to be fixed up, missing punctuation, and even places where your partner needs to add a word or take a word out. When you're done, give the book back to the writer, and writers, go ahead and fix those things up!"

■ **LINK**

Celebrate how writers fixed up their writing. Encourage partners to try this work moving forward.

"Wow, writers! You found so many places to fix up! From now on, try to read super-closely when you're looking for fix-up spots, and know you can use a partner to help you see more."

The writing center haz
Many things it haz pens,
paper, and revision flaps.
in writing workshop you
can tak what you need
you need it

the paper in the writing
center iz different some
hav a lot of lins. It is fun
to pick!

Gerty's writing

Possible Coaching Moves:

▸ *"Check for words you know in a snap!"*

▸ *"Reread this part again. Does this sound like how a book would talk?"*

▸ *"Talk with your partner if you can't find all the fix-its."*

MID-WORKSHOP TEACHING ✦ Using the Room to Help You Write

"Writers, have you ever seen a carpenter with his toolbelt on? He might have a hammer hanging from his belt, and a ruler, and tons of tools. Well, I wish that there were toolbelts for writers, because writers need tools too!

"You know, the whole entire room holds so many tools for you. There are words all over this room that can help you spell. If I was writing about the block area, where could I get help spelling *blocks*?" The kids pointed to the sign near the blocks. "Awesome. Now I have a harder question. If I wanted to spell *clock*, where could I get help?"

The kids looked at the clock, but there wasn't a label beside it. I went and collected the word *blocks* from the block area and brought it to the meeting area. "*This* could help me spell *clock*. Can you see why?"

The kids talked and realized that *clock* rhymed with *block*. "What if I wanted to spell *rock*? Where could I find help?" The kids called out and pointed at the "Blocks" sign.

"You know, you can even use your friends' names as tools." I pointed toward the name chart. "What if I wanted to write *thin*? Whose name could help me? Yes! Thatcher!

"Remember there are so many tools all around the room, and you can use all of them to fix up your writing."

CONFERRING SUPPORTS ✦ Common Punctuation Errors

You might notice . . .	To coach with more scaffolding . . .	To remind or coach with less scaffolding . . .
The writer has punctuation that conveys a visual break, not a meaning break (for example, after each word, or at the end of each line)	• "Punctuation shows a reader where to pause and take a breath. Listen to how I read your writing. Is that how you want it to sound?" • "Read your piece with the punctuation that you have. What do you notice? You are pausing a lot. Take out the punctuation that you don't need!"	• Provide an example: "Hmm, . . . I'm looking at my book, and I only had a period where I really needed it. You've got some extras. Fix it up!"
The writer has written a piece with no punctuation	• "Punctuation tells readers where to pause and that an idea is complete. It would sound weird if we didn't pause at all! Listen to how I read this." • "Read it. Where do you stop to take a breath? That's where the punctuation should be!"	• "Is your piece missing punctuation? Add it in!" • "Your reader won't know where to pause, where to stop. Add some punctuation."

You might notice . . .	To coach with more scaffolding . . .	To remind or coach with less scaffolding . . .
The writer has sentence fragments	• "A period shows where the idea stops. Let's read here. Is that a complete idea, or do you need the next part of your writing before you put a period?" • "Listen to how I read this. Would you want your reader to sound like that? Where should the punctuation go?"	• "Reread your writing, and stop when you get to a period. Is that a full thought? If not, move that period and finish your idea."
The writer has used a period where there should be a different end punctuation mark	• "It's great that you put some end punctuation here. I'm not sure it should be a period though. Let me read it the way you have it, and then with different punctuation. Will you decide which works best?" Read as written, as well as the correct way, and let the student decide which one sounds right. They can then quickly change the punctuation.	• "You've got a lot of end punctuation here—that's what strong writers do! Let's reread, though, to make sure it's the right type of punctuation. If not, change it to make it sound the way you want it to!"
The writer could use punctuation to enhance meaning, e.g., finding some places where exclamation marks would be appropriate	• "Punctuation can make people read with expression. Why don't you take this exclamation mark and move it to different places in your draft?" Hand the student a small sticky note with an exclamation mark on it. "You and I can take turns reading it the way the punctuation tells us to read it, and we'll see which works best."	• "You've worked really hard to use punctuation. Is there anywhere that you could make your reader sound excited? Or ask questions? Reread, and change the punctuation if you need to."
The writer has random capital letters	• "Every new sentence should start with a capital letter. Check your writing to make sure that there are no capitals in the middle of a sentence unless the word is the name of a person, place, or thing." • "I see a capital letter here. Does it belong there?" • "There's an extra capital letter here. Fix it; change it to a lowercase letter."	• "Check for capital and lowercase letters. Make sure that you don't have any capital letters in places where they don't belong!"
The writer has no capital letters or does not use a capital letter after a period or other end mark	• "Sentences need a line leader, so we use a capital letter at the beginning. Did you do that here?" Point to places where the child has made this error.	• "Check that all your sentences begin with a capital letter."

SMALL GROUP ✦ Getting Ready for Visitors' Questions

For this small group, you'll need your completed demonstration text, "The Key Ring."

■ RALLY

Remind students of the questioning nature of little kids. Connect this to the preparation needed for the visitors.

"Have you ever noticed that sometimes, when you're around little kids, they ask a lot of questions? They're always asking things like, 'Why does something go like that?' or 'How does that thing work?'

"It can be frustrating, but here's the thing: Our visitors are going to do the same thing! They're going to come in here, ready to hear your books, and they're going to ask tons and tons of questions! And we need to be ready to answer them!"

■ TRY IT #1

Read aloud one of the demonstration texts and pause to allow students to ask questions. Answer their questions as they are asked.

"Let's try it out together first. I'm going to read my book, and, while I'm reading, your job is to pretend to be one of those kids who is coming. Think about what they're going to want to know. When you have a question for me, give me a thumbs up so that I can answer it!"

I read the demonstration text out loud. While I read, I paused to allow a few students to ask questions, which I answered along the way. Questions included "What can you check out at the library?" "What do the different keys open?" "Why are the keys different colors?"

"Did you see how we were doing that? You were pretending to be the visitors, and you were thinking about what they might ask and I thought about how I'd answer them!"

■ TRY IT #2

Have students read their books to their partner, stopping for questions and answers as they read.

"Now it's time for you to try it with your partner. One partner is going to read their book out loud, and the other partner is going to ask questions along the way. Readers, make sure that you also answer those questions, so that you're ready for all of the visitors' questions!"

■ LINK

Leave the group but guide them to continue this work together.

"Writers, I have to scoot away. You can finish this work, and make sure that you switch too! Keep at it! The visitors are coming soon!"

> **Possible Coaching Moves:**
>
> ▶ *"Oh, what a great question! I bet some of our visitors will want to know that!"*
>
> ▶ *"I've noticed you haven't asked a question yet. Can you think of one?"*
>
> ▶ *"Remember that the visitors are going to ask lots of questions. Help your partner practice by asking lots too!"*

 The Visitors Are Here!

Welcome the kindergarten visitors to the classroom. Pair each first-grader with a kindergartner and encourage them to read their book aloud to their partner.

I asked students to bring the book they'd fixed up with them to the carpet. "I see that the kindergartners are all gathered outside, ready to learn!"

Before ushering the kindergartners in, I said, "Just like when you meet with your writing partner, you'll need to hold your book in between you and your kindergarten partner, and make sure you read in your proudest, but not too loud, voice. As soon as the kindergartners come in, their teacher and I will pair you up. And then you'll teach your own little student!"

As the kindergartners entered, I partnered them up with a first-grader who would read their book aloud to them. They found spots around the room, and the first-graders proudly began reading. The other teacher and I walked through the room, supporting and giving feedback.

After just a few minutes, I said, "Visitors, give the first-graders a round of applause! And first-graders, pat yourselves on the back. I bet your kindergarten readers have learned so much, and you've also shown them how they can teach people with their own writing. Great job!"

Writing about the Whole Wide World

Dear Teachers,

You and your students will be relieved that now, at last, they can write about the whole wide world of topics. To rally them and inspire them to come up with their own topics of personal expertise, you'll send them to perhaps the most inspiring part of the classroom: the library! Armed again with topic wands, your students will look through your classroom's bins of information books to figure out which books are *not yet* in the library, and to consider which books they can write. You'll want your students to say things like, "I don't see any books about pet cats, or baby sisters! I need to write those books!"

Don't worry if your nonfiction library feels limited or is mostly digital. You need not reorganize or restructure your library for the purposes of this bend. If your library doesn't feel like it's optimally set up, you might just go to the school library. Alternatively, students might simply look through their nonfiction book baggies to find potential topics.

Much of your students' success in the rest of this bend hinges on the topics that they choose in the first day of the bend. You'll want to help your students choose topics that are of a just-right size—not too big and not too small—and you'll want to make sure that they all plan some subtopics as well. Rally them to create several covers in the beginning for books they'll write and revise across the bend.

Across the first half of the bend, you'll teach students ways to lift the level of their writing. You'll start this work with illustrations. Across the rest of the bend, you'll teach about definitions, diagrams, pictures, comparisons, introductions, and conclusions. Throughout the bend, we call these moves "techniques," as they are things that your writers will do to achieve a specific end.

This is intricate and important work that lays the foundation for much of the information reading and writing that students will do throughout school. You'll find that the mentor text, which has been written specifically for this unit—*Cake* by Hareem Atif Khan— uses the teaching techniques that you'll show your students. Because *Cake* is featured as an online resource, you can print and provide multiple copies to students, and you'll want to carry it around as part of your own toolkit. You'll also craft your own demonstration text about dogs across the bend.

Remember that your library and your kids' book baggies are also full of many other mentor texts. Help your students ask, "What is the author doing to make sure that I learn a lot? How does this author teach their readers? Can I try those things too?"

All the best,

Lucy and Casey

Nonfiction Writers Get Inspired by Reading Other Authors' Work

In This Session

TODAY YOU will launch a new bend in this unit by rallying kids to get ideas for writing not only from things around them, but also from books! You'll use a topic wand again, this time showing how a writer can touch a book to spark ideas for topics that he also knows about. Books on bugs might spark thinking about bug bites or other animals like dogs, and lead to a book about these topics. Mid-workshop, you'll nudge the kids to transition from making covers to actually writing a book, encouraging them to conjure up mental images of the topic in order to think of important details to include. In the share, you'll invite partners to share information about their new topics.

TODAY YOUR STUDENTS will look at books to generate topic ideas and make covers for those books and then they'll write one. Generating topics and creating covers is important for the rest of the bend so that kids have a few ideas-in-waiting in their folders. As they write their own book today, they'll touch and tell across the pages, then sketch and write. Some students will complete a book today, and some will require a second day. At the end of workshop, partners will learn about each other as they discuss their topics.

Getting Ready

YOU WILL NEED . . .

- your topic wand from Bend I.

- several bins of information books to use as inspiration for topics.

- blank booklets to quickly jot ideas on each cover. You'll quickly sketch the cover for the book, "All About Dogs." An example of this cover can be found in the online resources. 👆

- to display the "How to Write a Teaching Book" chart from Bend I. 👆

- several empty book bins, ready to be labeled with new topics.

STUDENTS WILL NEED . . .

- their topic wands from Bend I.

- blank booklets with covers on their tables. For this bend, you'll want to stock your writing center with booklets that have smaller illustration space and more lines to write on than those in the previous bend. 👆

- access to the classroom library nonfiction book bins.

Ensuring Access

YOUR ULTIMATE GOAL TODAY is for kids to plan new information books and write one. The topics many kids write about will be less concrete than they were before. This is a small, more sophisticated step, but it allows students to draw on their personal expertise, so all your writers should be able to do this work.

- Your students will explore book bins during the active engagement. If you're concerned that your book bins do not have enticing topics, or that the topics may not inspire ideas in your students, feel free to simply place some of your most engaging, high-interest books in the middle of the carpet and you can help kids use each to spark zillions of topic ideas.

- Anytime you bring in books as models for students, it can be especially inclusive for MLLs to have books, whether physical copies or digital, in other languages. Be particularly cognizant, too, about inclusivity of topics in the books you bring out. For instance, if there are books about holidays, make sure you have a true variety of holidays from different cultures represented.

- Be fascinated by the things your kids know about and can teach you and invite the children in your classroom to show this same enthusiasm for learning from each other. Some kids will know how to use Kool-Aid to dye their hair, some will know how to ride a scooter. Create space in which peers can be fascinated by these topics and children will come to believe they are authorities on topics of interest to others. How empowering for our youngest students to be able to say, "The things I do every day are things that other people want to learn about!"

Nonfiction Writers Get Inspired by Reading Other Authors' Work

CONNECTION

Tell students that they are starting a new part of the unit. This time they'll be inspired not by the things in the classroom, but by the books in the library.

"Remember at the very start of this unit you took your topic wands and discovered topics all around you—the coat closet, the water fountain, the block center . . . You discovered that even the trash can could be a topic to teach about." I reached out with my wand as if touching each of those areas of the classroom.

Pointing my topic wand toward the library, I said, "Today starts a whole new part to our unit. I've been thinking of the big thing I want to teach you and it's this: there's something in this room that can help writers find new ideas for books." I began tapping the book bins nearby with my wand.

"Books!" several voices called out.

◆ **Name the teaching point.**

"That's right! Today I want to teach you that writers are also inspired by *books*. You can get ideas for your next book by looking at the topics that other authors write about. You can also get ideas for books by noticing topics that no one yet seems to have written about— those are topics that are calling out your name!"

TEACHING

Demonstrate looking at a book bin and getting ideas for your own books, books that could join those in the bin. Highlight topics on which you have personal expertise.

"Watch how I use these books to help me come up with new topics." I tapped a book bin with my topic wand and read the label on the front of it. "Transportation! The authors of all these books wrote about trucks and trains and boats and jets. I bet we could write a book to add to this bin. Maybe our book could be about buses. Some of us take buses. And you know what? Skateboarding is a kind of transportation too. My nephew likes to ride a skateboard and I watch him do tricks." As I thought aloud, I jotted each idea on the cover of a topic book, mentioning to the students that I would add the sketches—the subtopics—later.

I touched my topic wand to another bin and read the label aloud: "Bugs! Hmm, . . . I don't know very much about bugs, so I couldn't write a book about bugs. But I do know about other animals, like dogs! I have one at home. I could write about how dogs sleep and what they eat." I jotted the idea on the cover of another topic book. "Before I write a book on dogs, I want to remember some things about dogs that might go in my book." I scribbled a picture focused on dogs at night, and another showing dog food.

Point out that writers can look for the books that haven't yet been written, emphasizing especially topics on which you have personal expertise.

I looked at the other bins. "Hmm, . . . I can also think about things that aren't yet written, books that aren't yet in our library, but probably should be. Like, there aren't any books here about laundromats. And I know a lot about them because we have three near my apartment. I could write a book on laundromats." I glanced at the class. "You know, I'm looking

at Darron and wondering whether our library has books on paper airplanes, because if not, I know someone who could write one!"

I looked around at the other bins. "You know what other topic is missing? Gymnastics! I love gymnastics. I could teach readers what you need to wear, and all about the balance beam, and I could even have a page about cartwheels. Maybe I could start a new bin and fill it with books that teach about gymnastics. Or maybe we could make it a sports bin and you could help me fill it up?" I held up my pile of books with ideas jotted and sketched on the covers.

ACTIVE ENGAGEMENT

Invite partners to use topic wands to point at book bins and imagine books they could write, or books that haven't been written. Invite kids to share possible topics.

"Ready to try this? Scoot around to the edges of the rug so you can see the bins." I gave students a moment to rearrange themselves and put the nonfiction bins in the middle of the rug. "Partner 1, topic wand in the air! Use it to point to a bin of information books. Think of a book you could add to that bin. Then, it's Partner 2's turn to point and be inspired. Get started!"

After a minute or two, I called the group back together. "I'm going to use my topic wand to learn about the topics you've all thought about. When I point to you, will you share one of your book ideas?" I pointed to a number of students with my wand, inviting them to share their topics.

"Babysitting little sisters." "Double dutch." "Jouer à se déguiser. [Dress up.]" "Planets." "Donuts."

"And many more," I said, once students had shared.

LINK

Send kids off to sketch a few covers and then write books, reminding them to touch and teach, then sketch and write.

"You're full of so many great topics! I left a bunch of new booklets on the middle of every table, and there are more in the writing center. Grab a few blank booklets and make the covers for books about your new topics. Then choose the one you'll write first and get started." As I spoke, I gestured to the "How to Write a Teaching Book" chart from Bend I reminding students of the familiar process. "Remember to touch and teach across the pages, and then sketch and write.

"If you aren't sure of a topic, stay here on the rug, so we can work together. Otherwise, get started."

BEND II

SMALL GROUP ✦ Generating New Ideas

For this small group, you'll need blank booklets with covers and copies of the "All That You Know and Do Can Be a Topic!" chart.

■ **RALLY**

Introduce another way writers can generate ideas to write topic books.

"Writers, today we learned that the topic books we write about can be inspired by the books in our classroom library. But, that's not the only way to get new ideas. I made a chart of some things that can inspire your thinking and writing!"

■ **TRY IT #1**

Set up partners to use the anchor chart to generate new ideas.

"Watch as I read the chart and see if it can help me spark some new ideas."

I pointed to a question on the chart. "'Where do you go often?' . . . Hmm, . . . I go to the grocery store a lot, and I go to school, and sometimes I even go to the park with my friends. Each of those could be a topic for a brand-new book!"

I finished reading the chart, thinking aloud about potential topics. "Now it's your turn to try! With a partner, point to each part of the chart and answer the question. Then you can say, 'That makes me think that I could write about . . .' and see how many new ideas you can come up with for your topic books."

■ **TRY IT #2/LINK**

Invite writers to create book covers for a few of their ideas, planning subtopics as they go.

"Wow! Writers, you've found some terrific topics. You're ready to start making some book covers. Don't forget that when you make a cover, you need to think about what, exactly, you'll teach. If I'm writing a book about the grocery store, I want to plan a part about the aisles in the grocery store, a part about stuff that you can buy . . . "

Once students made a few covers, I sent them off, reminding them to touch and teach, sketch, and then write their new books.

> *Possible Coaching Moves:*
>
> ▸ *"Say something you will teach about your topic."*
>
> ▸ *"What else can you teach about your topic? Can you sketch an example of __________?"*
>
> ▸ *"What does that look/sound/feel like? That could be a part that you write about in your book."*

Q&A ✦ Choosing Topics across This Bend

Q **My kids have limited life experiences. How will they generate expert topics?**

A If your kids go to school, to their homes, and to the park, they are full of topics. How empowering for our youngest students to be able to say, "The things I do every day are things that other people want to learn about!" When working cross-culturally, it is particularly important to take the time to build awareness of the funds of knowledge present in your writing workshop. The teaching of writing begins with helping your writers see that yes, indeed, they have so much to write about!

Be fascinated by the things your kids know about and can teach you and invite the children in your classroom to show this same enthusiasm for learning from each other. Some kids will know how to take care of younger siblings, some will know how to play a video game. Create space in which children can be fascinated by peers' topics and they'll come to believe they are authorities on topics of interest to others.

"Writers, remember how, when you were writing about your objects from home, you used magnifying glasses to see all the teeny, tiny details of your objects so you could add those details to your writing? You made covers today about things that aren't in the classroom and are just starting to write one of those books now. You can't use a magnifying glass on your video game, or your skateboard, or your dad's blueberry pie.

"But here's the thing: writers have good imaginations. Even when you are writing teaching books, you need to use your imagination. And in your imagination, you *can* sit close to your topic and look closely at it. And you can then write with true details by putting down exactly what you see.

"You have just fifteen more minutes for writing. If you're still working on covers and haven't started writing any books yet, choose the book you want to write first, and start writing like the wind. Go, go!"

CONFERRING SUPPORTS ✦ Building Momentum and Getting New Work Going

Your students are starting some important new work today. Whenever you launch new work, put on your roller skates and move quickly through the room, sprinkling compliments. This structure can help you visit each table.

Get started with some research	Pull up to your first table and sit with a student. Be on the lookout for anything that you can compliment. Carry miniature copies of the first bend's anchor chart. Celebrate anything a student has carried over and provide a copy to kids who'd benefit from marking parts of the chart they're working to transfer.
Give a compliment	Stop the writer and give a compliment. You might say, "I see you using the word wall to help you write that snap word! It is so amazing that you are using your resources. Keep it up!" or "You're the kind of writer who has a lot to teach! You've written a page about one part of your topic already."
Let the table know, and make sure all the kids try it	Once you have the writer's permission, tell the whole table about the wonderful work that writer is doing: "Friends, can I tell you about what Rebekah is trying? She's made three covers, and now she's writing a page about different parts of her topic. Do this too!" After coaching for a moment or so, you can move on to the next table or you can linger for a bit to offer lean prompts.
Watch, note ways you can compliment or nudge	If you have time, watch as kids get started, and be ready to use gestures (a thumbs up, perhaps) or brief comments to support. If a child rereads as a way to get started, then you can admire that. If a child pauses while spelling a word, admire that.

Possible Compliments

Possible Teaching Points

"Sakina, you chose a topic that you're really an expert on. I know that you have a big sister, so you know so much about being a little sister. You can teach so much!"

"You don't have much punctuation here. Make sure that you read your writing back to yourself and add periods and exclamation points where you need them!"

"Before you began writing, you planned what would go on every page. That will help you write a great book."

"Your pictures are very elaborate, but I'm not sure how much they teach. Next time try adding labels or diagrams!"

"You used expert words like *hand-me-downs*, *siblings*, and *compromise*! That shows that you really know your topic!"

"You seem to have some of your snap words confused. Let's work on learning *your* and *you're*."

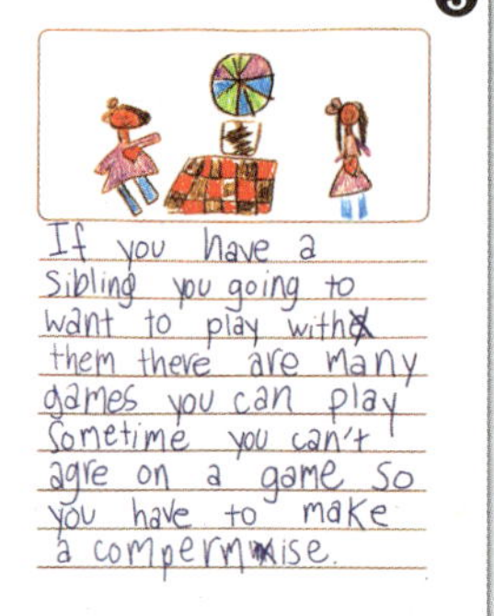

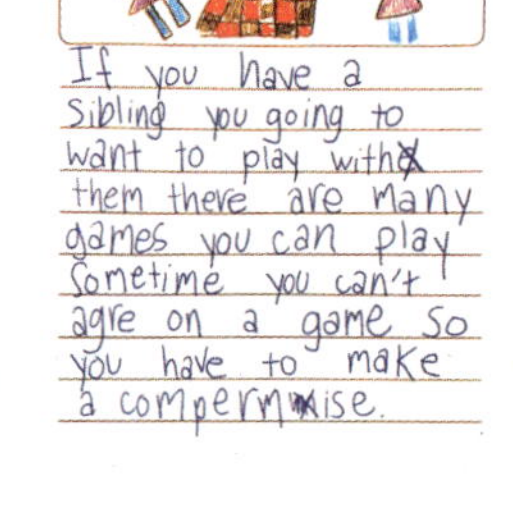

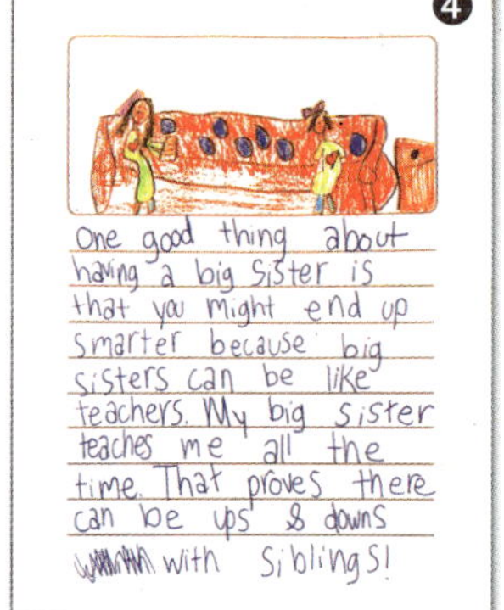

BEND II FIG. 1–1 "Little Sisters" by Sakina 

"You filled up the pages, and you wrote this entire book. That's about how much we want first-graders to write, so keep it up!"

"You have lots of big words, and I wonder if your reader knows all of them. You can give definitions of words like *compromise* and *siblings* to help your reader."

 Learning about Partners

Share some things you learned about your students by hearing about their topics. Recruit partnerships to share their books as a way to get to know each other.

I called students over to the rug, asking them to bring the book they wrote or started to write. "Writers, did you know that, among you, there is someone who helps his family cook roti every weekend? There is someone who has a snake that lives in a tank in their house, and there's even someone who is an expert on gardening because they help in their building's garden. I sure didn't know those things, but I do now. Your books taught me not only about your topics, but also about *you*! Would you be game to do the same kind of learning about your partner's topics, and about your partner?

"Right now, will you share the book you wrote today, even if it isn't finished? Listening partner, after you hear the book, ask about the writer's relationship to the topic. Learn about the writer *and* about the topic. Go ahead and get started!"

PHONOLOGICAL AWARENESS AND PHONICS EXTENSION ✦

For this extension, show a phonological awareness video. 

This video begins with a round of making words, where students will write a word, then manipulate a sound in that word to create a new word. In this activity, students will both add and delete phonemes to make new words. A new game is then introduced, called "What's the Snap Word?" In this activity, the instructor segments a snap word and then students blend it together and call out the word. The video ends with writing by analogy and using snap words to write. The instructor shows students the snap words *just*, *now*, and *went*, then dictates new words for students to write, using parts from the snap words shown.

Spelling by Analogy as You Write

In This Session

TODAY YOU will teach students that writing topic books involves some brave work with spelling. You'll begin by challenging students to help you write words that are similar to words on the word wall, using those words as clues for spelling. After you work with students to spell some tricky words you want to add to your book, you'll send them off to work on their own books. You'll remind them of the spelling strategies they learned in the previous unit with the "How to Spell Tricky Words" chart. Some children will finish books they started in the previous session. Others will start new books. Either way, remind them to be resourceful spellers, and also to be willing to approximate.

TODAY YOUR STUDENTS will either begin a new book, or finish the book they started in the previous session. They will work with the word wall to spell unfamiliar, but similar, words. After working with spelling using their whiteboards at the meeting area, students will transfer the skills they have learned to their own work. As they write, they will continue to use the word wall, spelling chart, and other spelling resources throughout the classroom. They'll also draw on all they know about writing information books, and you'll need to remind them of this so today's whole focus isn't on spelling alone.

Getting Ready

YOU WILL NEED . . .

- a new version of the "Our Spelling Toolbox" chart, with three strategies.

- a whiteboard and dry erase marker.

- your demonstration text, "All About Dogs," specifically, the "How Dogs Sleep" page. An example of the demonstration writing for this session can be found in the online resources.

- the "How to Spell Tricky Words" chart from Unit 1.

- the "Make a Plan for Writing" chart (see Share).

STUDENTS WILL NEED . . .

- whiteboards and dry erase markers.

Ensuring Access

YOUR ULTIMATE GOAL TODAY is to rally kids to write a lot, while keeping spelling in mind. In particular, you'll teach that the word wall can help them spell unfamiliar words. You'll also remind them to draw on all they already learned to sketch, say aloud, write, and reread.

- You'll probably need to help your students get started by deciding if they're adding to a book or using the covers they made previously to spark ideas for a new book. Sketching what they'll write about on any given page is a way to get writers started.

- For some students, you might treat today's session as a reminder to use the word wall to correctly spell misspelled snap words. You might say, "The word wall can make your spelling so much better. Can you use it to spell that word?" This connects students to the work of the entire class, while making sure they spell in ways that are appropriate to their developmental level.

- If you're using the Units of Study in Phonics, your students probably have personal word walls, and you may be blacking out words as they learn them. If students have a huge bank of snap words, channel them toward using their visual memory and their phonological knowledge to think about word parts that might help. You might say, "You know a word by heart that would help. Think of a word that has a part that sounds like that tricky word. Use that part to help you." You could also say, "You know this word by heart, but check the word wall to see if looking at it can help you find a powerful word part."

- You may seize this opportunity to teach some of your youngsters to apply all the phonics they are learning. If some are not signaling when a vowel is long, coach them to do so. If some aren't hearing a vowel at all, or the second letter in a blend, coach them to do so. Remember that writing workshop is a time for them to draw on all they have learned during phonics, thereby cementing that learning.

Spelling by Analogy as You Write

CONNECTION

Celebrate the number of words on the word wall by playing a game. Name a word wall word, ask students to jot it on their whiteboards, and end with a challenge.

I asked students to gather with their whiteboards and markers. "I came in this morning, writers, and I glanced at the word wall—there are so many words on it! This is a class that knows a lot of words! Let's play a quick game to celebrate all that you know. I'll give you a word, and you can use the word wall to write it on your whiteboards. Ready? Use the word wall to write the word *yes*. Hold up your board when you've got it." I gave a quick thumbs-up or "okay" signal to those who wrote it. We repeated this with the words *play*, *his*, and *run*. "Hmm, . . . these are easy for you. Let me give you a trickier one. Can you use the word wall to write the word *free*?"

I gave students a minute to try, and then said, "I heard some of you say, 'That word isn't on the word wall!' And you're right. But I want to teach you a neat trick about the word wall."

◆ **Name the teaching point.**

"Today I want to remind you that every word on the word wall can help you spell tons of other words. When you want to spell a tricky word, you can look at the word wall and think, 'Do I see parts that could help me?' Then, you can use those parts, along with everything else you already know about spelling, to write that word."

I tapped the third strategy on the "Our Spelling Toolbox" chart, "Listen for parts you know."

TEACHING

Demonstrate spelling the tricky word that you asked students to write on their whiteboards.

"Watch how I use the word wall to help me spell that tricky word you just tried: *free*." I picked up a whiteboard and marker.

"I know that the entire word *free* isn't on the word wall but let me see if there is a *part* on the word wall that could help me." I walked over to the word wall, running my finger under the words. "Oh! *Free* sounds a lot like *three*. I hear the same ending part. Let me look at *three*. It looks like that sound is made with a *ree*." I wrote this part on my whiteboard, then sat back down with the kids.

"What else do I need to add?" I said the word *free* slowly: /Fff/-/rrrēēē/. I'm missing the *F*." I quickly wrote it, then reread my word. "Even though the word *free* wasn't on the word wall, there was a word there that helped me spell it!"

Model using parts from the word wall to write a new page in your book.

"The word wall is super-helpful when you are writing. When you run into a tricky word, you can think, 'Do I know of a word on the word wall that can help me?' Watch how I do this as I continue writing my book about dogs." I projected page 2 about how dogs sleep.

"This is my page all about how dogs sleep. So far, I've written:

Some dogs like to sleep next to their owners. Sometimes they sleep on the

"I want to write that they sleep on the ground. Let me check the word wall to see what will help me spell *ground*." I scanned the word wall and said the word *ground* slowly. "/Grrr/ . . . /ou/ . . . That little part—*ou*—sounds a bit like *out*. *Out* has an *ou* part, the *ou* vowel team, so I bet *ground* does too. Let me try it." I wrote the letters *grou* on my paper. "/Grrr/ . . . /ou/ . . . /nd/ . . . That last part reminds me of another word on the word wall." I pointed to *and*. "*And* has that *nd*, and I bet that *ground* does too. I'm going to add *nd* to what I already have." I quickly wrote those letters.

"Now, let's read what I have so far." I pointed under each word as we read it together.

Some dogs like to sleep next to their owners. Sometimes they sleep on the ground.

ACTIVE ENGAGEMENT

Recruit students to help you spell a few other words. Coach as they work, and briefly review the word-wall words students used to help.

"Okay, I want to say a bit more about how dogs sleep. I want to say that dogs make a snoring sound." I wrote the beginning of the sentence on my paper and paused. "Hmm, . . . can you help me spell *snoring sound* on your whiteboards? See if there are parts on the word wall that will help you!"

Once many kids had written the words, I said, "Some people told me that *for* helped them spell snoring, since you hear *or* in both words. Other people used *going* to help with *snoring* since they both have the same ending sound—*ing*." I wrote *snoring*, spelled correctly, on my paper.

"Let's think about that other word, *sound*. I heard people say they used some of the same words to help them that we used earlier, like they used *out* since both *out* and *sound* have an *ou* part. Someone else said *and* helped them with *sound* because the two words have the same *nd* sound at the end." I added *sound* to my paper.

LINK

Rally students to reread, plan, and then to write about their topics, using the word wall to help.

"Writers, remember that you want your books to teach as possible, and you'll want to make them really readable. One way to do that is to spell tricky words as best you can, and you can use the word wall to do that. Or you can use this familiar chart!" I displayed the "How to Spell Tricky Words" chart from Unit 1.

"There are other ways that you can help your reader learn lots too. You might add punctuation, or check your vowel sounds, or make sure that you fill every line of your book with information. Before you get started today, will you pull out the book you'll be working on, and if you are still finishing yesterday's book, reread it to remember what you already wrote. If you are starting a new book, or if you are adding on, touch the page you'll write first and think, 'What will I draw here? What will I say?' Then get started, remembering to use the word wall to help you spell. If you finish writing this book, you can pick up another one that you've planned. Just make sure you write, write, write, and teach, teach, teach this entire time."

Spelling by analogy may be a tough skill for MLLs in the earlier stages of language development. Pay attention to their specific spelling needs. Depending on what you notice, you might encourage them to read and practice writing words from the word wall during this time or practice hearing sounds in words.

Remember that the big goal in all of this is flexibility. Your hope is that students leave this lesson thinking about the various things they can use to help them spell words. Emphasize that many different strategies can help spell words.

QUICK TIPS ✦ Helping Your Writers Write with Information

- Remind writers they are writing *teaching* books. It helps to imagine teaching a bunch of kids about the topic. Think, "What will they want to know?"

- Encourage kids to pretend to be readers of their writing and to ask questions. Questions that start with *how*, *why*, *where*, *when* can help a writer say more.

- Encourage writers to write with detailed information. One way to do that is to look at or imagine the topic and to describe parts of it in detail.

- Remind writers that when they come to a new page, it can help to think, "What will I teach here?" and to sketch that, then to say aloud what they'll write and write it.

MID-WORKSHOP TEACHING ✦ Helpful Word Parts throughout the Classroom!

"Writers, I have to stop you. I was walking around the room, admiring as you found parts on the word wall that could help you, when Talia pulled me aside and pointed to our morning meeting chart." Here I pointed to the *sh* in the words *share time*. "Talia said, 'You know, this could've helped you with the word *shake* too.'" I paused dramatically. "I couldn't believe it! What an important thing that Talia noticed! It's not just the word wall that can help you spell. It's *all* of the words in this classroom!

"So, if you're spelling a word and listening for the parts, the word wall can help you out, but so can this entire classroom. Can everybody point to a place in this classroom where there are tons of words, words that you could check for any helpful parts, like Talia just did?" Students pointed to the flow of the day, today's morning message, and library bin labels.

"Yup. There are so many words here, with so many helpful parts. Keep going, and, if you run into a tricky word, remember *all* the places you can look!"

For this small group, you'll need an "about the author" page. You can use one from your classroom library (we reference Dino Martins's page in *You Can Be an Entomologist!*), or you can show a student's example, such as Jack's in the online resources or one from your own students.

■ RALLY/ACTIVATE

Engage kids in an inquiry around what is included in a nonfiction "about the author" page.

"Have you ever noticed how toward the back of many of your information books, there is a special page that tells about the author? When you are a reader of nonfiction, it's probably pretty important to you that the author knows a lot about the topic, because if they haven't studied it they might not have all the facts right, or be able to actually teach you very much. Let's take a look at an 'about the author' page a student wrote and see what kind of information we can learn about him."

After a few minutes, I showed writers an "about the author" page for a professional writer and recorded what students noticed on a small chart.

"One of you said this page is helpful because it tells why we should listen to Dino Martins teach about bugs. I agree. It helps us understand that he's an expert on the topic. He teaches about bugs because he's an *entomologist*, a scientist that studies insects, so he knows a lot about them. It wouldn't make sense to read a bug book by someone who doesn't like or know anything about bugs."

■ TRY IT #1

Channel kids to interview each other about the books they've written.

"Right now, with the person beside you, try figuring out some of the things that can go on your 'about the author' page. One of you can be the interviewer and ask things from the chart, like 'How do you know so much about rocks or baseball cards . . .' or whatever object your partner brought, and the other person will answer. When you've asked and answered a few of the questions, switch roles."

■ TRY IT #2/LINK

Invite students to create their own "about the author" page. Then set them up to teach their writing partner how to create one too.

"After you finish your book, you can write your own 'about the author' page! Remember, this page will tell people why they should listen to what *you* have to say about your topic. Maybe you'll choose to meet with your writing partner later and use the chart and your own 'about the author' page to teach them how to make one of these important pages too."

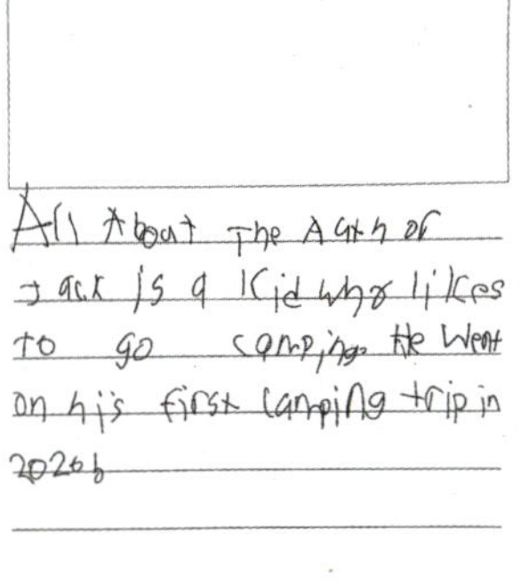

BEND II FIG. 2–1 Jack's "about the author" page

> **Possible Coaching Moves:**
>
> ▸ *"Ask your partner to tell you more."*
> ▸ *"Say, 'Why is that part important?'"*
> ▸ *"Ask if your partner can add anything else about that."*
> ▸ *"Do you want to know more? Ask your partner."*

 Writers (and Partners) Make Plans!

Channel students to share today's work and plan for tomorrow with their partners.

Once students were seated, I said, "Some of you finished your book today and even wrote an 'about the author' page. Others started your second book. Why don't you and your partner make a plan for what comes next in your writing life? To make a plan, decide who'll go first, and that person will put their book in the middle. If you're the one going first, tell your partner what you did, and then say what you might do tomorrow. Maybe your partner has ideas about another page you could add before you start a new book. Think together about how you'll make the new book even better than this one." I revealed a chart with these steps.

As students wrapped up their plans, I invited them to write their plan on a sticky note. "Make sure you jot down your plan on a sticky note, or you put a sticky note as a reminder on the book cover or page that you want to write!"

PHONOLOGICAL AWARENESS AND PHONICS EXTENSION ✦
Tongue Twisters with Blends and Digraphs

Do a quick rhyme with students. Then invite them to substitute other blends and digraphs to create new, nonsense words.

"Friends, it's almost time for lunch! Before we go to lunch, I want to do a quick tongue twister with you. I packed a snack, and everything in my snack starts with /ch/."

I said out loud:

> I chop cherries,
> Cheese, and
> Chocolate chips
> For a tasty snack.

I then said: "Let's say that I wanted to change the words a little bit, and instead of things that start with /ch/, I want things that start with *pl*. It would sound like:

> I plop plerries,
> Pleese, and
> Plocolate plips
> For a tasty snack.

"That would be really silly, wouldn't it!? Now let's try packing a /sh/ snack." We repeated the tongue twister a few times, each time substituting a different beginning blend or digraph.

Helping Readers Learn More by Giving Examples

In This Session

TODAY YOU will teach students how to fill up the blank spaces in their books with lots of information. You'll notice how a new mentor author adds examples to the words on the page to teach more—and then do that work in your book about dogs. You'll then channel students to touch and teach across the pages of the book they'll write today, planning places to include examples. In the mid-workshop teaching, you'll teach kids that they can also add more to a book by teaching readers how to do something. In the share, you'll invite students to compare their current writing to their very first piece and then you'll invite them to bring a photograph of their topic to school in the next session.

TODAY YOUR STUDENTS will teach as much as they can by adding examples in the words of their books. Most students will start a new book today, although others that started the second book of this bend already will continue working on that book. Even though the focus of the minilesson is examples, your students should call on all the skills and tools they have learned about thus far. After the mid-workshop, some students might add to their books by teaching readers how to do something, either by way of including steps or a "How to Use" page.

Getting Ready

YOU WILL NEED . . .

- to add a new sticky note to the "Writers Teach in Words and Pictures!" chart.

- a copy of *Cake* by Hareem Atif Khan.

- your "All About Dogs" demonstration text. You'll demonstrate adding examples to the third page. An example of the demonstration writing for this session can be found in the online resources.

- to add "How to Use" pages from Bend I to the writing center.

- to gather photographs of each student's topic before the next session (see Share).

STUDENTS WILL NEED . . .

- their writing plan from the previous session.

Ensuring Access

YOUR ULTIMATE GOAL TODAY is to give your young writers a concrete way to teach their readers more.

- By providing students with the strategy of adding examples, you are not simply saying, "Add more" or "Write with details." You are telling your students exactly *how* to do that. In that way, this work is already engineered for access.

- All students benefit from multiple exposures to the same concept, so consider carrying *Cake* and other familiar nonfiction books with you as you confer. As you meet with students, be on the lookout for those who do this work in their own writing—those pieces might next become a part of your toolkit, inspiring other students!

- Some students may require additional support to grasp the concept of an "example" of something. As you teach, use sentence stems such as 'one time . . .' or 'for example,' and statements such as "Be really specific!" or "Say what, exactly, you mean."

- MLLs who have command of writing in another language can be invited to write (at least in part) in that language, and those who are not yet writing letters and sounds on the page can continue the work from the previous session by teaching more through drawings. Having concrete ways to add more will help kids feel confident to write with more fluency and stamina.

- During today's share, students will celebrate the ways they are writing with increased volume. Especially if you have students who are still teaching primarily through pictures and labels, be ready to celebrate the ways their pictures have gotten more complex and detailed or the ways their labels have gotten longer so that they now include more letters and sounds. You might find other writers who began this unit writing about a new topic on each page and are now writing about different parts of a topic across a few days of writing. Celebrate writing growth in the many forms it takes in your classroom.

- If you teach writing workshop in Spanish, or if you have students who speak and write in Spanish, today you might use *Pasteles* by Hareem Atif Khan as a mentor text.

Helping Readers Learn More by Giving Examples

CONNECTION

After writers choose the book they will work on, explain a challenge that writers run into: lots of blank space because we run out of things to say about a topic.

"Writers, take a minute to remind yourself of the writing plan you made with your partner yesterday. If you haven't yet looked through all your covers, choose the book you want to work on first today, and put it on top of your folder." I gave kids a minute to do this.

When most kids had chosen a booklet, I continued. "Will you flip through your book and look at all those pages? They look pretty different than your booklets did at the beginning of the year and even of this unit, don't they? The picture boxes are a little smaller, and there are way more lines. It can be hard to fill them all up sometimes.

"Let me teach you a way you can fill up entire pages, even these new, long pages, with lots of information."

◆ **Name the teaching point.**

"Today I want to teach you a major way writers teach more about their topic. They give examples that help readers understand exactly what they're talking about."

I started a new "Writers Teach in Words and Pictures!" anchor chart and added the first sticky note.

TEACHING

Use a mentor text to show how writers include examples to teach more. Demonstrate how you write a new page by first leaving out and then including examples.

"I know what you're probably thinking. Examples! That sounds tricky! If you're thinking that, you're right. This is a really grown-up way of teaching people. I brought in an extra special guest teacher to help us . . ."

Students glanced toward the door. "Nope, the guest teacher isn't coming in the door. She's right here!" I set a copy of *Cake*, by Hareem Atif Khan, on the easel, quickly pointing to the author's photo. "This is Hareem, and I brought her here to show us how to become better information writers. Can I show you how Hareem used examples to teach us a ton about cake? After we study how Hareem did this, we can try it in our own writing."

I projected a page from Hareem's book and read it aloud.

> Cakes come in many different flavors. There are chocolate cakes and vanilla cakes with sprinkles. There are strawberry cakes and pineapple cakes. There is even a Black Forest cake. A Black Forest cake has cherries, chocolate, and whipped cream. What flavor do you like best?

"It would have really been a bummer if Hareem just said 'Cakes come in many different flavors' and didn't tell us about the different flavors. If she just turned the page and wrote about something else. But she didn't do that. Instead, she gave *examples* of different flavors of cake—chocolate, vanilla with sprinkles, strawberry, pineapple, Black Forest cake. Because Hareem gave examples, we learned so much from just this one page."

Picking up my booklet about dogs, I continued, "Will you help me try this same thing in my book about dogs? I want my next page to be about places you can walk your dog." I projected the third page with a sketch of someone walking a dog. The lines below were blank. "Maybe it should go like this."

You can walk your dog lots of places.

I wrote the one sentence, then put my pencil down dramatically.

"What do you think? Am I done?" Several kids called out, "No," so I continued. "Oh, you're right. I forgot to include *examples*. What are examples of places where you can walk a dog? Let's see. I walk my dog around the block. Sometimes I walk my dog to the park. I even walk my dog to the vet's office. Let me add those examples to my writing." I quickly added on:

You can walk your dog lots of places. You can walk your dog around the block. You can walk your dog to the park so it can run around. You can even walk your dog to the vet's office for a check-up!

"Do you see, first-graders, that looking at another author's book helped me learn a new way I could say more, by giving examples?"

ACTIVE ENGAGEMENT

Invite kids to consider what examples they might include on each page. Set partners up to listen for these examples.

"Ready to try? Pick up the booklet you plan to write today. If you have a new book, you know that the first thing you do when you start a new book is plan. You touch and teach across the pages. This time, when you touch and teach each page, do what Hareem did when she wrote about cakes. Give examples so that your readers learn a ton! If you're adding to a book you already started, you can touch and teach the blank pages. Try this by yourself first." I gave kids a minute or two to touch and teach across the pages of their booklets, whispering as they wrote in the air.

"Ready to teach your partner? Partner 2, will you touch and teach each page in your book? Partner 1, listen for your partner to give examples. If you don't hear examples, say '*Stop!*' and remind them. Partner 2, start touching and teaching each page."

LINK

Encourage students to include lots of examples as they start a new book or continue with an old book.

"Writers, today most of you will start a new book. A few of you may be returning to yesterday's book to write one more page or add more examples. Either way, remember: to teach your readers more, it helps to give lots of examples.

"Give me a thumbs up if you are ready to write." Around the room, children so signaled and soon two-thirds of the class had dispersed. I channeled the remaining writers to work together on the carpet to help each other gather ideas and plan for their writing, and I eventually sent them to their work spots as well.

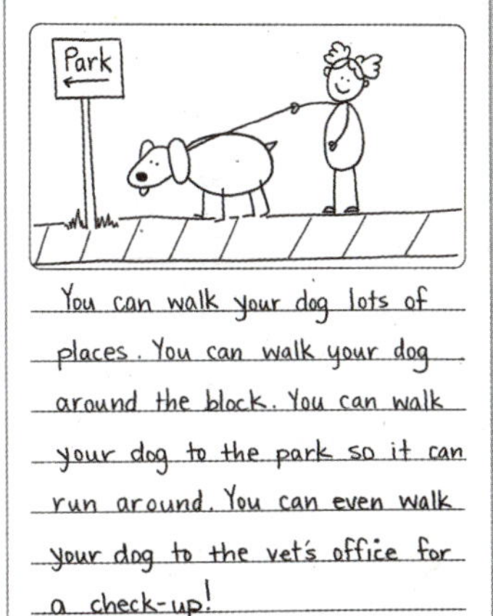

Consider using a digital toolkit to share the different demonstration texts from this unit. You could save your demonstration texts as PDFs on your device, and show students how you revise them, right on your device. This makes it even easier to use the same text many times to teach different things, since you can quickly erase your markups!

Emphasize that the start of all of these sentences is similar: "You can walk your dog . . ." This gives MLLs an authentic example of how they can use sentence stems in their own writing.

Children learning a new language can typically understand more in that language than they can produce. Remind students in the early and intermediate stages that they can practice giving examples in their own language if they choose, allowing them to actively practice this important concept.

Possible Coaching Moves:

▸ *"Say, 'For example . . .'"*
▸ *"That's one example. Can you give another example?"*
▸ *"Tell me more. Where exactly?"*
▸ *"What, exactly?"*

Throughout these minilessons, we talk frequently about the volume of writing kids are expected to be producing. We harp on that for their sake and yours. One of the most serious problems we have seen in primary classrooms is that sometimes teachers teach a tiny part of the writing process in a day's minilesson, and then kids go off and only do that one tiny part of writing. Adding examples is not a day's work, but one of many things that your students might do on this day. Kids also need to be writing new books, trying everything that they've learned about information writing.

SMALL GROUP ✦ Adding Examples

For this small group, you'll need a demonstration piece. We use "The Park." Show it to kids before—and after—you add examples. Both versions of this demonstration piece can be found in the online resources.

■ **RALLY**

Suggest using "For example . . ." as a sentence starter when giving examples.

"During our minilesson today, we looked at a page from Hareem's book where she used examples to add information to the pages of her book. Here is a little tip. When you get to a place where you want to add an example, you can write the words, 'For example . . .' Then you tell an example."

■ **TRY IT #1**

Recruit students to help you use "For example . . ." in your demonstration text.

"Let me show you how I do this in my book. I'm writing about the park. This is what I have so far : . . .

> *There is lots of equipment at the park.*

"Now I'm going to push myself to add an example. I need to say some of the equipment at the park. *For example,* . . . there is a slide, a swing to swing on, and even a basketball hoop.'

"See how I added the words *For example* and put some more details onto the page?

"Can you help me add more examples to this park book? I have a few pages that you and your partner can work on together. Read the pages together, then try to use the words *For example* to teach even more on each." I gave children more pages on which I'd written only the first sentence, leaving space for examples. They didn't actually write the words they proposed, as I wanted to channel them to their own books.

■ **TRY IT #2/LINK**

Ask partners to work together, trying this strategy in one partner's book, and then another.

"Why don't you try this with your own book now? Put Partner 1's book in front of you. And Partner 2, your job is to help Partner 1 remember to say 'For example' and teach a lot of information. Then you'll switch. Go ahead and get started."

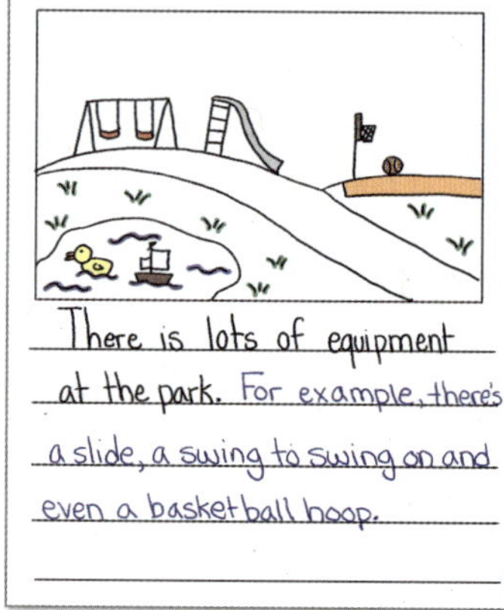

Page 1 of "The Park" with teacher revisions

Possible Coaching Moves:

▸ "Remember to say, 'For example . . .'"

▸ "That's one example. Can you give another example?"

▸ "That page was so short. Try it again."

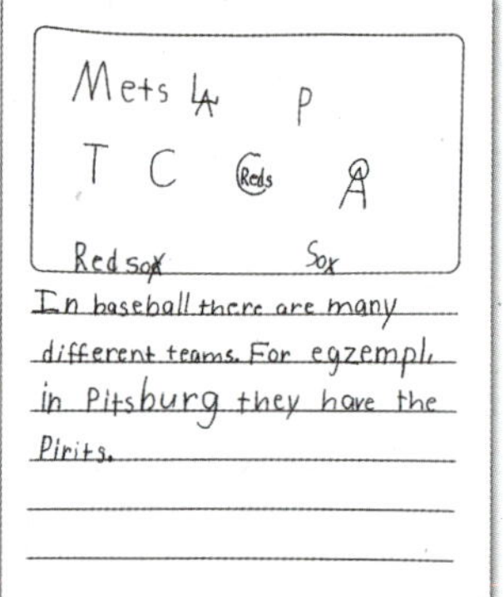

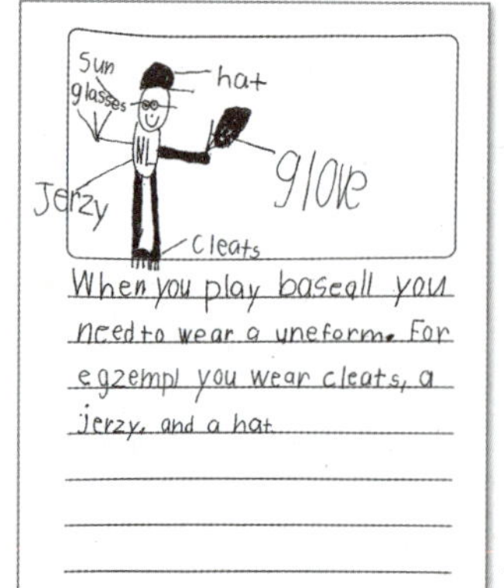
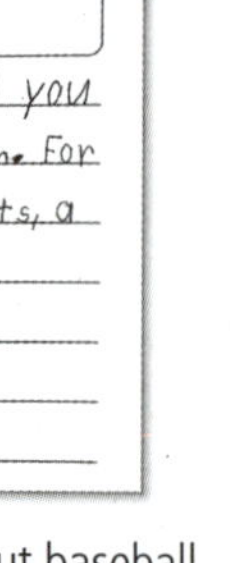

BEND II FIG. 3–1 Lucas adds examples to his writing about baseball. 

"Writers, today you learned that you can add onto your writing by adding examples. If you write that dogs can learn tricks, you can add 'for example,' and then what might you say? Yes! You might give examples of tricks dogs can learn.

"I want to remind you that you can also teach your readers how to use something. If you know how to use a scooter or how to use a bug catcher or how to use sprinkles to decorate a cake. You might even want to add a whole 'How to Use' page to your book!" I showed an example from the writing center.

CONFERENCE ✦ Turning Too-Small Topics into a "Different Kinds" Book

■ **RESEARCH/DECIDE**

Research the writer's process thus far, checking in on books he plans to work on next. Follow up to learn more.

I pulled up next to Jack. I noticed that his folder has quite a few books with prepared covers. "Wow, Jack!" I said. "It looks like you have tons of ideas for fabulous books."

"Yes! I'll write a book about The Incredible Hulk®, a book about Spider-Man®, and maybe a Captain America® book." As Jack held his books up, I saw that he had only sketched a subtopic in one or two boxes on each cover.

"Jack, I notice that you only have one box drawn for The Incredible Hulk book, and one box for Spider-Man. . . ."

I probe a bit more, because there could be many reasons that Jack hadn't chosen any subtopics. Does he know enough about each topic—each superhero—to write a whole book on each?

"I know. I'm going to teach about how The Incredible Hulk is really big and green. And I'm going to tell about his purple pants. He has strong muscles."

"Okay, so you'll describe The Incredible Hulk on one page. How about the next page?" I tapped another one of the empty boxes on the cover.

Jack says, "I'm not sure about the next page."

Compliment the writer and set up the teaching point.

"Jack, the details that you plan to write about The Incredible Hulk's purple pants will help readers learn a lot! It is great that you know readers want specific information."

It can often be helpful to connect the compliment to the teaching point. This provides more of an organic feeling and underscores the importance of the teaching point.

■ **TEACH**

Introduce Jack to a new structure, and show him an example.

"Jack, I'm not sure you have enough specifics for a whole book of details about The Incredible Hulk, and a book about Spider-Man, so I have a suggestion. Have you ever heard of a 'Different Types . . .' book? Look at this 'Different Types of Fish' book. When you look at the table of contents, you can see that one page teaches all about starfish, another page teaches all about goldfish, and still another page teaches all about beta fish.

There are some different ways that you might provide the student with an example. You might carry around a "Different Types . . ." book from your classroom library, or you might write your own. You could even use Jack's superhero book, included in the online resources, as your example!

"I'm thinking that you could write a 'Different Types . . .' book too. Look in your folder and see."

Jack went through his folder and found the unfinished books about superheroes. "You know," he began, "I could have a whole superheroes book. And one page can be about The Incredible Hulk, and another page about Spider-Man . . ."

Have the student name the parts of his new book.

"That sounds like a 'Different Types . . .' book that so many people would want to read! Let's say the different parts out loud! That'll help you make sure that you get all of the right information down on the pages!"

Jack began rehearsing his book out loud.

■ LINK

Send the student off to begin his book, reminding him that he might write other "Different Types . . ." books.

"Okay, Jack! You're ready to go off and write this book. It'll be so interesting to read about a different hero every page. And remember that there are lots of other 'Different Types . . .' books that you could write too!"

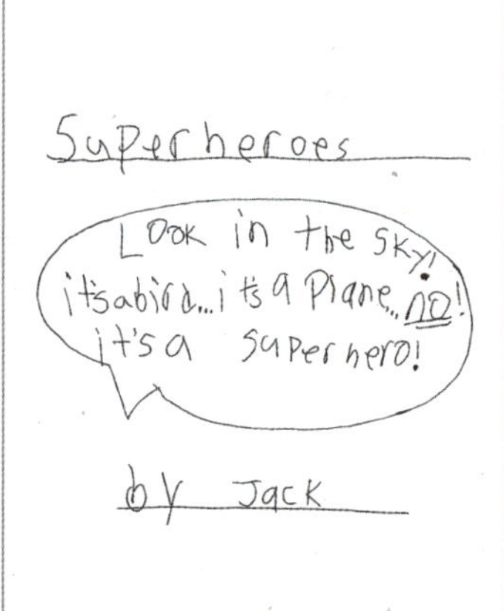

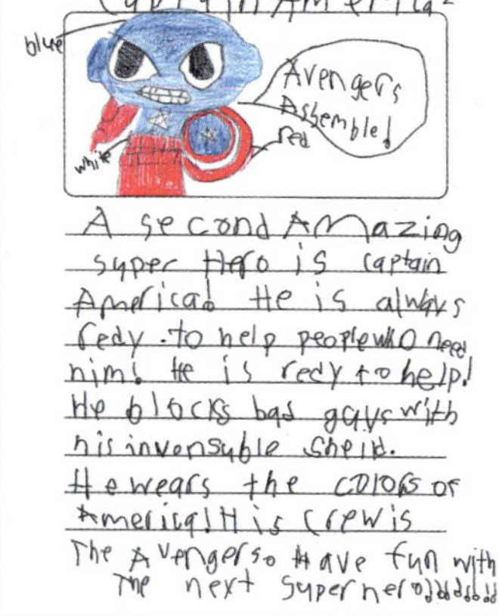

BEND II FIG. 3–2 Jack's piece about superheroes

BEND II

 # When Writers Write with Detail, They Write a Lot

Channel students to compare their writing from the beginning of the unit with their current writing. Rally them to write even longer in their next book.

"Writers, some of you are saying that your hands are already hurting because you wrote so much! Right now, get out the teaching book you wrote on the very first day of this unit, and get out whatever book you just finished. Read through both books to see if, and how, your writing is growing longer. Show your partner what you notice.

"Thumbs up if today's writing is a lot longer than the first book you wrote in this unit." Many children put their thumbs up. "Great. Give yourself a pat on the back because longer is one big part of better. And if your books haven't yet begun to get longer, the next book you write could be the longest book you've ever written, which would be really exciting."

Invite students to bring a photograph from home to use in their writing tomorrow.

"You already know that writers make their writing longer by adding more details. One way you can come up with more details is by studying photographs of your topic, which is what we'll do tomorrow. If you'd like, you can bring a book with photographs of your topic or actual photographs of your topic to school tomorrow. Like, maybe you have a book about planets or a photograph of your cat. But don't worry if you don't have any books or photographs of your topic at home—I'll make sure to have a photograph for each of you to study of the topic you wrote about today."

PHONOLOGICAL AWARENESS AND PHONICS EXTENSION ✦ "What's the Blend that You Hear?"

For this extension, you'll need a copy of the "What's the Blend that You Hear?" lyrics. 

Sing "What's the Blend that You Hear?" to help your students recognize blends.

"I have a quick song for us to sing. It goes to the tune of 'London Bridge,' but we're going to change the words, so that we can practice listening for blends."

> What's the blend that you hear,
> That you hear, that you hear?
>
> What's the blend that you hear,
> In . . . *snack, snack, snack*?

"Give me a thumbs up when you think you know what blend it is!" I paused to give students time to think, then continued with the next verse.

> /Sn/ is the blend that you hear,
> That you hear, that you hear!
>
> /Sn/ is the blend that you hear,
> In . . . *snack, snack, snack*.

We repeated the song with a few more words with initial blends: *scoop, crown, treat, clap, fries, slip, dream*.

Studying Photos or Pictures Can Help You Say More

In This Session

TODAY YOU will provide your students with another way to do research. You'll teach students today that they can look at photographs to learn more information to add to their books. You'll demonstrate this during the minilesson with your book about dogs, and, during the active engagement, you'll set students up with photographs where they can do their own research. You'll provide a quick mid-workshop interruption on adding definitions to pictures, giving students yet another way to elaborate. During the share, you'll set students up for a gallery walk to receive feedback on their books.

TODAY YOUR STUDENTS will conduct their own research by using photographs. Using resources provided by you, or from their homes, students will look carefully at a photograph, think about what they're noticing, and add that information to their books. Because you'll channel them toward certain resources, your students will most likely begin today by adding information to a book they'd previously started. Some students, though, will move on to another book once they've added a bit of information.

Getting Ready

YOU WILL NEED . . .

- a photograph showing different types of dogs, for your own research.

- to match students to photographs or books about their topics. Label the photographs or books with each student's name, and place them in bins in the meeting area.

- your demonstration text "All About Dogs." You'll add a new page describing the different sizes and colors of dogs. An example of the demonstration writing for this session can be found in the online resources.

- to add a new sticky note to the "Writers Teach in Words and Pictures!" chart (see Mid-Workshop Teaching).

STUDENTS WILL NEED . . .

- a photograph from the classroom library, or from home, about a topic they've been writing about.

- sticky notes and pens for feedback (see Share).

Ensuring Access

YOUR ULTIMATE GOAL TODAY is for your students to study a visual source closely and add new information to their writing.

- You'll want to work hard to make sure that your students all have a relevant photograph or book to study during the active engagement and at the start of work time. Remember that it need not be a perfect match. For example, your students who are writing about Mars will still benefit from looking at a book about planets. You might also have students bring in photographs from home as part of a homework assignment.

- Your MLLs may notice many important details in their photographs, but may not be able to describe them accurately in English. As students orally rehearse during the active engagement, you might pair them with a more proficient partner who can help them name the things they point out. Remember also the power of translanguaging, and know that your students might add some details in a first language.

- Finding information from photos can provide a special challenge to students with visual processing disabilities. You might consider providing a simple, uncluttered photograph to those students, or you might teach them how to fold or cover parts of the photo, to draw their attention to certain areas and teach them to focus on one part at a time.

- Consider the many photographs and information books you're providing to students today. Make sure the content is appropriate for the students in your class.

Studying Photos or Pictures Can Help You Say More

CONNECTION

Share a photograph that goes with your demonstration text, showing how a picture can tell a lot about a place or thing.

"First-graders, hurry to the meeting area! If you brought a photograph with you, bring it to the rug." I'd lined up a few different nonfiction bins at the front of the carpet, making sure that kids' topics were represented across those bins. Once students had gathered, I said proudly, "I have something really special to share with you."

When all the children were in their spots on the rug, I said, "Close your eyes. I'm going to teach you something really important about different kinds of dogs. Are you ready?"

Eyes closed, they nodded.

"Um, there are different kinds of dogs. There are, um, dogs that have . . . ears. And there are dogs with tails." Then I paused and commented on my teaching by saying, "Isn't that interesting? Can you guys get a real clear picture about all the different kinds of dogs?"

"No!" several children announced in unison.

"Now look! Everyone, open your eyes!" I revealed a photograph, showing a few different kinds of dogs at a dog park. "Is what I said about many kinds of dogs more clear now?"

"Oooh!" many students exclaimed. Eyes widened and heads nodded. Tonia said, "That's much better."

I continued, "Yes, the photograph gives you lots more information, doesn't it? Writers, they say a picture is worth a thousand words. That means, when we look at a picture, we instantly know a whole bunch of stuff about the place or the thing, because we can *see* it."

✦ Name the teaching point.

"Today I want to teach you that writers find photographs or pictures that are connected to their topics. Writers then research by looking closely at these, mining them for specific details that will teach people even more about their topics. Then they put into words what they've learned and add this to their writing."

TEACHING

Demonstrate studying a picture and transferring information to your text.

"Writers, I want to show you how I use my photograph of different kinds of dogs to help me add more to my book about dogs. Let me study this photograph. Hmm, . . . The first thing I notice is the different sizes of the dogs. Some of these dogs are small, some are medium sized, and some are big. I'll make sure to include that in my writing. 'Dogs are different sizes.' And I could put that in the picture too!" I quickly drew my picture and jotted my words on the lines of page 4.

"The next thing I notice, writers, is that dogs are different colors. This dog is golden, this dog is black, and this dog has spots. That's more information to put into my book! I can add this to my words and my picture!"

The saying that a picture is worth a thousand words illuminates the power the photographs can have for helping writers learn that outside sources can help them say more.

BEND II

Recruit kids to join you in using the photograph you brought to elaborate.

"As I write this next part, think about what other information you notice in the picture. Then turn and talk with the person next to you." I recorded what we had noticed so far in my book while children talked quietly about the other details in the picture.

Before long, children noticed that some dogs had fluffy tails, while others had short tails. Students also shared that all of the dogs had four legs. I added this information to my book before moving on.

Debrief in a way that highlights the transferable work students have been doing.

"Writers, do you see how we didn't just give any ol' details? We gave *specific* details. We named the different colors of fur that we saw.

"Photographs and pictures tell us a lot of information—if we look closely. My own dog doesn't have spots, but looking really carefully at the picture reminded me to add that detail into my writing."

ACTIVE ENGAGEMENT

Recruit children to describe their pictures in detail to partners.

"Writers, now it's your turn to give this a try with the pictures that I've set out at the end of each row. When you look through your bins, you'll notice that I've stuck some sticky notes to each book, or to each photograph, with your name on it. I've picked something that will really help each of you with the book you've been working on. If you brought some pictures in for homework today, look at them." I gave students a moment to look through their bins and take out a photograph that would help them with their research.

"Let's take a minute to just look really carefully on your own. Study the picture, really zoom in if you need to. Then, describe your photograph to yourself with as many *specific* details as you can." I gave students a moment to study, then continued: "Now, partners, you can show your photographs to each other."

Debrief, emphasizing strategies writers can use other days and in other books.

"Writers, I want to share some things I overheard that I think might help all of you. First, I heard Wilder describing his picture. Soccer players were moving to protect the goal. He didn't just tell about the people, he told about the *actions*.

"I also overheard Madeline telling Theo all about her photograph of the beach near her house. She told about the objects that were there, like shells and rocks, and she also described the objects so that Theo could really picture them. She said there were *pink* shells and *big* rocks. She used *color* and *size* to help describe her picture. Those details really help readers get a picture in their minds. Nice work."

LINK

Send students off to continue drafting their information books.

"Writers, I know you have so much you want to do today, so I'm going to send you off now. And remember, doing this kind of research can help you make all of your books better. This is just one way to make sure your books are as chock-full of information as possible." I sent students off.

Digital tools might make the logistics here a bit easier. Students can look at photos that you have saved to a file on their devices. If you do not have devices available to students, remember that digital tools could make finding these images easier, and you need not limit the photos you choose to the ones in your classroom library.

STUDENT WORK ✦ Studying Sara's Exemplar Illustration

Sara's information book about camels is one potential "exemplar illustration." You can print this illustration from the online resources and mark it up using the labels suggested below, or you can use the labels to mark up illustrations from your own students.

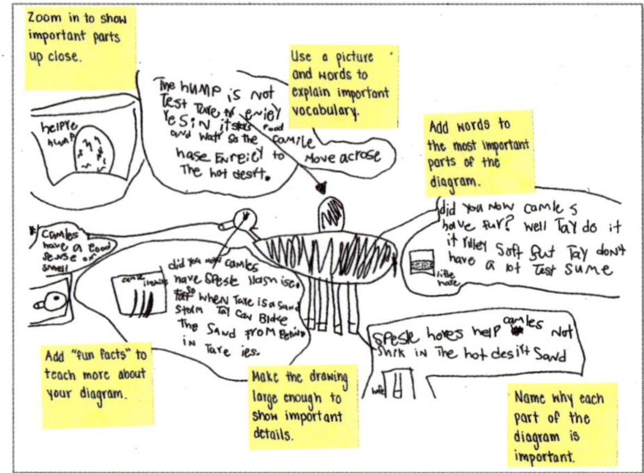

BEND II FIG. 4–1

Writing Move	You might say . . .
A "zoom in" box to show important parts of the camel up close	"Can I show you what Sara did? This picture has a part that has a bit more detail. There's this special box that shows the camel's hump. It's like a magnifying glass—it lets you zoom in and see up close."
"Fun Fact" boxes	"Sara's illustration has something that'll be so fascinating to readers, but that might not fit in the lines. So, she used a Fun Fact box to teach a little bit more about it. See where she wrote, 'Did you know . . . ?'"
Pictures and words to teach important vocabulary	"If you look at Sara's illustration, you can see that she taught her readers about the word *hump*. She told a bit about what it means, and why it's important. She said, 'A hump is . . .' and 'It does something important by . . .'"
An explanation of why each part of the diagram is important	"Sara did something really cool here. After she made her diagram, she told why each part of her diagram was important. See here how she wrote about the camel's special hooves?"
A diagram that is large enough to show important parts and details	"Do you see how Sara's diagram is so big, it fills a whole page? Since it's big, she could include lots of important information, with words and with the picture."

"Writers, can I interrupt you for a moment? As you look at pictures and read your labels, your interesting words are popping up. Isabella wrote, 'Soccer players wear cleats. Soccer players always wear shorts.'" Isabella nodded.

"But the thing is—some people don't know what cleats are. And that's true for the words many of you are using.

"Writers, if you use a special word like *cleats*, you have to give a definition, which means you explain to your reader what the word means. One way you can do that is with a word box." I drew a box at the bottom of the easel. "Inside a word box, you explain what the word means, like this." I wrote the word *cleats* and then made a colon and wrote:

> *Cleats are shoes you buy at a special store. They are pointy on the bottom.*

I said the words as I wrote them, ending with, "Do you see how I made a box at the bottom of the page and explained what cleats are? You can also draw the thing you define and label it.

"Will you take a moment to reread and see if you have places where you can give a definition? In some books, writers put the word they're going to define in bold letters."

I added a new sticky note to the "Writers Teach in Words and Pictures!" anchor chart.

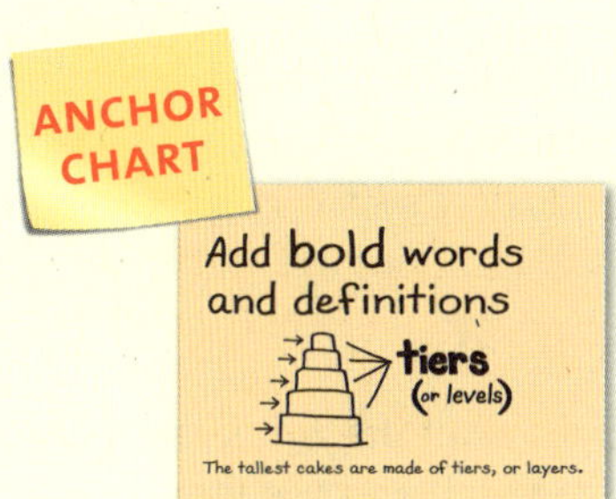

Your students will be using the lingo of their topic as they write, labeling soccer shoes as cleats and using the correct names for players. Now is a good time to help kids also use academic vocabulary to talk about their books. To support this, tell kids that just as a soccer player uses soccer vocabulary, writers use writing vocabulary. Give partners some words on sticky notes and ask them to label the books they've written and those they need with these words. Here are some: *lead, introduction, publication date, caption, illustration, diagram, text box, subheading, heading, glossary, index, example, quotation, statistic, detail,* and *summary*.

CONFERENCE ✦ Consistently Representing Blends

■ RESEARCH/DECIDE

You might study a writer's draft before a conference begins. If you decide to study phonics, tell her why. Compliment the writer.

Before conferring with Abigail, I had studied her writing and noticed that she inconsistently represented blends. She sometimes wrote blends, which signified that she had an understanding of them and could hear the sounds within them. Other times she only wrote the first sound and left off the second letter in the blend altogether.

"Abigail, I came over to talk to you because I have been studying your writing. Specifically, I have been studying *phonics* inside of your writing—meaning, what you know about letters and sounds that helps you spell. I noticed that you make sure to write a letter for every sound you hear, even in long words like *batteries*." I pointed to the word and ran my finger under the letters as I read it. "And in *afternoon*."

■ TEACH/LINK

Highlight what the writer knows about phonics, showing an example, and encouraging her to use that knowledge consistently.

"I also noticed that sometimes, when words have blends, you write the whole blend, both letters. Like in *clock*. See you wrote *cl* for /cccllll/ -ock. But other times, the blends trick you! The second sound in a blend can be sneaky. And sometimes, because it is sneaky and not as loud as the first sound, you miss it and forget to write it altogether. Here's the thing, though; you didn't let the *L* in *clock* sneak off and get away. Are you game to reread your writing and see if you can make sure that none of the other letters in blends sneak away?"

Provide the writer with a process she can follow to edit her writing.

"Here's a tip for any time you are writing: reread your writing out loud. You will want to go slowly so you can hear when a word has a blend at the start. When you hear one, check it! Take a look at what you wrote. If you see the blend there, give yourself a thumbs up. If you don't, fix it up!"

I coached Abigail as she started rereading her writing to hunt for blends. When she reached the word *press*, she paused.

She said, "I think I missed a letter."

"Say the word and run your finger underneath. Which letter did you miss?"

"/Prrreeesss/. I need an *R*. There." Abigail pointed.

"Yup! *Pr* as in *press* is a blend. That *R* was sneaky, but you didn't let it trick you! Abigail, now that you have the hang of this, I'm going to leave you to work. Before I do, remember: you are very talented at hearing sounds in words. Blends can be tricky! Sometimes those sounds are harder to hear. Make sure to listen extra closely when you're writing or rereading your writing so that you can record all the letters in each blend. After you fix up the blends, decide: will you keep rereading and fixing up blends? Or will you write some more and make sure to spell blends correctly while you write?"

<blockquote>
I choose to focus on a phonics principle that the writer is using with inconsistency.

My compliment leads into my teaching. In this way, I leverage the things the writer is doing well so that she can see how the new work connects to her strengths.

It's important to leave some work for the writer. Here, I highlight the place where Abigail uses the blend, but I didn't point out where she didn't use blends.
</blockquote>

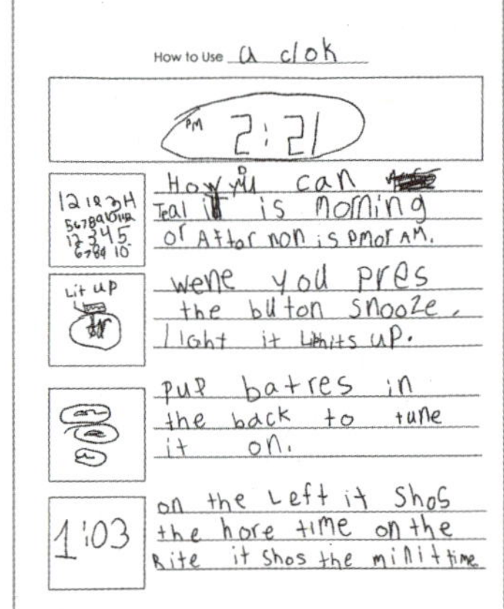

BEND II FIG. 4–2 

<blockquote>
It's important to let writers know how the new phonics work is connected to work they have already solidified.

Notice how I end by providing choices for Abigail.
</blockquote>

Getting Feedback Helps Writers Write Books that Stand on Their Own

Explain that authors can't always stand by their books to answer questions. Set up a gallery tour for students to learn whether their books can stand alone.

"Writers, there have been lots of times when you read your writing to each other and talk about it. But you know what? Our library sure would be crowded if every book had an author next to it, ready to explain the book. When we write books, we have to make sure they don't need us to explain them to readers.

"We're going to try something today. You're going to leave your book out, and you're going to let your book stand on its own. Your book needs to do the talking! That means that readers will read the book without you there to help. This is kind of like a test to see if your book can teach without your help. Clear your workspace of everything but your book for today's gallery tour." I moved through the room, leaving sticky notes on each table for students to give feedback to one another.

Once the room was set up, I said, "Are you ready? You'll walk through the room, reading your friends' books, and then give them feedback, tell them what you think. There are sticky notes and pens on every table to share your feedback. You can tell your friends what they're doing well, and you can even jot questions in spots where you wish they had given you more information." As students read one another's work, I encouraged many to leave questions for writers or to use the classroom charts to make suggestions.

"Now that you've had a few minutes to read others' books, move back to your seats so you can read the feedback your friends left for you. Are there places where readers asked questions that show they would like more information in your pictures or words? If so, stick that feedback on the page where you plan to do that work tomorrow."

PHONOLOGICAL AWARENESS AND PHONICS EXTENSION ✦

For this extension, show a phonological awareness video. 

This video begins with an onset-rime word-building activity. Students will read the rime *-ick* and will be presented with a collection of initial consonants and blends to build words. The video moves on to a round of making words, where students will write a word, then manipulate a sound to create a new word. In this activity, students listen for initial and medial phonemes that have been added, deleted, and substituted to make new words.

Learning from Mentor Illustrations

TODAY YOU will again teach your students that information writers teach through both words and pictures. You'll ask, "How do the illustrations in teaching books help writers teach more?" and use the mentor text *Cake* to answer that question, while coaching students to add pictures to their own books. In the mid-workshop teaching, you'll demonstrate alternating between writing and drawing in your own book. In the share, you'll display illustrations that partnerships found in their nonfiction book baggies to showcase more examples.

TODAY YOUR STUDENTS will probably start new books. They'll need to generate new topics, which should be easy by now, and to plan what their pages will be about. Then you'll help them realize they can use different illustrations to teach more. They'll make drawings that show steps or kinds, and add arrows and labels and other visual details. Mid-workshop, students will practice a new way to increase the volume of their writing: adding to the picture, then adding those same things to the words. In the share, partners will study their book baggies to uncover more examples of teaching illustrations.

Getting Ready

YOU WILL NEED . . .

- a copy of *Cake* by Hareem Atif Khan.

- to add two new sticky notes to the "Writers Teach in Words and Pictures!" chart. ✋

- your "All About Dogs" demonstration text. You'll add to the fifth page (see Mid-Workshop Teaching). An example of the demonstration writing for this session can be found in the online resources. ✋

STUDENTS WILL NEED . . .

- their reading book baggies (see Share).

Ensuring Access

YOUR ULTIMATE GOAL TODAY is to rally kids to start new books while also celebrating assets that aren't always given their due in a writing workshop. Illustrations are an important part of a book and studying the decisions an artist has made conveys that you value drawings—and value those who love to draw. The message is that writers make choices on purpose, based on their intentions. Some of your kids may already be adept at teaching through illustrations; this is a great session to hold them up as leaders, particularly kids who don't often take on that role.

- A challenge today will be that writers may need to think of ideas for their new books and to plan the pages they'll write using your suggestions for new sets of illustrations. Give time to helping them come up with pages and encourage kids to help each other.

- For students who need support adding labels with more sounds to their pictures, you might try the "Be a Word Wizard!" small group from the *Small Groups to Support Phonics, Grades K–1* book. Kids tap a place where they want to place a label, stick the label on the page, slide their finger across the label as they slowly say the word(s), and then write the word(s), recording as many sounds as they can. This supports students with word placement, draws attention to handwriting, and can make labeling more enticing. This is helpful work for MLLs, especially, who need extra support to develop phonemic awareness and decoding skills in a new language.

- You'll highlight some academic vocabulary today, including *diagram*, *caption*, *close-in*, *highlight*, and *label*. Attaching the words to the visuals in the book is especially helpful for MLLs. Be sure to point clearly to these text features as you discuss them.

- If you teach writing workshop in Spanish, or if you have students who speak and write in Spanish, today you might use *Pasteles* by Hareem Atif Khan as a mentor text.

Learning from Mentor Illustrations

CONNECTION

Suggest that kids still have a lot more to learn from studying books.

"Writers, today most of you will begin a new book. Will you look back at the cover ideas you came up with earlier and decide on a topic for today's book? If you don't have a great idea in your folder, think of something you do that you could teach all of us." I gave kids a moment to think.

"Friends, did you know that you are surrounded by teachers? And I don't just mean me, or my teacher friends in the teacher lounge. If you look carefully, you'll find teachers everywhere!"

I placed *Cake* on the easel. "We already looked at this book, and we learned tons about how to add examples to our books. To do that, we studied the words Hareem used. Today, let's study her pictures because I think she can show us how to make our pictures teach people things."

◆ **Name the question that will guide the inquiry.**

"Writers, today we are going to do an inquiry. Let's explore the question, 'How do the illustrations help writers teach more?' We might notice some special techniques or tricks that authors of teaching books use, to give their books teaching power. Then, we can try those same techniques in our own books."

TEACHING

Take writers through a guided inquiry to investigate the illustrations in *Cake*. Listen in and coach, eliciting their comments and collecting these on a chart.

"*Cake* can show us lots of ways to make our illustrations the best they can be. So, let's look closely, and try to notice what Hareem has done, and then see if we can try some of the same things in our books. Are you ready to look and learn?"

I displayed page 10 from *Cake* and read it aloud. "What has Hareem done in her illustrations to teach us? Turn and tell your partner what you notice." The children talked and I listened in, then, after a minute, summarized.

"I heard some of you say that she drew her topic, pointed to parts of the topic with arrows, and wrote labels for the names of those parts so readers would know what those things are. The fancy name for this kind of illustration is a *diagram*." I added a sticky note to the "Writers Teach in Words and Pictures!" anchor chart that captured this point.

"Let's study a few more illustrations and see what else we notice." I flipped to page 7 in the book and channeled students to study the illustrations. Touching the page where Hareem had sketched the steps in the cake-making process, I said, "Writers, Hareem has done something very different on this page. Instead of one big picture, she used three little pictures." Touching the next page, I said, "And on this page, she's just got one big picture. Will you look, and think again, 'What is the author doing in these illustrations?' This time, also ask, '*Why* might she be doing this?'" I read the main text on both pages, then channeled kids to talk while I listened in.

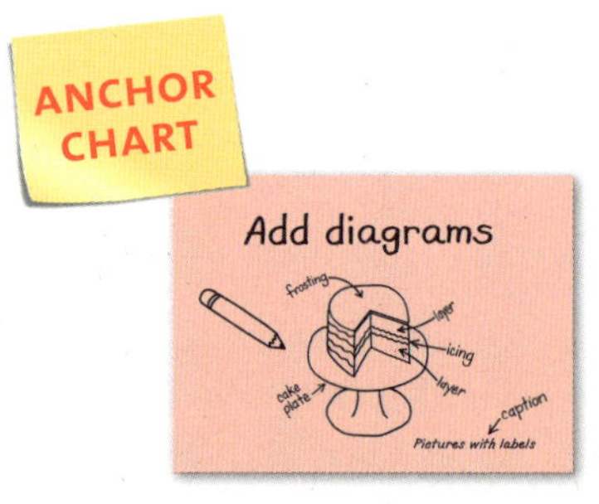

Cakes can be simple or fancy. Some cakes have layers. Frosting acts like a delicious glue to hold these layers together. The tallest cakes are made of **tiers**, or levels.

"I heard many of you saying that her pictures teach the steps you need to follow to bake a cake." I added another new sticky note to the "Writers Teach in Words and Pictures!" anchor chart.

ACTIVE ENGAGEMENT

Ask kids to mark where they can add diagrams and pictures in the book they wrote yesterday.

"Ready to plan how you can use pictures, just like Hareem?

"First, will you think, 'What will I teach about my topic?' and then write a word or draw a small picture on the top of each page to show what will go on that page. Help each other.

"Now writers, will you look over your pages and think, 'Can I put pictures of how to do something on one of these pages?'" I showed Hareem's "How Are Cakes Made?" page. "Think, 'Can I show different kinds of something on a page?' Tell your partner your ideas."

LINK

Set writers up to get new books started.

"Most of you will probably want to start by sketching and then by touching each page and saying aloud what you'll write on that page. After you write a page, look back at your picture and think whether you can make it teach even more."

As students began, I walked around, voicing over and complimenting what I saw: "I see lots of labels showing up in pictures!"

Diagrams are a concrete and powerful way for students to include labels in another language (potentially alongside an English label as part of a bilingual book). Encourage students to plan in any language they choose. Make sure that you regularly and publicly celebrate their strengths as speakers of multiple languages—how beautiful to have so many tools for communicating and teaching!

SMALL GROUP ◆ Using Pictures to Teach Even More in the Words

For this small group, you'll need a demonstration text. We use "All About Pizza." 

■ RALLY

Remind writers of the ways they've learned to elaborate in pictures. This can help them teach even more in the words of their books.

"Writers, today you learned you can add things like diagrams, examples, and steps to your pictures. Those pictures certainly help your readers learn more. Here's the thing, though: detailed pictures can help you as a writer too. Writers can reread a page, study the picture, and then ask, 'What else could I teach in my words that I've already taught in my picture?' And then they add it. That helps them teach even more on each page!"

■ TRY IT #1

Study a page of the demonstration text together. Invite partners to brainstorm what else you could teach and add to your book.

"Let's try this in my book about pizza. On this page, I am teaching about different kinds of pizza. Let's read the page, study the picture, and think about what else I can add." I read the page aloud.

"Now let's look at the picture. I drew pepperoni pizza, cheese pizza, mushroom pizza, and Sicilian pizza." I touched each part as I mentioned it. "Hmm, . . . what else could I teach in my words on this page? Turn and tell your partner, and as you do put a finger up to signal each new sentence I could write.

"Oh, what great ideas! Let me add your sentences to my page."

■ TRY IT #2

Have students study a few pages of their own writing, adding to the words as they go.

"Now it's your turn to try. Reread your writing, study the picture, and ask, 'What is here in my picture that I could add to my words?' Once you've found some things you can add to your words, go ahead and add them! Then turn the page and try it again."

■ LINK

Remind writers to continue using their pictures as a way to add more details to their teaching books.

"Writers, remember, when you add labels, examples, and steps to your pictures, you can use your pictures to teach even more in your words. You can do this in all the teaching books you write. Touch something in your picture, say more about it, and then write it down. Before you know it, your books will be full of new information!"

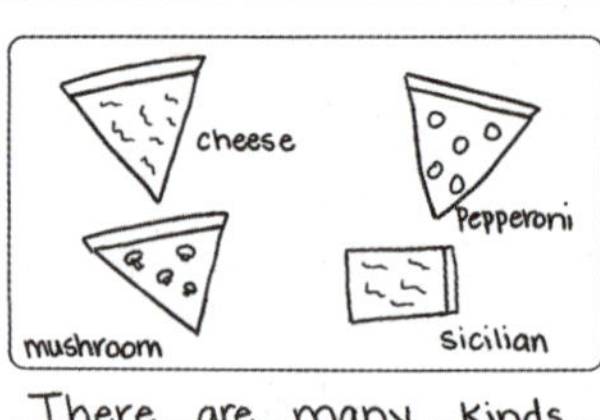

Possible Coaching Moves:

▸ *"Touch something in your picture. Have you taught that in the words yet? Say it, write it!"*

▸ *"Keep going. Touch something else in your picture. What else can you teach?"*

▸ *"Say more about that. Can you give an example?"*

▸ *"As soon as you've rehearsed, get started writing!"*

MID-WORKSHOP TEACHING ✦ Tapping into the Power of Drawing and Writing Together

"Writers, you've been studying what authors do in their illustrations and thinking, 'I can do that.' You're learning from the things that writers do! I've actually been learning from a lot of you, the writers in this room, and I want to show you something that I've seen.

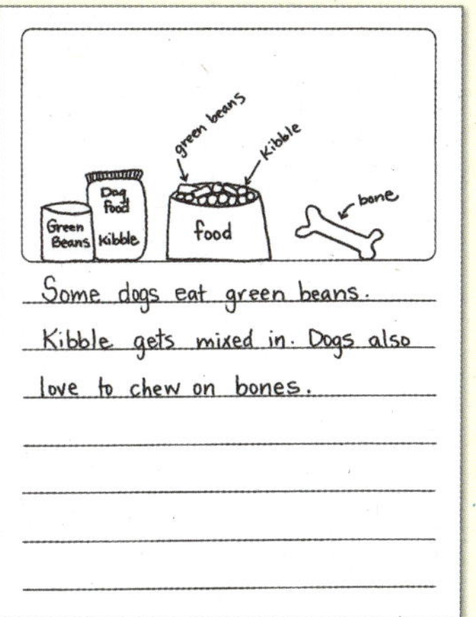

"I've seen many of you switch off between drawing, writing, drawing, writing, drawing, writing in an amazing way. I've been trying to learn from you and to do the same thing. Watch how I do it." On the fifth page of my "All About Dogs" demonstration booklet, I quickly drew a can of green beans going into a dog's bowl on the first page. Then I mumbled some words to myself as I wrote them:

> Some dogs eat green beans.

I took two seconds to add a sketch of dry dog food in the dog's bowl. Then I mumbled and wrote:

> Kibble gets mixed in.

Then I sketched a bone and said, "You know what I will write next . . .

> Dogs also love to chew on bones.

"This switching between drawing and writing is what many of you are doing and it is very writerly. I bet that when you draw, new ideas come to your mind!"

CONFERRING SUPPORTS ✦ Using Pictures to Write with Detail

If you notice . . .	Then you might . . .
Students who look at their work quickly and then announce, "I'm done!"	• Coach these students to make a plan for how they'll look at their work. You might suggest they look at each part of their illustration first, then review their writing. • Help these students slow down. You could say, "Focus your eye on this one little part of your picture, then touch it. What can you write about it? Then move to the next little part. Work slowly so you notice all you can!"
Students who draw their pictures out of order	• Coach these students toward organizing their pictures into a sequence. "I noticed that you talked about putting on a helmet before hopping onto the bike. Is that how your writing goes? No? Then I bet it'd be so helpful for your reader if you put that picture first."
Students who draw only the big outline of a picture	• Say, "You've got the big outline of your picture. You're ready to add in details, so you can teach more. What could you add to the middle/inside?"
Students who've added labels to their picture and haven't yet added any sentences	• Do a bit of quick coaching. "Make sure that you use your pictures and labels to say more in your writing too. Look at your picture and ask yourself, 'How can my picture help me teach more with my words?'"

 Looking to Our Book Baggies for More Writing Mentors

Invite partners to study the illustrations in the books in their reading baggies, noticing how writers are teaching through them.

"Writers, I know this is unusual, but will you put away your *writing* folder and get out your *reading* book baggie? Bring that with you to the rug."

Once kids were gathered with their book baggies, I continued. "Earlier, we studied Hareem's book, *Cake*, with a big question in mind: How do the illustrations in teaching books help writers teach more? We noticed that Hareem used a special kind of illustration called a *diagram*—that fancy picture with all the arrows and labels—and that she also had pictures that gave examples or showed steps. Just like we learned from Hareem, I bet we can learn a ton about illustrations from the books in your baggie that will make the books you're writing even better.

"Will you pull out one of the nonfiction books from your baggie? Put it between you and your partner and study the illustrations super-closely. How do the illustrations in that book help teach more? You might find diagrams or pictures that give examples or steps, or you might notice new ways the illustrations teach. See if you can get ideas for how to teach even more in your books."

I gave partners a few minutes to study together. Then, I asked a few partnerships to share the illustrations they'd found with the class, and how these had given them ideas about making their own books better.

PHONOLOGICAL AWARENESS AND PHONICS EXTENSION ◆ "What's the Middle Sound that You Hear?"

For this extension, you'll need a copy of the "What's the Middle Sound that You Hear?" lyrics.

Sing the "What's the Middle Sound that You Hear?" song, adding the final step of changing the vowel.

"I know that you sang 'What's the Middle Sound that You Hear?' in kindergarten. Now that you're in first grade, though, we're going to find the middle sound in a few words, and we're going to change the vowel from a short vowel to a long vowel. Let's try it out!" We sang:

What's the middle sound that you hear,
That you hear, that you hear?

What's the middle sound that you hear,
In . . . *cap*, *cap*, *cap*?

I gave students a quick moment to figure out the sound, then continued:

/a/ is the middle sound that you hear,
That you hear, that you hear.

/a/ is the middle sound that you hear,
In . . . *cap*, *cap*, *cap*.

"Now comes the special first-grade part. Say *cap* again. Now change /a/ to a long *A*." Students shouted out *cape*. We continued with a few more rounds with *mad/made*, *tap/tape*, *hid/hide*, *not/note*.

Revising by Using Comparisons to Help Readers Picture Things

In This Session

TODAY YOU will teach students that writers use comparisons to help readers picture and understand their topic. You'll share an example from your mentor text to illustrate this concept for kids and then coach students as they try out different comparisons for your demonstration text. In the mid-workshop teaching, you'll remind students to describe exactly how something looks. During the share, you'll share specific compliments about a child's writing and then coach students as they do the same.

TODAY YOUR STUDENTS will work to add comparisons to their writing that help readers picture things. Most kids will continue drafting the books they began in the previous session, although they can also revise those books and others to bring out more comparisons and descriptions.

Getting Ready

YOU WILL NEED . . .

- a copy of *Cake* by Hareem Atif Khan.

- your demonstration text, "All About Dogs." You'll need to write the first sentence on the sixth page prior to today's session. An example of the demonstration writing for this session can be found in the online resources.

- to add two new sticky notes to the "Writers Teach in Words and Pictures!" chart.

STUDENTS WILL NEED . . .

- revision toolkits on each table.

Ensuring Access

YOUR ULTIMATE GOAL TODAY is twofold: to guide writers to use comparisons to teach their readers and to help students recognize all that they have done so far—and write even more—by using the anchor chart as a guide.

- Making comparisons is easier the more examples you have, so if a student is struggling, you can prompt him with quick fill-in-the-blank comparisons, like "soft as a _____," "hard as a _____," "loud as a _____," "quiet as a _____." Using objects can help too. You might put a rock, feather, bell, and teddy bear in front of a child and invite him to use those objects to create comparisons. These exercises will be especially supportive of MLLs in the early and intermediate stages of English acquisition.

- Remember, your goal is that kids use the anchor chart to lift the level of their work. There's no expectation that kids will try every single thing listed on the chart on every page or even in every book. Instead, you'll hope to see that kids try a bit more as writers than they have before.

- In the share, you channel students to give each other feedback. Digital tools can provide another opportunity for students to share and respond to each others' writing. You might set your students up with Flipgrid or a Padlet where they can record themselves reading their book. Other students can respond and give feedback, either through another video, or a written comment.

- If you teach writing workshop in Spanish, or if you have students who speak and write in Spanish, today you might use *Pasteles* by Hareem Atif Khan as a mentor text.

BEND II

Revising by Using Comparisons to Help Readers Picture Things

CONNECTION

Ask writers to use the anchor chart to note places where they've tried strategies. Let students know that you'll teach them a new strategy.

"Writers, you've learned tons and tons of ways to teach your readers so much!" As I spoke, I gestured to the "Writers Teach in Words and Pictures!" anchor chart.

"Before I teach you something new, let's see which of these ways of teaching you've already tried. Will you and your partner read the first sticky note on the chart and then look for places where you tried it out? Show each other these places. Say 'I did it!' or 'Look at what I tried here!' Then, check the next sticky note on the chart and see if you tried that out too." I gave partners a few moments to talk and study their writing.

"There is something I haven't taught you yet, something that could help you teach your readers *even* more."

◆ **Name the teaching point.**

"Today I want to teach you one more way to make sure that your book teaches a lot. You can help your reader picture whatever it is you are writing about by comparing that thing to something that readers know well."

TEACHING

Tell a story that illustrates how using a comparison can help readers understand something that is unfamiliar to them.

"Writers, can I tell you a story? The other day my computer froze." I began to dramatize the moment. "I clicked on the mouse and nothing happened. I pressed on the keyboard. Still nothing." I held my head in my hands. "I have a friend who is good with computers, so I called her, and she said, 'I know what the problem is. So much information has been traveling into your computer that it is like there are too many cars on a road, so there is a traffic jam and nothing can move.'

"Writers, when my friend said it was like there was a traffic jam of information inside my computer, I could picture what she was saying. And nonfiction writers do that all the time. They compare something that is hard to picture with something that is easier to picture."

Show an example of how a mentor author uses comparison to help readers picture something.

I placed page 3 of *Cake* under the document camera. "Hareem used comparisons—saying that two things were *similar*—to teach us about cake. She wrote:

A cake can be as soft as a pillow.

"I'm thinking that if I had a reader who'd never tried cake, they might not know about the texture of cake. But, they've probably felt a pillow many times. Hareem's comparison would help them know what cake feels like! She compared something harder to picture—what cake feels like—to something easier to picture—a pillow."

Finish writing and sketching this page in your demonstration text after the minilesson.

As always, consistent gestures for new vocabulary will help students grasp it more easily. You might move two hands up and down like they are balancing two items to show compare. *Don't worry if the meanings of these words are not solidified yet, since your model (returning to these gestures throughout) will help clarify them for students.*

Set writers up to try making comparisons, first using your text, then playing a game.

"I'm still writing my book all about dogs, and the part I'm working on is about what dogs like. Here's what I have so far." I displayed page 6.

Dogs like baths.

"I was just about to write about dog's fur when it's wet. How many of you know what that is like? You do? So what comparison might you use to help readers know what soggy dog fur is like?" I asked. "When a dog is wet, its fur is *like* . . . Tell your partner what comparison might work." I gave kids a moment to discuss.

"So many interesting ideas that could make my page about a dog's fur more special! I could say a dog's wet fur is *like* a soggy carpet, or it's *like* when you accidentally put a stuffed toy in the washing machine . . ."

"I'm definitely going to add one of those comparisons into my book, but first, let's play a little game. Pretend you are writing a book about airplanes. What could you compare an airplane to?" The children talked, generating the obvious connections to birds and kites. "Let's try one more," I said. "What about if you were writing about the *Tyrannosaurus rex*? What might you compare its teeth to?" I gave students time to generate a few comparisons.

LINK

Add to the anchor chart. Encourage students to use everything they know as they write new books today.

"Writers, let's add this new strategy to our 'Writers Teach in Words and Pictures!' chart." I added the new sticky note to the anchor chart.

"Don't forget that your job is to teach readers as much as possible about your topics. You always have some choices. I know you'll finish your book today. You might also decide that you want to go back and revise a book you wrote before to add in comparisons. Off you go!"

When teaching a new technique, students are more likely to transfer it if they both see examples of it and practice it in multiple ways.

If you have a class with many MLLs, you may want to quickly show visuals of things like a pillow and a dog's wet fur to make these examples of comparisons more concrete.

You can provide MLLs with a sentence frame to support this work: "_____ is like ___." Write this frame somewhere that is visible to students throughout today's session, in addition to expressing it verbally.

SMALL GROUP ✦ Adding Comparisons to Topic Books

For this small group, students will need a mini-version of the anchor chart, "Writers Teach in Words and Pictures!" Each partnership will need a copy of Gerty's writing, "All About Scooters," and the "Add Comparisons" process chart.

▪ RALLY/ACTIVATE

Invite writers to go on a strategy hunt with their partner to spotlight places in their writing where they've tried something from the anchor chart.

"Writers, as I was looking at your writing, I noticed you teaching your readers lots of information in your topic books by trying out several different strategies from our chart. With your partner, put one book in the middle and use this mini-copy of the chart to help you find places in your writing where you've tried one of these strategies. Then switch!"

▪ TRY IT #1

Invite writers to add comparisons to a shared text with their partner.

"One thing you all are ready to try is adding comparisons, just like Hareem did in *Cake*! When you add a comparison, you help your readers understand something that they might not be familiar with." I read over the "Add Comparisons" process chart with the group.

I passed out a copy of Gerty's writing to each partnership. "Right now, work with your partner to help Gerty add comparisons to her writing! That will help Gerty teach more information to her readers."

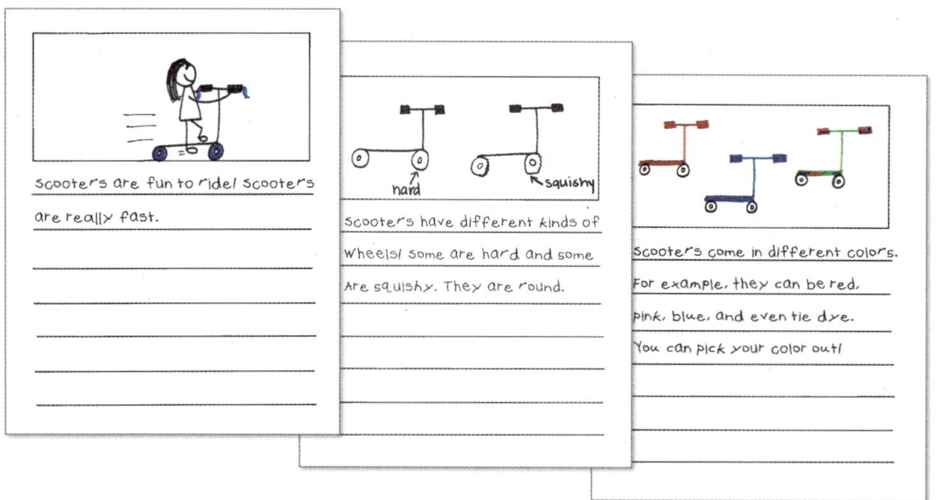

▪ TRY IT #2/LINK

Transition writers to work on their own writing. Build repertoire before sending students off with their own copy of the chart.

"Now try it in your own writing! Using the chart, reread a part of your writing, picture that part in your mind, and see if you can teach your readers by adding a comparison!

"Writers, as you keep working today, remember that you can help your readers understand something they are less familiar with by adding a comparison! This is one more way you can teach your readers even more in pictures and words."

Possible Coaching Moves:

- "*Reread that part again, then stop and think!*"
- "*Close your eyes. What do you see? What is it like?*"
- "*Try out some comparison language! 'Like a . . .' 'As _______ as . . .'*"
- "*Keep reading. See if there is another spot you can try it.*"

"Writers, that magnifying glass in the writing center is reminding me of one more way that writers teach in pictures and words. It's something that I already see many of you doing! You've been adding *exactly* how something looks, right? You look closely at the details—the size, the shape, the color—and then add those details to your writing." I added the new sticky note to the "Writers Teach in Words and Pictures!" anchor chart.

"If you finish your book, instead of starting a new one, you might want to reread and revise. One thing you can do is reread, looking for places where you haven't yet described exactly how your topic looks. Decide what details you want to add, and then dig into the small revision toolbox on your table to grab a flap or whatever else you might need. Or, you can even just add on to the bottom of the page!"

SMALL GROUP ✦ Supporting More Descriptive Vocabulary

For this small group, you'll need chart paper and a marker. You'll also need sensory picture cards. 

■ **RALLY**

Tell kids you will help them describe things in their books. Draw a face to illustrate sensory details.

"Writers, I want to give you a tip. When you want to describe something, you need to write not only with your hands but also with your. . . ." I let my voice trail off as I drew a face with eyes, a nose, a mouth (with a tongue), and ears.

■ **TRY IT #1**

Give kids pictures of items that can be described with sensory details and channel partners to generate sensory words.

"I'm going to give you and your partner some picture cards. Will you come up with the *best* words you can to capture the sight, smell, taste, sound and feel of the items?" I gave students a few minutes to come up with a list, and I recorded some of the words they used. I suggested some, too, and recorded those as well.

■ **TRY IT #2/LINK**

Channel kids to add descriptive vocabulary to their own books.

"Look at the words you have used! Will you go to a page in one of your books where you could use words like these to describe your topic? And after this, aim to use your eyes, ears, nose, hands, and tongue to write!"

© peresanz/Shutterstock/HIP

© ozgurdonmaz/iStock/Getty Images/HIP

© Hero Images/Getty Images/HIP

© Alamy/HIP

CONFERRING TOOL ✦ An Annotated Student Exemplar

Prepare an Annotated Student Exemplar Piece

You might start by transferring over our annotations from page 1 to pages 2 and 3 of Bella's piece. You could continue marking up the piece with annotations on the following pages as well.

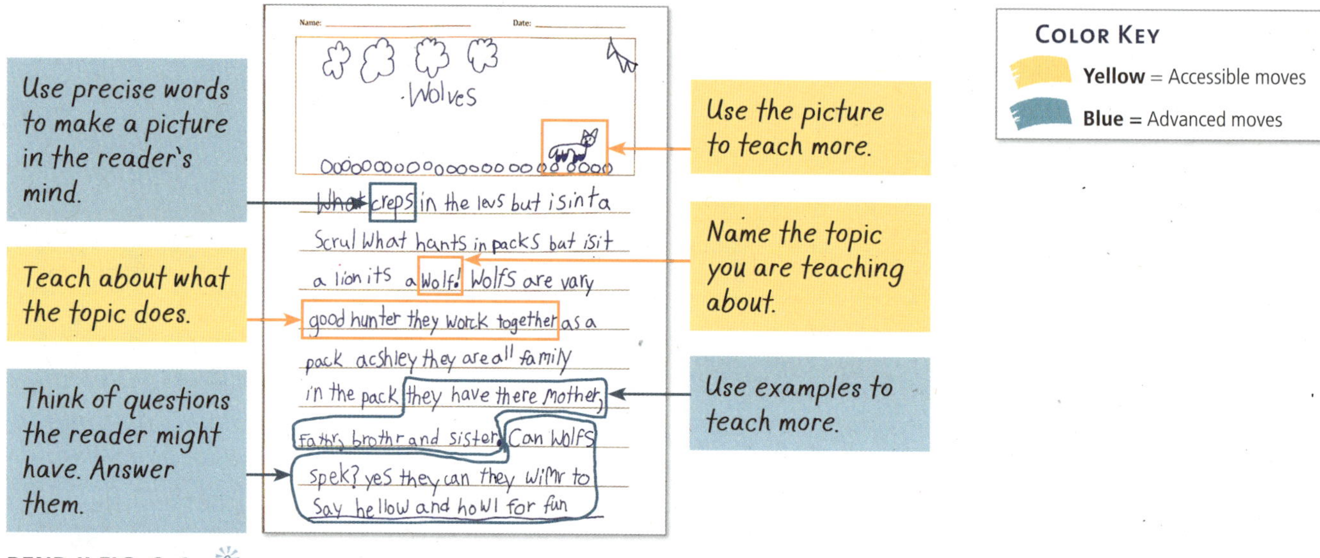

BEND II FIG. 6–1

Use an Annotated Student Example while Conferring

Research and decide: Once you have prepared your annotated exemplar, pull up next to a child to confer. After talking with the child for a few minutes about what she is working on as a writer, you could prioritize one area to teach into.

Teach, introducing the exemplar piece: You might say, "I have an information book, written by a writer your age, that I'm dying to share with you. Bella wrote all about wolves. Can I show you what Bella tried that I think you could do too to make your writing even more powerful?"

Showcase what the writer did and theorize about how she might have done it: If you want to teach the student to use questions in his writing, you might say, "Here's what I was dying to show you. In 'Wolves,' Bella is really thinking about how to teach her readers a lot about her topic. She even imagines what questions her readers might have and answers them in her writing—like here when she says, 'Can wolves speak?' and then answers it, 'Yes, they can whine to say hello and howl for fun.'"

Coach the writer to try the same move: "I bet you could try this same move in your writing. Can you find a page you'd like to work on? Start by rereading, then ask yourself, 'What questions might a reader have after they read this page?' You can ask that question and answer it, right there, in your writing." Spend a minute coaching the writer as he tries this out.

Leave the writer to continue writing: At the end of the conference, you might restate your teaching point, by saying, "Bella's piece is so full of powerful teaching moves. Do you want a copy of it so you can keep learning from it on your own? Fabulous."

 # Noticing and Complimenting What Your Partner Did Well

Remind students that strong partners give each other feedback. Demonstrate this, and then set students up to give each other feedback using the anchor chart.

I asked students to meet me in their rug spots with their folders and pens.

"Yesterday, you worked with your partner, and your partner gave you feedback on whether your book was clear, whether your book taught a lot. That's one kind of feedback that makes your writing better.

"There's another kind of feedback that can make your writing better, too, though, and that's compliments. Compliments are the kind of feedback that you give when you say things like, 'It's amazing that you . . .' and 'You did such a good job of . . .' and 'I noticed that you . . .' When you give a compliment, you want to tell your partner what, exactly, you liked about their writing. Watch how I do it."

I asked for a volunteer, projected their writing, and studied the first page along with the anchor chart. "Wow! You did such a good job of using lots of diagrams!" I tapped the chart and the piece of writing to emphasize that I was looking for things represented on the chart.

"Did you see how I did that? I was very specific, and I used the chart to help me give a compliment. You can do that too. Partner 1 can go first. Read your partner's piece, look at the chart to see what they did well, and give a compliment!" I gave students a few moments to give compliments, coaching students who were having difficulty. Halfway through, I channeled students to switch, so both partners received some positive feedback.

PHONOLOGICAL AWARENESS AND PHONICS EXTENSION ✦

For this extension, show a phonological awareness video. 

This video begins with a round of making words. This activity will reinforce hearing long-vowel sounds and writing CVCe words. Students manipulate the initial sound and vowels across a set of words. The video moves on to reading by analogy. The instructor shows the words *trunk*, *scream*, and *stray*. Students then read a new set of words. They will find that the given words they've just read—in particular the phonograms and vowel teams—will help them read the new words. The video ends with writing by analogy using the words *saw*, *like*, and *make*.

Using Familiar Charts to Help Teach as Much as Possible

In This Session

TODAY YOU will guide students to research, think, and write even more by bringing their attention back to the "Writers Teach in Words and Pictures!" chart. You'll model how to use a chart as a tool by going through each item on it and considering whether that item gives you an idea for what more you can teach your reader, and then trying a few strategies in your book. You'll also emphasize how the anchor chart can be used as a tool as you send students off with their own mini copies of the chart. During the mid-workshop teaching, you'll ask students who are still revising to move on to writing new pages. Make sure to set aside enough time at the end of the workshop for students to celebrate each other's work today.

TODAY YOUR STUDENTS will use the "Writers Teach in Words and Pictures!" chart to help them revise their books and write even more. They might use revision flaps to add more text or they might add new pages to their books. In the share, writers will review each other's work and put sticky notes next to the parts that show exemplary teaching.

YOU WILL NEED . . .

- the chart, "Writers Teach in Words and Pictures!"

- your "All About Dogs" demonstration text. You'll need to sketch and label a picture of a dog on the seventh page prior to today's session. An example of this page can be found in the online resources.

- sticky notes.

- a purple revision pen to revise the fifth page of your "All About Dogs" demonstration text about the foods dogs eat. An example of this revised demonstration text can be found in the online resources..

STUDENTS WILL NEED . . .

- individual copies of the "Writers Teach in Words and Pictures!" chart.

- revision tools stocked in the writing center.

- several "Lots of Teaching Spotted" sticky notes (see Share).

Ensuring Access

YOUR ULTIMATE GOAL TODAY is to help students use a chart as a tool for revision. This is a challenging lesson and you can expect that some writers will need extra support. But there's plenty of other productive work they can do!

- Encourage students to place the mini-anchor chart next to them while they work. For those who may not recall the items on the chart, you may ask them to review the chart with a partner before they work independently. For students who need support using the mini–anchor chart effectively, you may need to model—or have another child model—the process: 1. Check a strategy on the chart; 2. Reread your writing, seeing if there is a place to do more of that work; 3. Write; and 4. Revisit the chart for another technique to check.

- Some students, including MLLs in the early stages, may first express their ideas through complex drawings and diagrams and then in sentences. Make sure to appreciate the teaching they are conveying with drawings as well as sentences.

- For students who are stuck revising, you may want to remind them of their options with the different page types, review how to use flaps for revision, or send them back to observe and research their topic, to come up with more ideas to write about.

Using Familiar Charts to Help Teach as Much as Possible

CONNECTION

To rally kids to enjoy making choices today, talk up the pleasure of a smorgasbord.

"Writers, over the weekend, I went to a party and there was an ice-cream sundae bar, where everybody could make their own ice-cream sundaes! Each person got a bowl of ice cream. There was a list of all the choices for toppings: whipped cream and sprinkles and gummy bears and cherries and chocolate chips and so many more! I got to read down the list and choose the toppings I wanted, the ones I thought would make my sundae the best it could be. It was hard to choose—all the toppings looked so tasty—but eventually, I picked the toppings that seemed just right for me: whipped cream, sprinkles, and gummy bears.

"That got me thinking. Writing a nonfiction book is a lot like making an ice-cream sundae. We have to make choices about what our nonfiction books need, just like I made choices about what toppings my ice-cream sundae needed. As writers, we don't have a list of toppings to choose from . . . but we do have a list of choices that'll help us make our object books really strong!" I tapped the "Writers Teach in Words and Pictures!" anchor chart.

◆ **Name the teaching point.**

"Today I want to teach you that writers make choices about what will make their books the best they can be. Charts can remind writers of possible choices. Writers read the chart, choose what their book might need, and then add that into the book."

TEACHING

Put the chart on your teacher's chair, suggesting the chart has become the teacher. Invite students to join you as you read the chart and think about what you have and haven't yet tried.

"In a way that means you don't need me, do you? Look!" I got off my chair and clipped the anchor chart to it, so the chart replaced me. Then I sat on the floor at the feet of this new teacher. "Let's read our chart, and make sure we know our choices, okay?" I used my pointer and led the children in reading the chart.

"Wow! This chart gives us so many choices of different ways we can teach. Watch how I use it to help me make my book the best it can be." I took out my book about my dogs and stood beside my chair and the document camera.

"Will you read off each choice? Then I'll see if I already have each choice in my book and if I don't, you can tell me if I should add it."

I pointed to "Add diagrams" and the class read it aloud. I looked over my booklet and displayed page 7, on which I'd sketched a dog and labeled its parts. "This is a diagram, and it has pictures with labels." I wrote the word *done* on a sticky note and stuck it onto the first item on the chart.

While this analogy is great fun and may be helpful for many students, don't spend too long trying to make sure it is understandable if some students are confused. Focus on the heart of the lesson: supporting writers' independence to make choices in their writing.

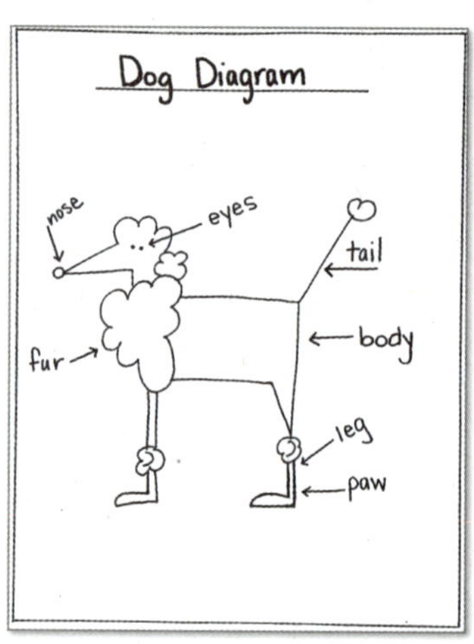

BEND II

We moved on to the second item on the chart, and I shook my head, no. "I don't have any pictures that show steps yet. But I could teach you how to train your dog to sit. I could definitely use pictures that show steps there! Does that seem like a good idea?" I asked the kids, and when they said, "Yes!" I added a To-Do sticky note to that item on the chart.

The children read the next item. "I do have examples." I stuck another "done" sticky note on the chart and then moved on to the next strategy. "Hmm, . . . my book doesn't have any bold words or definitions yet, but I don't think I'll need them. I've got lots of size, shape, and color words. I bet I can add more comparisons. I could add them on almost *any* page!"

Demonstrate revising your book based on the decisions you just made. First, revise by adding comparisons.

"Page 5 of my book tells about the food dogs eat. I tell that some dogs eat green beans with kibble and they like to chew on bones. But I don't describe the food. I could say the kibble looks like. . . . Hmm, . . . what could I compare it to . . . ? I know! A bowl of peanuts."

I pulled out a new sheet of paper. "I think I should also add a new page to tell the steps for teaching dogs to sit."

Debrief, emphasizing the transferable steps involved in what you just demonstrated.

"So, writers, did you see how that went? First, I read through the chart, remembering what I could do in my book. Then, I thought, 'Which of these things will I add to my book?' I thought about places in my writing where I could add those things, and also about new pages that I might add to my book. Then, I started writing."

ACTIVE ENGAGEMENT

Recruit students to study the chart and decide what they want to revise or add to their own books. Then, ask them to begin working as you coach.

"Now it's your turn. First, take out the book you are working on." I gave students a moment to do so. "Will you read through our anchor chart and think, 'Which of these things could I add to my book?' You might check in order like I did. Choose what you'll add to make your book the best it can be. Maybe start with one or two things." I left a little space for students to read the chart and start making choices.

After a minute to read the chart and check their books, I said, "Now, see if you can add those things to your book in lots of places! I have some flaps right here." I held up a basket. "I'll come around to help. If you finish adding things, you know what to do—turn to a new page, and think, 'How can I add these things, right from the start of my writing?'" I moved from student to student, coaching them to add the things they'd chosen.

LINK

Restate the teaching point. Distribute individual copies of the anchor chart, and emphasize how it can be used as a tool as they draft and revise.

"Remember, charts give you choices of all the things you can add to your book. I think you're ready to keep using this chart to make your books even better on your own!"

I distributed mini-copies of the anchor chart to each student. "Make sure to keep it front-and-center today as you add one thing and then another to your book. And there are also flaps in the writing center if you need more as you are working."

As students scooted back to their seats and began writing, I gave a few fast voiceovers to convey the importance of today's work: "Speedy, speedy! There's lots to do today!"

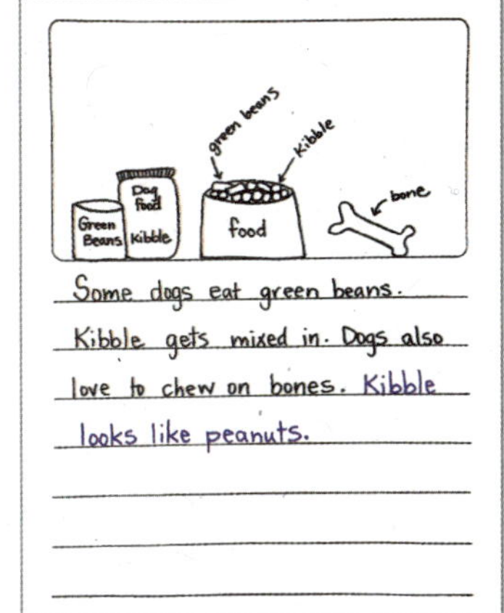

Notice that we are demonstrating the thinking involved in both revising an old page and drafting a new one. Your students will be at different places in the writing process right now, and we want all students to engage in this work, whether they are drafting, revising, or both!

We do not expect students will add everything from the chart. This is a repertoire chart, one that lists options. We want students to make intentional decisions about how they'll elaborate, not to add all of the options willy-nilly.

CONFERRING TOOL ✦ Using Charts in a Variety of Ways

1 Choose One Goal to Weave across the Whole Book

Support the writer in selecting a strategy from the anchor chart, perhaps one they have yet to try or one that they've only tried once. Push them to see how they can try that same strategy across the many pages of their books.

2 Empower Partners to Give Tips Using an Anchor Chart

Set partners up to put one child's book and the anchor chart between them. Invite students to read the book together, naming compliments and giving tips from the chart. The writer may circle the strategy that was offered as a tip or get started adding new teaching right away, before switching with their partner.

3 Check Each Page across the Whole Chart

Invite students to use the chart as a checklist. They may place the first page of their book beside the anchor chart and check to see the kind of teaching they've used on that one page. Students may check off the strategies they've tried on the chart and then push themselves to try out strategies they have yet to try before repeating this process on page two of their book.

4 Cut and Sort to Create an Individualized Goals Chart

Cut the anchor chart into individual strategies prior to pulling up next to a writer. Invite the writer to look at each strategy alongside their book, reflecting on which strategies they've already tried and which they have not, sorting the cards into two piles. Plan to use sticky notes, glue, or tape to add the strategies to this new T-chart, which you will leave with the child as they work.

MID-WORKSHOP TEACHING ✦ Drafting New Pages

"I just looked around the room, and guess what? So many of you are acting on your plans from today! You're revising your pages to teach your readers more. I love that many of you are grabbing a whole new page from the writing center. Before you write that new page, look at your anchor chart and think, 'What do I want to make sure to do on this page?' In this way, the chart can help you right from the start. It can help you decide how you want your new page to go!

"I can't wait to see if some of you add new pages to not just the book you've been working on recently but also to books from earlier in the unit."

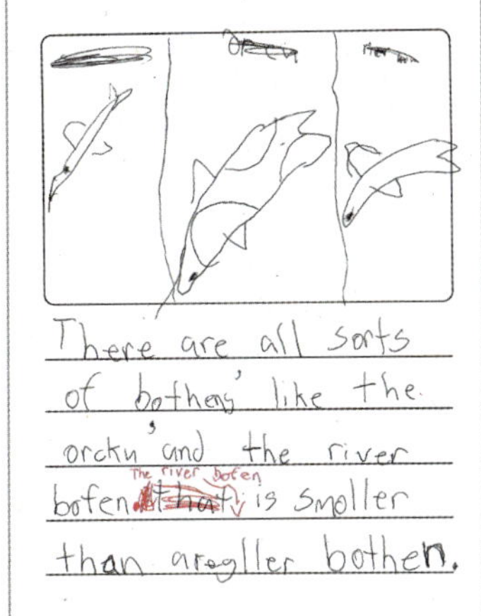

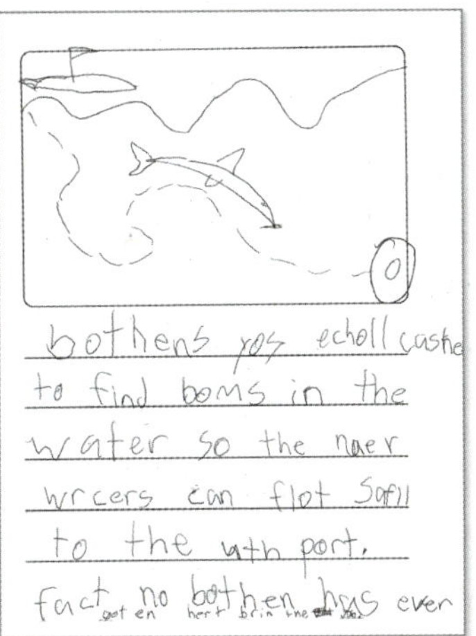
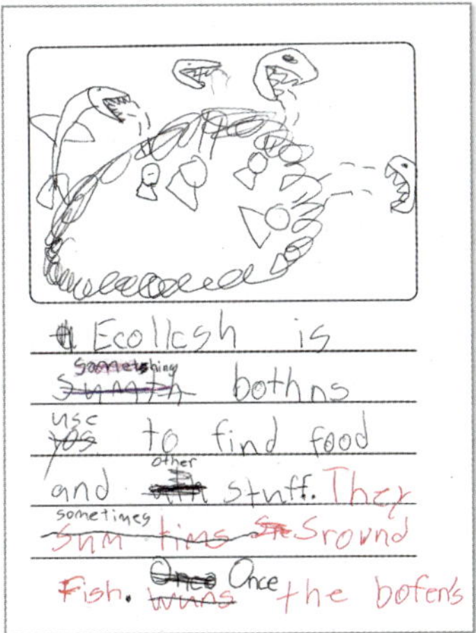

BEND II FIG. 7–1 Elyse's piece about dolphins 

■ RESEARCH/DECIDE

Ask a few broad questions to gain a sense of where the writer is in the process.

"Hey Elyse. How's it going?" Elyse shrugged and responded that things were good. "Great! Tell me a bit about what you are working on."

Elyse flipped through her pages and pointed at the labels in her pictures. "I'm trying to teach a lot." She continued to flip through the pages, and I could see that her book was mostly done.

"Will you show me a page where you are especially proud of all that you have taught?" Elyse flipped to a page about different kinds of dolphins, where she'd divided her picture box into thirds to draw pictures of several different kinds of dolphins.

I could have done a bit more research, but after noticing a trend I decided on my teaching point.

Compliment the writer, making sure to name out what, specifically, is going well for them in their writing.

"Elyse, you've done so many marvelous things in this book. As I look through this entire book, I notice that you're the kind of writer who includes lots of expert words—look at this page alone. You talk about the orca and river dolphin, and on another page, you use giant words like *echolocation*. You don't shy away from those words!"

I attached my compliment to a page the writer was especially proud of, and, as I complimented, I made sure to point out something specific and replicable. I wanted my compliment to make the child continue to do that thing.

■ TEACH

Offer a "just in time" tip to the writer that is transferable to other books and in this case, other genres.

"Can I give you a tip before you move on to your next book?" Elyse nodded. "Something writers do when they finish writing a book is check to make sure they've spelled snap words correctly so others can read their writing easily. You can do this by rereading your writing, hunting for snap words. When you find one, stop, find it on the word wall, check it and fix it if you need to. Then keep hunting to see if there are more words that need fixing!"

Typically, a student's work presents many teaching opportunities, and many things—development, structure—often feel more high-priority than spelling. However, it's critical that students spell snap words correctly, particularly as they prepare to publish, so we focused on this teaching point today.

Invite the writer to try this out right away, coaching her with lean prompts related to the teaching point.

Elyse nodded her head and began to look at her writing. "I found one. Here's *are* and *all*."

"Yes, those words are snap words! Check them!" Elyse glanced at the word wall, then gave a thumbs up.

It's important for Elyse to check all of the words, not just the words that are spelled incorrectly. Confirmation and checking reinforce correct spelling and orthographic mapping.

"You're right. You spelled those correctly, and it's so important to check all of the snap words. Keep going. Let's check the next page."

Elyse read the next page out loud, then said, "I see this word. I don't think that this is how you spell *their*."

Time is, however, of the essence, so I wanted to balance the work of practicing with giving Elyse the opportunity to actually fix some of her misspellings.

I said, "You could be right! Find it on the word wall, check it, fix it! Keep going." Elyse looked up at the word wall and found the word *their*. She crossed out *thar* on the page and rewrote it correctly, then turned the page.

I coached Elyse as she continued to read, identifying snap words, checking them, and fixing them up.

Name the work the writer has done and that you hope the writer will continue to do. Leave a visual behind as a reminder.

"That was hard work! You just fixed up three or four different snap words in your book, which will make it even easier for readers to read and understand. Remember, you can do this with any book you write. You can hunt for snap words, check them on the word wall, and then fix them! Let's say the steps together on our fingers. Ready?" Elyse repeated after me: "Hunt, check, fix!"

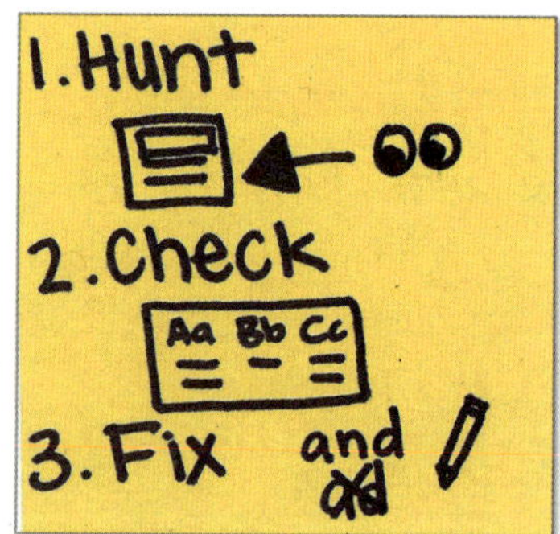

I used a playful process to help the writer remember the strategy.

I jotted the three steps on a sticky note along with a small visual of the word wall to remind Elyse of the work we did together.

Executive functioning skills play a major role in the development of independent writing skills. We talked to school psychologist Ellen Kelty MA, NCSP, to get some tips on responding to predictable, executive functioning challenges that children may encounter during writing workshop.

Q **What exactly does executive functioning mean?**

A According to The Child Mind Institute, "Executive functions are mental skills that we use all day, every day to get things done." Executive functioning plays a role in kids' ability to goal-set, plan out a task, manage time and materials, and prioritize.

Q **What are some predictable challenges that kids experience around executive functioning during writing workshop?**

A Executive functioning challenges can manifest in a variety of ways during writing workshop. For some, time management can pose a particular challenge. You might notice those children struggling to move quickly from one part of the writing process to the next. Others may encounter difficulty with organization of materials and may struggle to organize the writing they are doing across days. Their folders may appear messy and they may struggle to find what they need to write. You may also notice some children who struggle to organize the information in their writing.

Q **What are some ways to support students with executive functioning challenges?**

A Some predictable ways of supporting executive functioning include: giving students checklists to break down the concrete steps of each part of the writing process, giving children additional time and visual reminders to organize their materials during a transition, differentiating organizational tools (for example a multi-pocket folder with pockets for each bend), and using timers to help children pace themselves throughout the workshop. It is important to explicitly tell children the rationale behind these structures so that they feel purposeful and not like unnecessary additional work.

Q **How can I use technology to assist with these executive function supports?**

A Remember that many of these executive function supports can be digital. Students might have different checklists on a tablet or other device, or they might have a visual timer on a device that they can set on their own. Use of a device to manage these supports may also help with organization.

BEND II FIG. 7–2 A laminated personal checklist can be reused each day with a whiteboard marker.

BEND II

 Teaching Treasure Hunt

Invite students to participate in a "Teaching Treasure Hunt" at their tables, searching through one another's books and celebrating each other's use of different strategies.

"Friends, for our share, you'll stay at your tables. That's because you'll be looking through one another's books, noticing and admiring the amazing things you've all done! It's as if you'll be going on a treasure hunt, noticing all the wonderful things you each did to teach more in your books!

"If you're going on a treasure hunt, you'll need these." I held up sticky notes labeled "Lots of Teaching Spotted" and began walking around the room, placing several on each table while I talked. "When people look at treasure maps, they sometimes say, 'X marks the spot!' These sticky notes will mark the spots where you found some teaching treasure in your friends' books—where they did a lot to teach as much as they could.

"Choose someone at your table to go first. Put that person's book, and the chart you studied today, in the middle of your table. Read that person's book together and stop and celebrate where you see them doing the things on the chart. Make sure to mark it with one of those special sticky notes. I bet you'll find lots of examples of great teaching in every book. Are you ready to hunt for treasure? Go!"

PHONOLOGICAL AWARENESS AND PHONICS EXTENSION ✦

For this extension, show a phonological awareness video. 

The video begins with dictation, segmenting words starting and ending in blends, then writing the word. The video ends with the onset-rime word-building activity. Students will read the rime, -ash, and be presented with a collection of initial consonants, blends, and the digraph *qu* to build words.

The First Page Begins the *Whole Book*

In This Session

TODAY YOU will teach students that the introduction of a book should set up their readers to know a little bit about the topic and what they're going to learn. You'll invite kids to help you study the mentor text, marking up the moves the author made in her introduction, and then you'll demonstrate how you craft your own introduction using similar strategies. Before sending students off to write, you'll set them up to try this work in their own books. Mid-workshop, you'll encourage students not to spend too much time getting one introduction just right—these sections also need to be revised and reworked, just like the rest of the book. In the share, you'll reveal ways students can end their books too.

TODAY YOUR STUDENTS will add introductions to each of their books, or start a new book altogether. They will learn that they might need to write lots of different introductions until they figure out the one that works the best. In the share, writers will learn how to write a conclusion too.

Getting Ready

YOU WILL NEED . . .

- a copy of the mentor text, *Cake*, and sticky notes to annotate the introduction.

- to add an introduction to your demonstration text "All About Dogs." An example of the demonstration writing for this session can be found in the online resources. 

- the "Ways to Say Good-Bye . . ." chart (see Share).

STUDENTS WILL NEED . . .

- blank pieces of writing paper (see Share).

Ensuring Access

YOUR ULTIMATE GOAL TODAY is for students to add at least one introduction and conclusion, though some students might decide to add these to all their books.

- If you have students who still need support writing conventionally, they might orally rehearse how their introduction and conclusion could go first. MLLs in early and intermediate stages may especially benefit from this increased opportunity for oral rehearsal and should be invited to try this in a different language if it helps them.

- Give students who need support emulating a mentor text their own copy of the introduction of *Cake* annotated with sticky notes. You could encourage them to pull the sticky notes off the mentor text and search for places for those labels in their own writing. If the child can't find a place for a sticky note in their writing, that's a sign they could add that.

- The next session marks the end of this bend, when you'll invite students to add their books to the classroom library. If you have students who wrote books that will be especially tricky to read conventionally, you might invite those kids to create audio recordings of their writing. You could then link these recordings to QR codes, so that someone could scan the code and hear the child reading their book aloud.

- If MLLs need additional support with introductions, pull a small group and guide them through the process of studying the introduction of a favorite, self-selected mentor text. MLLs benefit from repeated readings and study of familiar texts; if a child is particularly drawn to a certain book and reads it again and again, guide her to study it as a mentor! If you have mentor texts available in other languages too, you can draw upon these to make small groups especially powerful.

- If you teach writing workshop in Spanish, or if you have students who speak and write in Spanish, today you might use *Pasteles* by Hareem Atif Khan as a mentor text.

The First Page Begins the *Whole Book*

CONNECTION

Refer to the way morning meetings go—students greet each other and preview the day. Explain that book introductions are similar.

"Writers, I love our morning meetings. Those meetings get us ready for the learning that will happen all day long. We say hello to each other, and we always make sure to read the schedule and think about the things that we'll do across the day." I gestured to the classroom schedule as I mentioned it.

"When we say hello and talk about the schedule, it doesn't just help us get ready for the *first* thing we will do though," and I tapped the first item on the schedule. "It helps us get ready for the entire day. When we look at the schedule, we hear a tiny bit about what we're going to learn and how our day is going to go.

"Information books start the same way."

◆ **Name the teaching point.**

"Today I want to teach you that information writers include a special kind of 'morning meeting' inside of their books, called an *introduction*. The introduction says 'Hello' to the reader and explains a little bit about what they are going to learn."

TEACHING

Study the mentor text to see what the author does to begin her book. Use sticky notes to label the moves students notice. Convey the transferability of strategies.

"Of course, I am joking a little. It would be so silly if, at the start of an information book, all the readers gathered in a circle! But we could study the ways authors like Hareem say 'Hello' to their readers and set them up to learn a lot. Let's try it."

I opened up *Cake* to the introduction page and read it to students.

> What makes any day feel like a party? What does every birthday need? If you said "Cake!" you're right! If you want to learn more about this delicious food, keep on reading! Cake is the best!

"Hmm, . . . what does Hareem do in her introduction?" I paused to give students time to think, then said, "Turn and talk to your partner. How does Hareem say 'Hello' to her readers and let them know what they are going to learn?"

As students talked, I walked around the carpet with a stack of sticky notes, labeling things students noticed. Soon, I had labeled the questions at the start of the introduction, the part that tells what the reader will learn, the opinion, and the "Keep on reading!" prompt to build excitement.

Model using strategies from the mentor text to craft your own introduction for your demonstration piece.

"Now that I've learned about different ways information writers start their books, I'm going to go back to the start of my book and try writing my own introduction." I picked up my book on dogs, used a staple remover to pull off the cover, and then inserted a new page for

If your class does not have a morning meeting or daily welcoming ritual, you might just refer to your classroom's schedule and point out the first activity of the day. Or, you could remind students of what happens during breakfast, lineup, unpacking, or a similar arrival procedure.

It's unlikely that your students will notice these exact same things—that's okay. Feel free to write them down anyway. Especially when students are newer to studying mentor texts, they often need support naming what, exactly, a mentor author did.

In Bend I, you introduced kids to some simple sentence starters they could use to start an information book. If most kids are already writing introductory pages, you might instead show how you revise your introductory page in light of the mentor text study.

the introduction. "Since I'm adding this special new section, I'll need to add a new page. You'll have to do the same thing when you write your introduction.

"One thing I've learned is that I could start my book by asking a question. I could ask, 'Have you ever seen a dog?' I don't know about that, though, because people who pick up my books probably already like dogs. Hareem also started by giving an opinion, saying that cake is the best. Maybe I could start my book about dogs by saying, 'Dogs are such fun animals. They make great pets!' Oh, and just like Hareem did, I could tell my reader what they'll learn . . . 'Let me teach you all about dogs.'" I jotted this down on the first page.

"Did you see how I did that? I used Hareem's strategies to start my book. I chose to give my opinion about dogs and tell my readers what they're going to learn, but you could do other things. Some of you might decide to give a quick fact, some of you might ask questions, some of you might even tell your reader to 'Read on!'"

ACTIVE ENGAGEMENT

Channel students to think through ways they might begin one of their books. Invite partners to share and receive feedback.

"Now it's your turn. Get out one of your books that needs a special introduction. Start by rereading your book, thinking about how you'll say 'Hello' and get readers ready to learn a lot. I'm going to leave the page from Hareem's book up here; it might give you some ideas." Students worked and thought for a few moments.

"Now, Partner 2, turn and tell your partner about how you might start your book. And then, ask your partner what they think. Listening partner, Partner 1, if your friend could add something more, try saying something like, 'Why don't you . . .' to help your partner make their introduction even better."

LINK

Remind students of the choices that they have during today's independent work time, then send students off to write.

"Writers, before you go off to write today, remember that you have some choices. You've learned a ton about introductions, and you might add an introduction to the book you've been working on, then finish that book. You could go back to all of the books you've written and add an introduction to each of those books. If you don't have the space in your book, you can just staple another page to it, like I did." Here I pointed to the writing center to remind students of where the blank paper was stored.

"Or, you might be starting a new teaching book. If that's what you're doing, remember to make sure that it has an introduction too.

"Once you have a plan, give me a thumbs up." As students signaled they had a plan, I sent them off to write.

Dogs are such fun animals! They make great pets! Let me teach you all about dogs.

If you have time, invite partners to switch roles. It's not absolutely necessary that both partners get to share in every turn-and-talk. Here, both partners play an active role and benefit from this work.

Consider providing sentences starters from the "Ways to Start an Information Book" chart. Celebrate students approximations, and over time coach them to try specific strategies from the mentor text.

BEND II

Work Time

STUDENT WORK ✦ Compliments and Next Steps for Luca's Introduction and Conclusion

As students write, you'll notice them including introductions and conclusions, as Luca did in his piece about video games. Even though your students are approximating, be sure to find many things to admire, and many other things that you might teach into, just as we did for Luca's piece!

Possible Compliments

"Wow! What a powerful introduction! I notice that you told your readers right away what this book would be about, and you asked a question to draw them in. You also included a picture so they can *see* what you'll be teaching about. Your readers will be hooked!"

"There is so much excitement in your conclusion! It makes me want to go off and play video games! You've done a great job giving lots of knowledge and information in your book, then telling your readers what they can now *do* with their new learning. Your readers will really appreciate that!"

"When I read your introduction and your conclusion, I can tell that you're the kind of writer who's not scared of hard words, or of punctuation. You used tons of different punctuation to ask questions, or to show that something is really exciting. You should be very proud of that!"

Possible Teaching Points

"Can I tell you what might make your introduction even more powerful? You could think of a really powerful first line, something that would make your readers say, 'Wow! I need to read on!'"

Use the "Ways to Start an Information Book" chart from Bend I, Session 4 to give examples of powerful openings. 

"At the start of a book, readers want to know *who* the book is for. Is it for someone who wants to learn a little bit about video games, or is it for someone who already knows a little bit and who wants to learn about specific *kinds* of games? You can write a sentence or two to tell what, exactly, this book can teach someone."

"Just like your introduction says 'Hello,' your conclusion can say 'Good-bye' to your readers. Could you start this page by saying something like, 'Now you know all about . . .' or 'I hope you enjoyed learning . . .'?"

Use the "Ways to Say Good-Bye . . ." chart (which you will introduce to the entire class in the share) to offer a few options.

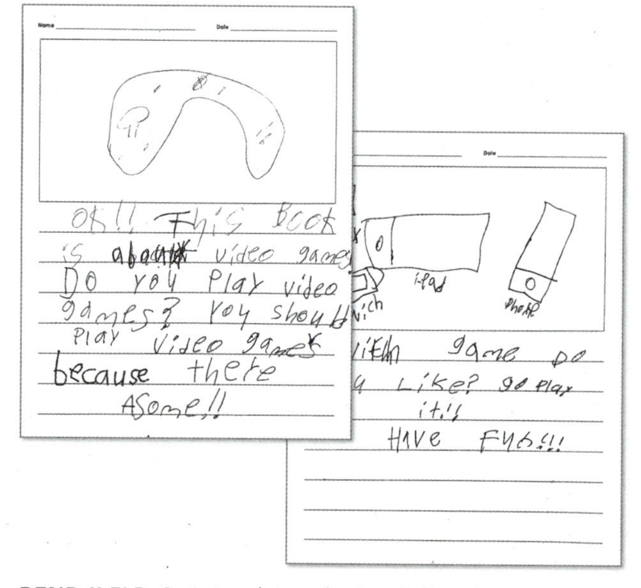

BEND II FIG. 8–1 Luca's introduction *(left)* and conclusion *(right)*

"Writers, I don't know about you, but sometimes I spend *a lot* of time picking out my lunch in the cafeteria. Today, I was standing with my tray, and I went to reach for a peanut butter and jelly sandwich. Then I said, 'No, not that, not today.' I thought about getting a hot dog but decided I didn't want that either. And, then, I finally saw what I wanted: a delicious slice of pizza! I put it on my tray, and I knew I had made the right choice.

"I'm telling you about how much time I spend picking out my lunch because writing an introduction is actually no different. You might write one introduction and then think to yourself, 'Nope, that way doesn't work.' That's okay! If you try one introduction that doesn't work, just cross it out and try out another way. You might need to try lots of different introductions until you have one that feels just right.

"You can do this work by writing down lots of introductions, or you can whisper them to yourself or your partner before you write them. Either way, remember—the best writers try lots of different introductions before they figure out which one is just right."

SMALL GROUP ✦ Rehearsing and Writing Many Introductions

This small group could be adjusted to work on introductions, conclusions, comparisons, sensory description, and more by using the same images but changing the supporting anchor chart.

To prepare, you'll need the "Ways to Start an Information Book" chart and photograph cards. You'll also need blank sheets of writing paper, staple removers, and staplers for students to add introduction pages to their books.

■ **RALLY**

Remind kids of the purpose and qualities of introductions.

"Friends, today you've been adding introductions to your information writing to help get your readers ready to learn when they read your books. Introductions are an important thing to consider for each and every information book you write, and authors always work to find the just-right words to get their readers excited and ready to learn.

"Remember this chart of sentence stems?" I showed the group the "Ways to Start an Information Book" chart. "Let's quickly revisit it together so you can use it in case you feel stuck."

■ **TRY IT #1**

Set students up to quickly, orally generate introductions for multiple topics.

"I was thinking that today we could practice quickly giving introductions to the topics we are writing about. I have a pile of cards for each partnership. When I say 'Go,' Partner 1 will flip over the top card, and I want you to each try saying a different introduction for the topic on the card. Once you've each given an introduction, Partner 2 can flip the next card. Remember, you can use the chart to help you out if you get stuck. Try to introduce the topics in lots of different ways. You ready? Go!"

Possible Coaching Moves:

▶ *Gesture to a new prompt on the chart.*

▶ *"Tell me more in this introduction. Try to use more than one of the things from the chart."*

▶ *"Can you say that another way?"*

▶ *"Use words to get your reader excited."*

■ TRY IT #2/LINK

Channel students to make a stack of all the books in their folders, then add an introduction page to each one.

"Wow! You're getting so strong at giving introductions that set readers up to learn a lot. In fact, I think you're ready to do this work with your *own* topics. Right now, your folders are almost bursting with books you've written about our classroom and about topics you know super-well. Will you make a little stack for all the books you think you could add an introduction to?

"Here's a stapler and a pile of blank pages for you to use to make your introductions. See if you can use all you know to add introductions to each and every one of your books. Try to add ones that get your reader excited *and* ready to learn all about your topics."

© Radius Images/Jupiterimages/Getty Images/HIP

© Comstock/Getty Images/HIP

© Comstock/Getty Images/HIP

Sample photo cards for generating introductions. Additional cards can be found in the online resources.

 Writers Say Good-Bye at the End of a Book

Tell students that writers also make sure to end their books and reveal a list of ways to do so. Give students a few minutes to write a conclusion for their books.

Once the kids had gathered with their folders and pens, I gestured back to the schedule. "It'd be pretty hard for us to leave school if we didn't have pack-up and good-bye time, wouldn't it? You'd probably be saying, 'I can't go yet. I don't have my coat on.' And when you got back home, you'd wonder why you didn't put all your things in your backpack. Yikes!

"Just like we can't finish our day without packing up and saying good-bye, you can't send your readers off without an ending. I've gathered up a list of ways that writers might end their teaching books." I displayed the "Ways to Say Good-Bye . . ." chart.

"Take out a book you worked on today and think about an ending you could add to your book. You can try one of the endings from our chart, or you can come up with your own. I'll circle around with extra pieces of paper if you need one. Make sure to say good-bye to your reader!" I scurried around the carpet, providing support to students who needed it, and passing out extra pieces of paper to students who didn't have any blank pages in their books.

After a few minutes, I said, "Wonderful work today, writers. Everyone, hold up your ending pages." Students proudly held their pages over their heads. "You know, I think you're almost ready to share these books with others. Put your book back into your folder, making sure not to wrinkle it. I'll think tonight about how you can share these special books!"

PHONOLOGICAL AWARENESS AND PHONICS EXTENSION ◆

For this extension, show a phonological awareness video. 

This video begins with a round of making words. In this activity, students listen for phonemes that have been added, deleted, and manipulated to make new words. Today's work with adding phonemes asks students to hear and write blends and the beginning and ends of words, as well as three-letter blends, like *spl* in the word *split*. The video then transitions to writing by analogy. The instructor shows students the words, *just, now,* and *went,* and dictates new words for students to write, using the words shown. The video ends with a celebration, reading a collection of decodable words and snap words and a message from the instructor.

Paying Careful Attention to Vowel Sounds as You Write

In This Session

TODAY YOU will use a letter from the Super Secret Detective Agency to remind writers of the silent *e* and lead them in a quick word sort to identify long and short vowels. You'll teach students that they should always pay attention to whether words have long or short vowels, and that writers use all their writing knowledge to represent those sounds correctly. You'll model how to stretch out vowel sounds and use the vowel chart as you add to your own book, then you'll send students off to fix up their own writing. In the mid-workshop, you'll coach students to edit their writing by playing "Find-It Fix-It." In the share, you'll celebrate their work by passing a bin around, asking each student to choose their strongest book and read the title as they place it in the bin.

TODAY YOUR STUDENTS will strengthen their phonics skills with a word sort to identify different vowel sounds in a set of words. When they go off to write they will work to fix up and finish the books in their folder by correcting spelling and punctuation and adding missing information. If they've finished checking their books, they can always start writing an entirely new book. In the mid-workshop, they'll pick a book from their folder and take just one minute—timed—to quickly look for and fix up spelling errors. In the share, students will celebrate their work in this bend by adding their strongest book to the classroom library.

Getting Ready

YOU WILL NEED . . .

- an envelope addressed to your class with the Super Secret Detective Agency's letter, a set of picture cards, and "The Case of the Silent *e*" chart.

- a pocket chart.

- sticky notes.

- the "Our Spelling Toolbox" chart, the version with four strategies.

- your demonstration text, "All About Dogs." An example of the revised demonstration text for this session can be found in the online resources.

- a purple revision pen.

- a timer (see Mid-Workshop Teaching).

STUDENTS WILL NEED . . .

- whiteboards and dry erase markers.

- their folders.

Ensuring Access

YOUR ULTIMATE GOAL TODAY is to support students in transferring what they've learned about long- and short-vowel patterns from phonics to writing workshop to help them spell words. Rather than correcting students' spelling errors, you'll want to encourage their attempts at generalizing spelling patterns.

- If students make errors with some logic (such as spelling *phone* as *fone*), make sure to praise their attempts. Say, "You're listening really hard and using everything that you know about words and letter sounds!" If there are times when students' spelling errors don't have clear logic underlying them, say, "Hmm, . . . say that word again. Is there anything that you've learned in word study that can help you spell that?"

- There will still be many words misspelled across students' books. When we encourage children to publish, we want them to make their work *public*, not *perfect*. If you notice a mistake, say, "Check that word. Does it look right?" If the word fits within the student's zone of proximal development, point out resources in the room that could help, and offer tips, saying, "Is there another vowel that could work?" Otherwise, allow spelling mistakes to remain, knowing that consistently correct spelling is a goal throughout all of elementary school.

- If your students are not familiar with the vowel and silent *e* charts from the Units of Study in Phonics, you could introduce these charts to students in this session, knowing they might need more time to understand them, or substitute in long- and short-vowel pattern charts from your existing phonics program.

- Producing language on-demand for the class can be stressful for some MLLs. Consider gathering those students together in advance of the share, inviting them to choose the book they'll add to the library and rehearse reading the title aloud.

Paying Careful Attention to Vowel Sounds as You Write

CONNECTION

Reveal a letter from the Super Secret Detective Agency, reminding students of the importance of paying attention to long- and short-vowel sounds.

"Writers, this is a bit strange." I held up the envelope from the Super Secret Detective Agency. "It looks like the SSDA sent us this letter, but it's addressed to *Authors of Room 103*. I'm confused because I thought word detectives were only on the job during reading and phonics workshop. Let's find out what a word detective might need to do during writing workshop!" I opened the envelope, took out the letter, and read it to the students.

```
First Grade Information Authors:


Remember: Silent E is still on the loose.

Do not forget to listen for long vowels and make
sure Silent E is doing its job in the words you need
to spell during writing workshop.

We have sent a few tools that can help. Look inside
this envelope!


The Super Secret Detective Agency
```

"Of course! A word detective needs to use what they know to spell hard words, especially when there are tricky parts like silent *e*." I shook the envelope, and a pile of picture cards fell out. "Hmm, . . . I wonder how these words are supposed to help us with silent *e*." I held up two pictures featuring long-vowel sounds, and one other picture with a short-vowel sound. "This one looks like a picture of a lime. And this is tape. And this is a cat. Lime? Tape? Cat? How am I supposed to find silent *e* with these pictures?" I shrugged.

The kids began to shout out that silent *e* would be at the end of a word with a long vowel. "Oooooh, you're right! I bet these words will help us think about long and short vowels. Look! There's also a copy of 'The Case of the Silent *e*' chart in here to remind us of how silent *e* usually works."

Lead students in a quick word sort to help them listen for long and short vowels.

"Let's go ahead and get our ears warmed up by listening for long or short vowels in these words. I'll hold up a picture card and say the word. Let's make one column of words with a long sound and another column for words with a short sound." I pointed to the empty pocket chart to indicate on which side of the chart each would go. "Your job will be to point to the side where we should put each picture."

I held the first picture card up. "This is a picture of a *lime*. /Līīm/." I looked toward the vowel chart and pointed to the long-vowel side. "It's a long /ī/!" I placed the picture card on the side of the pocket chart designated for long-vowel sounds.

If you use the Units of Study in Reading or the Units of Study in Phonics, your students will be familiar with the Super Secret Detective Agency from Word Detectives and The Mystery of the Silent e. If not, you might have the principal, the school's reading specialist, or another significant adult write this note to your class.

Digital tools can make this type of delivery both logistically easier and more exciting. If you are using another adult in the school, they might record themselves reading this message, and you could play the message for students on an interactive whiteboard.

This work leans heavily on students' phonological awareness skills. You can promote students' phonological awareness, and make the lesson multilevel, by saying the words slowly and stretching out the vowel sound.

Support MLLs who are working hard to develop their phonemic awareness in a new language to participate in this sort by first leading children through a review of short- and long-vowel sounds. Channel kids to quickly say each sound aloud with you, focusing on the shape of your mouth as you pronounce each, and point to the long- and short-vowel columns of the chart as you do so.

I held the picture cards up one at a time, and students said each word slowly, stretching out the vowel sounds, then pointed to indicate whether they heard a long vowel or a short vowel.

"Now our ears are warmed up!" I touched my ears. "Do yours feel warm? Mine do! Now we can use the SSDA's important reminder about silent *e* to spell words with long vowels."

◆ **Name the teaching point.**

"Today I want to remind you that writers pay attention to the vowel sounds they hear inside words they want to write. They use everything they've learned about vowels to help them spell those words. When you hear a long vowel, you can add a silent *e* to the end of the word. Then you can ask, 'Does that look right?'"

TEACHING

Demonstrate labeling the picture cards with long vowels. Show how you make predictable mistakes.

"So writers—or should I say *detectives*—let's put this reminder to use. Help me label these pictures using what you know about long vowels and silent *e*." I touched the long-vowel column. "We'll also check them, making sure the words look right."

I tapped on the first picture in the left column. "*Lime.* What letters do we need to spell it? /Lll-īī-mmm/.' I stretched the sounds aloud as kids called out the letters. I recorded *lim* on a sticky note and stuck it to the picture card. Then, I touched each letter to spell it aloud, "*L-I-M, lime.*" The kids protested that I had forgotten silent *e*. "Oh! Of course! Without that silent *e*, a reader might think this says *lim*. Even though you can't hear the *E* at the end, it does the important job of changing that vowel sound."

We moved on to spell and check the words *note, cube,* and *tape.*

"Okay, last word. Let's label *green.* I hear a long *E* in the middle of *green.* So that means I'll need a silent *e* at the end like all the others." I quickly recorded *grene* on a sticky note. Then, I pointed to the misspelled word and squinted at it for a moment. "Hmm, . . . does that look right to you? What do you think?"

Many of the kids shook their heads, some pointing to a nearby chart of color words. "But it's a word with a long vowel, *and* I used a silent *e*. But wait! Silent *e* isn't the *only* way to write a long-vowel sound. Sometimes you need a vowel team, like *ee* in *tree.* Let me try that." I crossed it out and wrote *green* above my first attempt.

"Does that look right?" The kids nodded to confirm. "It's a good thing we made sure to check and that we remembered to be flexible with vowels, trying them more than one way. And here's something exciting! Now that you're mastering checking for vowels, you have another tool in your spelling toolbox. I've added it to the 'Our Spelling Toolbox' chart." I gestured to the new version of the chart, with "Don't forget the vowels" added.

The completed vowel card sort

The truth is, it's easy for kids to not realize a silent e is missing because they have, in fact, recorded all the sounds in the word. It can help to coach kids to listen and look for VCe phonograms as they read and spell to offer continued support with this work. For example, you might coach writers to recognize the phonogram -ime in lime *rather than isolating the long vowel.*

Add to your demonstration text, pausing at a word with a long vowel. Coach students to write that word and then the next sentence on whiteboards.

I displayed my completed page about different kinds of dogs. "I've been thinking that I could make this page even better! Will you help me out with that? Great! Quickly get out your whiteboards and markers, so that you can help me write!"

After students were ready, I said, "I want to add here, 'They can be huge.'" I grabbed my revision pen and added a caret and the word *They*, then modeled checking the word wall for *can* and *be*, and stopped at *huge*. "Okay, I'm not sure how to spell *huge*." I said the word slowly, stretching out the vowel sound: /hūūūg/. "Hmm, . . . I need your help. Say the word out loud. Do you hear a long vowel or a short vowel?" I paused as kids listened for the vowel.

Then, I voiced over, "Yes! Me too! I hear /ū/, like in *unicorn*." Here I pointed to the vowel chart. "That means that it's a long vowel, so we'll need to make sure we show readers that it's a long vowel. Quick! Write the word *huge* on your whiteboards. Then, check it. Does it look right?" I gave the class a few moments to record the word as I scanned their boards. Then, I filled in the word on the demonstration piece, pausing before I added the *e* to say, "Let me add the silent *e* at the end.

"Yes! That looks right. Without the *E* this would say *hug*." I masked the *E* with my finger.

"So writers, did you see how we did that? When I got stuck on how to spell a tricky word, we listened for the vowel sound to decide if it had a short sound or a long sound. And when we heard a long sound like the *U* in *huge*, we tried spelling that word with a silent *e* at the end and checked to see if it looked right. That way readers would know this word is *huge*, not *hug*!

"Will you help me write the next sentence? I also want to add, 'Big dogs need space to run.' Work with your partner. Say the sentence, stopping at any words that feel tricky to spell. Listen for the vowel sound and decide how you'll write it. If you hear a long sound, you might add a silent *e*, but be sure to check that it looks right." I repeated the sentence, then gestured for kids to get started.

I called the group back together and elicited students' help as I recorded the sentence on my page. We paused to study the word *need*, realizing that the long vowel was represented with a vowel team, *ee*, like in *green*, rather than a silent *e*. Then, we went on to spell and check the word *space*.

LINK

Remind students of the importance of continuing this work in their own writing.

"Friends, when you go off to write today, continue this important work. Make sure that when you stretch words, you listen really hard for the vowel sound, and you think, 'Is that a long vowel or a short vowel?' And don't forget that the silent *e* usually signals that the vowel is long. So, when you hear a long vowel, you might need a silent *e* at the end of that word!" I gestured to "The Case of the Silent *e*" chart as a quick reminder to students.

"Your folder is getting pretty full of books, and that means that it could be a good time to make sure that your books are finished and as strong as they can be. So, today, take a quick walk through your folder and make sure that your books are finished, fixing up the spelling and filling in the lines as you go. And then, there might even be time for you to start a whole new book before our celebration at the end of workshop!"

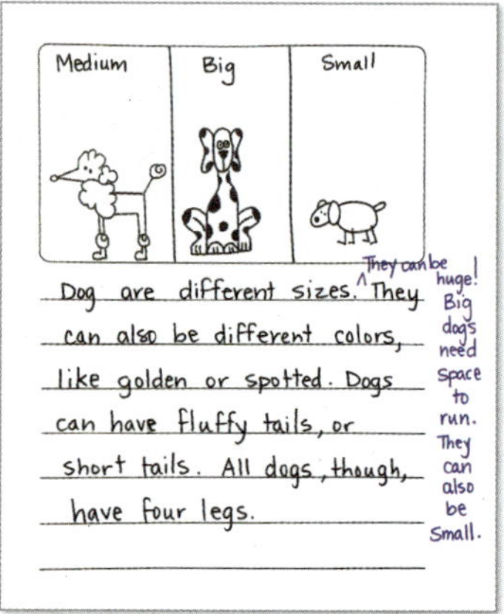

Don't belabor this modeling. Your hope is simply that students walk away knowing that careful spellers stay alert to different vowel sounds, drawing on their knowledge of long-vowel patterns like VCe to help.

Pay special attention to how kids tackle need *and* space. *Expect kids to approximate the use of VCe when spelling words with long vowels, perhaps spelling the word* need *with a silent* e *instead of a vowel team. Celebrate their ability to draw on spelling patterns and coach kids to be flexible, prompting them to check if a word looks right.*

Teachers, keep in mind—both now and when you work with MLLs in small groups and conferences—that the spelling strategy of asking if a word "looks right" may not be the most helpful for some. Students learning a new language are in the process of acquiring a sense of English spelling. Celebrate their growing phonemic awareness and approximations. As they read more and more, they'll have a larger bank of words that they recognize "look right."

SMALL GROUP ◆ Editing with Silent *e* in Mind

For this small group, you'll need whiteboards, markers, and copies of "My Vowel Chart" and Gerty's writing, "All About Bears."

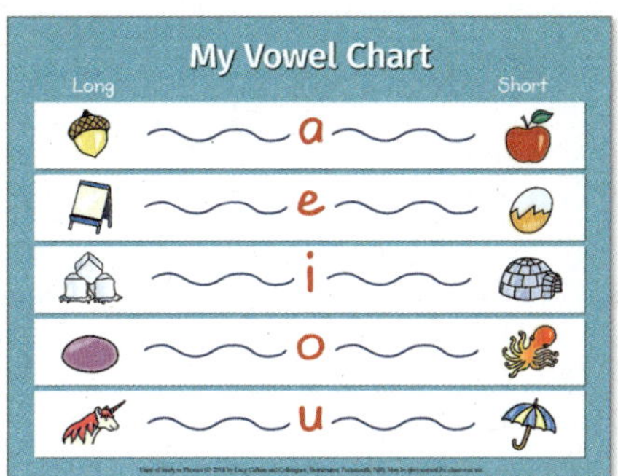

■ RALLY

Tell a story to emphasize the importance of rereading and checking for words that need the silent *e*.

"Writers, last weekend I brought home an information book that I wrote about bikes. I was very proud of it, so I gave it to my brother to read. He read the first page and stopped, looking a little confused. He said, 'Hold on a second, what do you mean, "You can *rid* on a bike?"'

"Of course, I *meant* to write 'You can *ride* on a bike.' But he was right—when I wrote the word *ride*, I left off the silent *e*. That little mistake made it so much harder for my brother to learn from my book. It's so important that we edit our writing carefully to make sure our words have the exact right vowel sound."

■ ACTIVATE

Call out a few words, some with a silent *e* and some without. Invite students to write these on their whiteboards before checking them.

I distributed whiteboards and markers to each student. "Let's practice writing a few words together. Listen as I say each word and make sure you use the silent *e* when you need to. If you need to, check the 'My Vowel Chart' as you write."

I said each word, gave students a moment, then wrote the correct spelling on my whiteboard and asked students to check their spelling against it: *cap, cape, hop, hope.*

■ TRY IT #1

Distribute a copy of Gerty's writing to each partnership to edit.

"Writers, my neighbor Gerty has a hard time knowing when to use the silent *e* in her writing too. She was hoping you could help her edit her teaching book about bears. I have copies for each partnership. Read her writing together. If you see a word where she mixed up the vowel spelling pattern, circle it on her paper. Then see if you can write the word correctly above it. Help Gerty fix up any places where she didn't use the long- and short-vowel patterns she knows."

■ TRY IT #2/LINK

Channel students to return to their own writing, paying careful attention to long- and short-vowel sounds as they do.

"You did a great job helping Gerty. Now it's your turn to try this in your own writing. Take out a book from your writing folder and reread it. As you read, use what you know about long- and short-vowel patterns to help you edit your writing. Remember that from now on, you can be your own editor, checking as you go!"

Gerty's writing

> *Possible Coaching Moves:*
>
> ▸ *"Say the word again and listen for the vowel sound. Is it a long-vowel sound or a short one?"*
>
> ▸ *"Does the word need an e at the end to make it look right and help you remember to say the long vowel?"*

Mid-Workshop Teaching ✦ A Minute to Play "Find-It Fix-It"

"Writers, you've been stretching your words out, listening really carefully for the vowel sounds, and recording those so that your reader can read each word. With all the hard work you've done, it'd really be a shame if only your current book got that treatment!

"We're going to have a Find-It Fix-It minute. I'll set the timer and you'll have one minute to read through another book in your folder, checking that you spelled all the words correctly. If you find places where you made mistakes, go ahead and fix them. Pull out the book you'll reread. Your Find-It Fix-It minute starts . . . now!"

I coached as students worked. "Keep reading! I bet there's some spelling to fix up in that book. Look at the vowel chart. Do you hear a short or long vowel?"

Once the timer went off, I said, "Now that the Find-It Fix-It minute is over, go back to your writing. Remember the work you need to do with those vowel sounds!"

Small Group ✦ Checking for Meaning Too!

For this small group, you'll need page 3 of the demonstration text, "All About Pizza." 

◼ ACTIVATE

Tell students that sometimes a quick check works for editing, and other times, they need to read slowly and carefully.

"Sometimes, when you are fixing up your books, you can do a quick check for things like misspelled words, or to make sure that there's punctuation at the end of every sentence. But other times, you'll need to read really carefully, asking yourself, 'Does all of this make sense? Am I missing anything here? Can my reader follow this?'

"And then, if the answer is 'No,' that means that you'll edit, so that your reader can say, 'Now I understand!'"

◼ TRY IT #1

Read your writing aloud. Have students signal when your writing doesn't make sense. Then, fix it.

"I'm going to read my writing, and if you find a place that doesn't make sense, that makes you say 'Huh?,' hold your hand up like a stop sign so that I can fix it!"

I read my writing, stopping when students signaled. I modeled fixing my writing, then reread it to make sure it makes sense.

◼ TRY IT #2

Channel students to reread their own writing and stop to fix up anything that doesn't make sense.

"Now it's your turn. Get out your writing and do a really careful read, making sure that what you wrote makes sense. If it doesn't make sense, fix it up!"

◼ LINK

Remind students to continue this work whenever they draft or edit.

"I'm going to send you off now with one last tip: You don't need to wait until the end of a book to make it make sense! You can reread and fix things up as you write."

BEND II FIG. 9–1 Mason fixes up his writing about books.

Possible Coaching Moves:

▸ *"Read that part again. Think, 'Does this make sense?'"*

▸ *"Something about that part doesn't make sense. How can you fix it?"*

▸ *"What can we add here to make your reader understand this part?"*

Choosing Books to Add to the Classroom Library

Celebrate the work that students have done in this bend, inviting them to choose which book they'll add to the classroom library during tomorrow's celebration.

"Writers, come quick! Make sure you bring your folders too. There's something new in our classroom library!"

When students were gathered, I pointed out the empty bin on one of the bookshelves, with the label *Class 1-103 Topic Books*. "You've worked so hard with your books to choose the most fascinating topics, to teach as much as you can, to make sure your words are spelled correctly. By now, your books are probably just as good as the ones in the classroom library. So, I thought, why not add them to the library? And I made a special bin, just for the topic book authors of Class 1-103!

"You'll add your topic books to this special bin during our celebration tomorrow. For now, will you go through your folder to find the book that you think is the strongest, the one that you worked the hardest on, the one you think so many people will just *need* to read? Put that book in the front of your folder, so you are ready to share it during our celebration tomorrow."

I gave students a minute to select their book. When everyone was ready, I said, "I cannot wait for you to add these topic books to our classroom library tomorrow!"

PHONOLOGICAL AWARENESS AND PHONICS EXTENSION ✦ Swap the Sounds

Lead students in a quick phoneme manipulation activity.

"Friends, we're going to play a game where we swap some sounds. Let's warm up our voices by singing the song.

> Swap, swap, swap the sounds,
> Add 'em, take 'em out.
> Moving sounds all around
> Is fun without a doubt!

"Today we're going to trade the sounds out. I'm going to say a word and tell you what sounds to switch.

"Say *cake*. Now change the first /k/ sound to /b/. What do you get?"

Students told me the word, and we continued with a few more rounds.

"Say *bake*. Now change /b/ to /sh/. What's the new word?"

"Say *shake*. Now change /k/ to /p/. What's the new word?"

"Say *shape*. Now change /sh/ to /t/. What's the new word?"

Dear Teachers,

We hope that your students are ending this unit with a folder full of writing that shows growth in terms of volume, understanding of information writing, use of different elaboration strategies, and teaching voice. We also hope that you've seen your students' stamina increase, and that students are approaching the spelling of particularly challenging words with gusto and bravery.

Most of all, though, we hope that your students end this unit with new understandings about how to study something closely and write their observations, and that your students see themselves as holders and writers of information. Your classroom is now full of writers who believe that they have things to teach, that they are experts on their own special

corner of the world and the things they care about most. Those same writers are saying, "Yes, I can be a teacher, and I can use my books to teach people everything that I know." We hope you use this celebration to instill one more powerful mindset in your students. Let this be the opportunity to convey that others care about the things they know the most about, that there are people in the world who want to learn about what they can *uniquely* teach. Those people are the ones you'll want to invite to this unit's celebration: students' parents or caregivers and anyone in the school who knows your class and will respond to their work with enthusiasm.

Before the Celebration

You might take some time (it doesn't have to be a large amount of time), outside of the writing workshop, to gather students in the library, surrounded by the different browsable nonfiction books that live there. You might say to students: "You've spent so much time writing books that teach your readers so much. Look at these beautiful books! These books also teach, just like yours! Do you think we can make our teaching books look this good? Let's each browse some books for a minute and notice what makes them beautiful." Then, you could send students to their seats with colored pencils, black felt-tip "publishing pens," sticky notes, "about the author" pages, and construction paper. Allow your students to color in their pictures, trace over their words with a publishing pen, and create a cover. Make sure they add an "about the author" page at the end, something they'll remember how to do from their work in *Small Moments*.

You'll want to arrange the room so that each student can have their own special "teaching spot," where each visitor can read their book and ask questions of the expert who is in front of them. You might also provision the hallway with a sort of "guest book," where visitors can leave compliments for the experts.

Remember that the setup need not be fancy, but you want to see your students, their handwriting, and their work all over it!

DURING THE CELEBRATION

Position each child in their special teaching spot and announce to the experts: "There are loads of people outside, all ready to read our information books and learn from the experts . . . us! As they walk around, you could say things to them like, 'Do you want to learn more about this? I can answer any questions you have!' Make sure that you stay close to your spot, so that you are there to actually answer those questions. Remember to talk in your proudest presentation voice." Then, let the visitors in!

As the visitors circulate, make sure that you do the same. Stop by to read each student's book, give your own compliments, and make sure that visitors do this too. Celebrations can be tricky for the child whose parents are unable to come, so put some extra effort into making sure that all children feel celebrated. As you see visitors leaving, remind them of the guest book and the opportunity to leave some concrete feedback for the experts to read later.

AFTER the CELEBRATION

After the visitors leave, you may want to give your students an opportunity to circulate, too, checking out their classmates' expert writing. Wrap up the celebration by inviting each student to add their books to a special basket in the classroom library. Your students will love reading each others' books and continuing to learn from the expertise of one another.

All the best,

Lucy and Casey

Gallery of Student Work

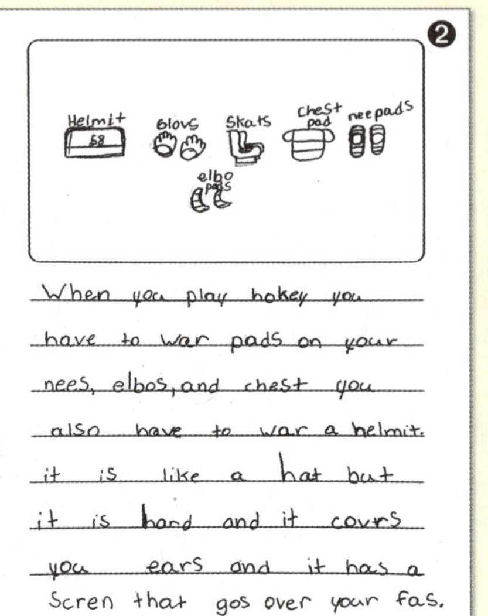

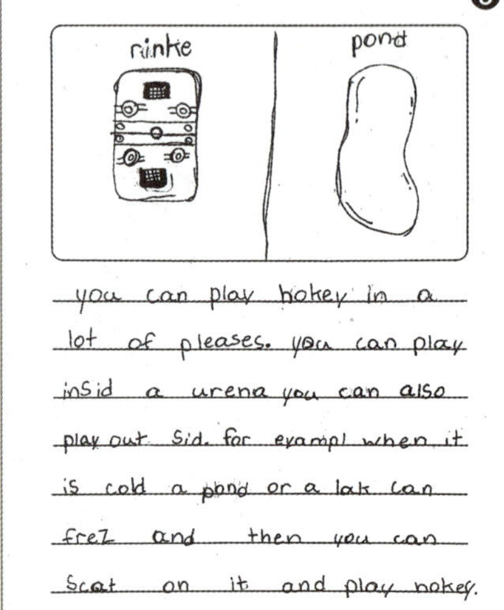

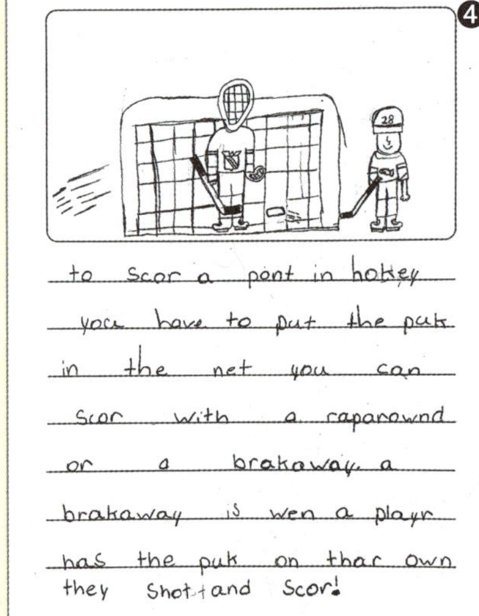

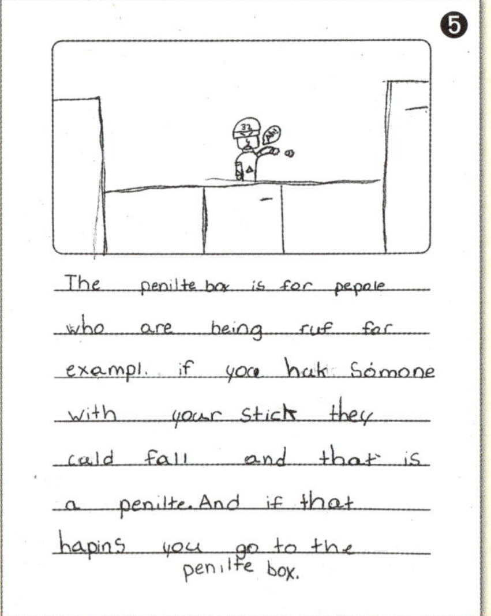

BEND II FIG. C–2 Ben includes different kinds of information in his book about Legos®, such as definitions and details. Ben's complete book can be found in the online resources.

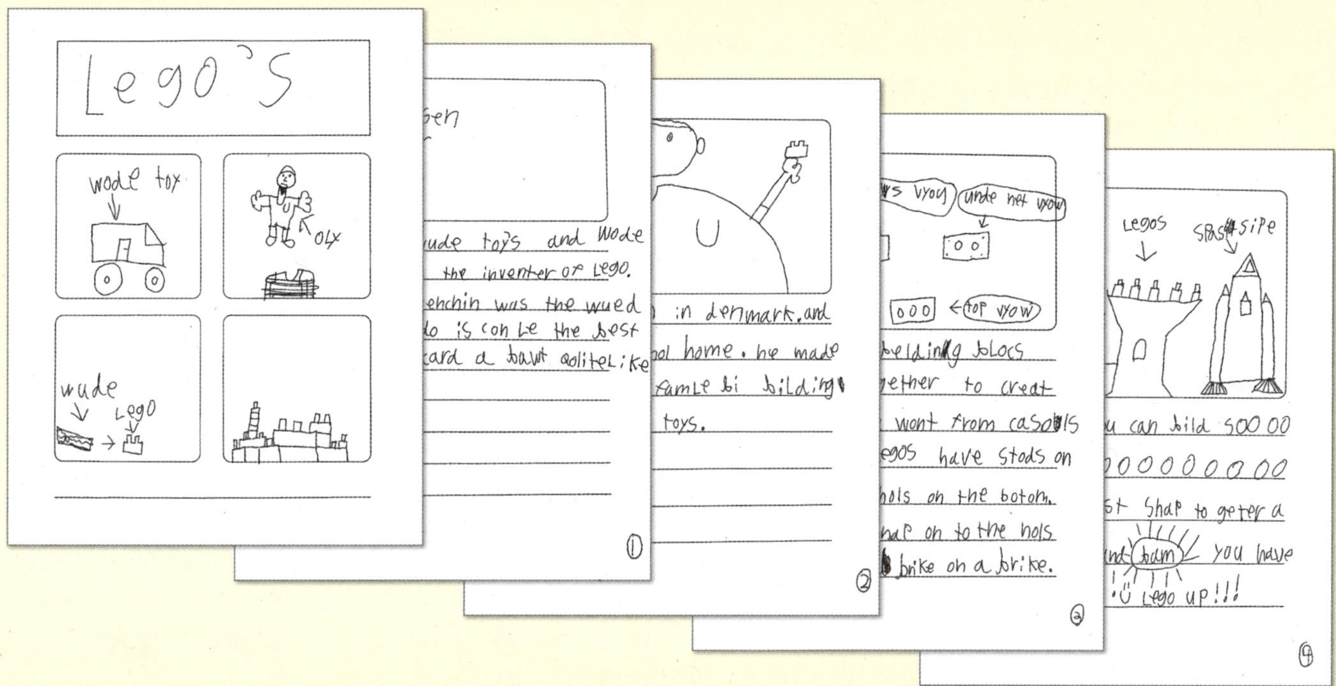

BEND II FIG. C–3 In "My Book About Dogs," Eleanor describes exactly how her topic looks. She also adds several examples across her book and shows steps. Eleanor's complete book can be found in the online resources.

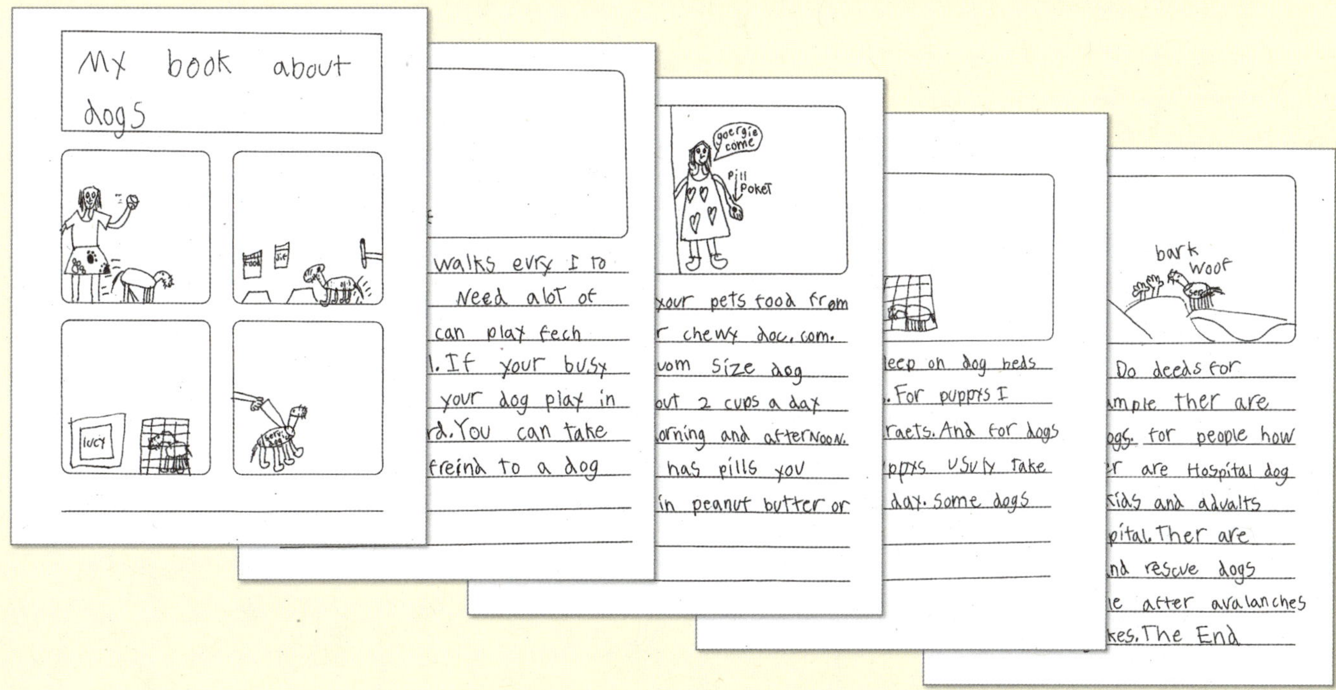

Anchor Charts in This Unit

INTRODUCED IN BEND I, SESSION 1

INTRODUCED IN BEND II, SESSION 3

Completed Teacher Demonstration Texts

All demonstration texts are in the online resources. 

"Stapler"

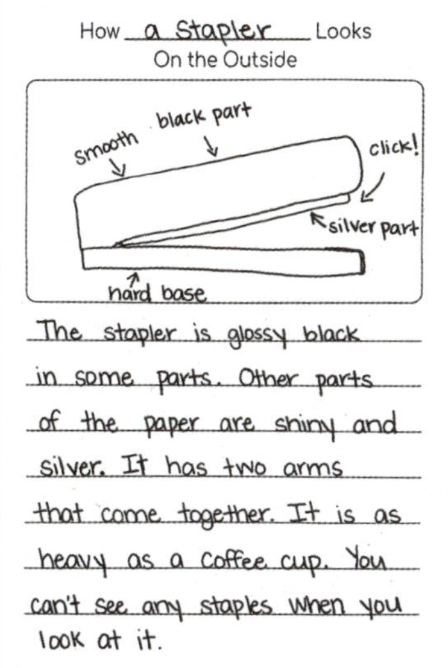

"All About Dogs"

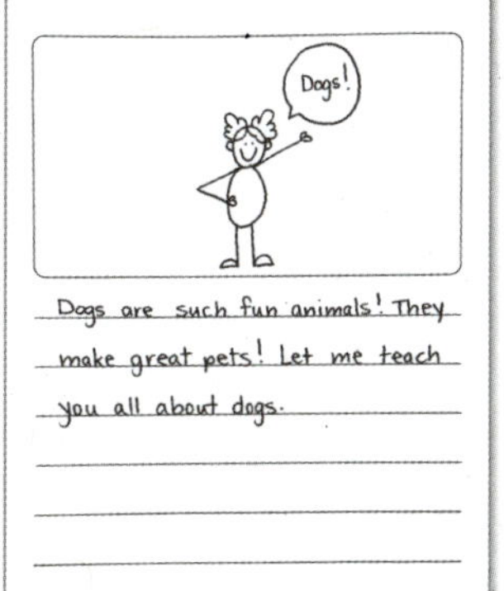

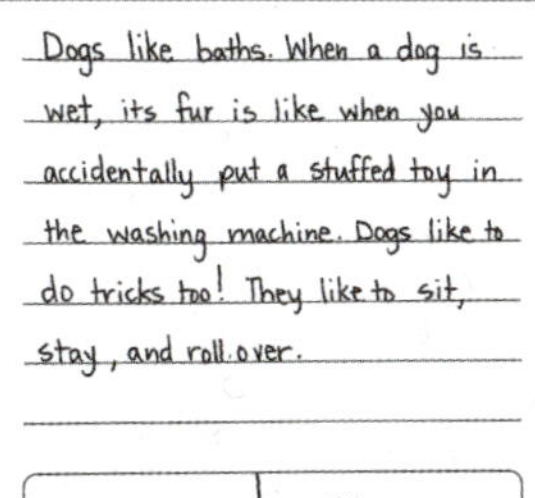

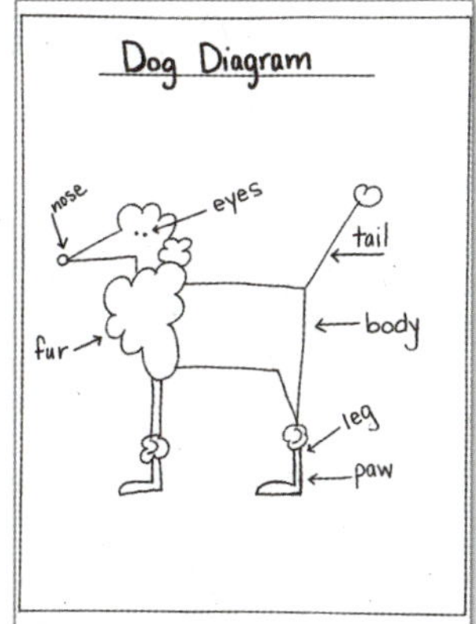

	SESSION / MINILESSON	WORK TIME	MID-WORKSHOP TEACHING	SHARE
	Bend I Writing Teaching Books with Independence			
1	**Finding Topics in the World at Your Feet**	**Voiceovers** ✦ Generating Momentum **Conferring Supports** ✦ Predictable Challenges **Conference** ✦ Thinking through Subtopics You Want to Teach Your Reader **Q&A** ✦ Teaching about Classroom Objects	Getting Topic Ideas from Friends	New Partners, New Energy
2	**Touching and Teaching before You Sketch, Then Write**	**Voiceovers** ✦ Independence and Productivity **Assessment Tool** ✦ Writing an Information On-Demand **Student Work** ✦ On-Demand Strengths and Next Steps	Channel Students to Complete Entire Books	Writers Work Hard to Fix Up Their Writing
3	**Predicting What Your Reader Will Want to Learn**	**Conferring Supports** ✦ Starting a Second Book **Conference** ✦ Transitioning to Information Books **Conferring Supports** ✦ Spelling the Best You Can	Listening Partners Ask Questions	On Every Page, Add Information that Wows Readers
4	**Researchers Look Closely to Discover and Add Details**	**Conferring Supports** ✦ Adding More in Pictures and Words **Student Work** ✦ Learning from Maya's Exemplar Book	Coach Kids to See and Think More through a "Writer's Eyes"	Details Matter in Writing
5	**Researchers Study (and Write about) How Things Look**	**Conferring Supports** ✦ Predictable Problems Can Prompt Reteaching **Conference** ✦ Looking Closely and Writing a Lot (MLLs in Intermediate Stages of Language Development) **Student Work** ✦ Analyzing Phonics Patterns in Abigail's Writing	Looking Closely at the Inside	Helping Your Partner See More
6	**Researchers Study (and Write about) How to Use Things**	**Small Group** ✦ Adding Tips and Warnings **Toolkit** ✦ Using the "Questions to Ask One Another" Chart to Say More	A Quick Gallery Tour to Learn from Your Classmates' Pages	A Quick Celebration of a Strong Start
7	**Using Sensory Details to Add Describing Words**	**Conferring Supports** ✦ Getting All Kids Writing about Their Chosen Objects **Small Group** ✦ Starting an Information Book **Small Group** ✦ Writing with Sensory Details	Choosing the Just-Right Word	Commas Can Help Punctuate a List
8	**Writing More Quickly, Using Words You Know in a Snap**	**Small Group** ✦ Using Syllables to Spell Multisyllabic Words **Voiceovers** ✦ Writing with Volume, Stamina, and Independence **Conference** ✦ Returning to Unfinished Books to Teach Even More	Writers Gain Momentum by Backing Up and Rereading	Tackling *Humongous* Words and Familiar Words with Courage and Confidence
9	**Getting Our Books Ready for Readers**	**Q&A** ✦ Editing and Preparing to Celebrate **Small Group** ✦ Finding Fix-Up Spots, and Fixing Them Up! **Conferring Supports** ✦ Common Punctuation Errors **Small Group** ✦ Getting Ready for Visitors' Questions	Using the Room to Help You Write	The Visitors Are Here!